The Rhetoric of Church and State

■

The Rhetoric of Church and State

■ ■ ■ ■ ■ ■ ■

A Critical Analysis of

Religion Clause Jurisprudence

■

Frederick Mark Gedicks

Duke University Press   *Durham and London 1995*

© 1995 Duke University Press

All rights reserved

Printed in the United States of America on acid-free paper ∞

Typeset in Aldus by Tseng Information Systems, Inc.

Library of Congress Cataloging-in-Publication Data

appear on the last printed page of this book.

For F.H.G. & S.A.B.

Contents

. . . . .

Preface

. . . . .

I first began thinking of organizing religion clause jurisprudence in terms of competing rhetorical discourses of church-state relations during the summer of 1989. At the time, I thought the idea might provide the basis for a short essay explaining several of the Supreme Court's more controversial decisions, such as *Lynch v. Donnelly* and *County of Allegheny v. ACLU*, that could easily be written before classes began in the fall. As I worked my way into the project, however, I encountered two complications. First, the manner in which the discourses seemed to interact was far more complex than I had anticipated. Several times I thought I had captured this complicated relationship, only to see it slip away in the application. At the same time, the explanatory power of the relationship, once mastered, was much broader than I had imagined. Far from explaining only two or three aberrational cases, it seemed to organize virtually all of religion clause doctrine. From an essay, the project evolved into a full-blown article, then into two, and finally, more than five years later, into this book.

Numerous people helped me bring the project to closure. Ted Blumoff, Gerry Bradley, Jim Gordon, and Steve Smith were kind enough to read the entire manuscript. Nancy Ehrenreich, Neil Kramer, Steve

Monsma, and David Smolin read and commented on one or more chapters. Dan Conkle, Mark Tushnet, and Richard Wilkins commented on drafts of essays originally published in law reviews that are included here as separate chapters. I received helpful criticism and comments from Milner Ball, Bill Marshall, and an anonymous reviewer who read and commented on the manuscript for Duke University Press. Portions of the project were presented at faculty colloquia at the University of Denver and Brigham Young University in January 1990, and at symposia at Capital University and Hamline University in October 1990, and at the University of Montana in September 1994, all of which also supplied me with valuable criticism and commentary. I received indispensable research assistance from Greg Call, Christine Jepsen, John Kelleher, Stan Mortensen, and Lisa Rowell. Trinyan Paulsen prepared the index. I owe special thanks to Dean Reese Hansen and the faculty research committee at Brigham Young University, who funded this project for three consecutive summers despite little evidence of progress toward publication. It goes without saying, but I will say it anyway, that none of these people can be held responsible for the final product.

Finally, I am grateful to Nicea, Alex, Annie, Abby, and Amanda for all that they bring to my life. They put up with too many distractions and disappointments while I was working on this project.

Most of chapter 2 first appeared in somewhat different form as "Public Life and Hostility to Religion," 78 *Virginia Law Review* 671 (1992), and a part of Chapter 6 was included in "RFRA and the Possibility of Justice," 56 *Montana Law Review* 95 (1995). The rest of the book has not previously appeared in print.

Introduction

. . . . .

The Religion Clause

Jurisprudence of the Supreme Court:

A Failure of Doctrine and Politics

. . . . .

Documenting the inconsistency of the Supreme Court's religion clause decisions is a virtual cliché in constitutional scholarship. The Court's decisions in this area have been described as "ad hoc,"[1] "eccentric,"[2] "misleading and distorting,"[3] "historically unjustified and textually incoherent,"[4] and—finally—"riven by contradiction and bogged down in slogans and metaphors."[5] No one, it seems, much cares for the Court's work in this area. Steven Smith has observed that "in a rare and remarkable way, the Supreme Court's establishment clause jurisprudence has unified critical opinion: people who disagree about nearly everything else in the law agree that establishment clause doctrine is seriously, perhaps distinctively, defective."[6] The intense and almost unanimous criticism of the Court's abandonment of settled free exercise doctrine in *Employment Division v. Smith*[7] suggests that this observation applies to the Court's free exercise jurisprudence as well.[8]

Although the doctrinal deficiencies of the religion clause decisions are legion, they basically reduce to three: failure to supply persuasive accounts of requirements of governmental neutrality and secular justification (under the establishment clause) and of freedom of religion itself (under the free exercise clause). The Court has long purported to ground its establishment clause doctrine in government neutrality between religious sects and between religion and nonreligion,[9] yet there seems to be no such pattern—of neutrality or anything else—in the decisions themselves. For example, the Court has held that states may provide buses to transport students to and from religious schools at the beginning and end of the school day, but not to take them on field trips in the middle of the day.[10] In another set of cases, the Court decided that supplying parochial school students with films and maps violates the establishment clause, but giving them textbooks does not.[11] In still another pair of decisions, the Court held that providing certain services on a parochial school campus is unconstitutional, but providing identical services in a mobile home directly across the street is constitutionally permissible.[12] Whatever principle governs the outcomes in these decisions, it is not neutrality.

For nearly as long as the Court has been committed to neutrality, it has insisted that government interactions with religion have a secular justification.[13] Yet its application of this principle has been unpersuasive. The Court has endorsed implausible secular justifications for religiously charged government practices like displays of the Christian nativity and the Jewish menorah (commemorating in traditional ways religious holidays that are now largely secular) and Sunday closing laws (encouraging family togetherness).[14] At the same time, it has rejected as religiously motivated certain government practices that have secular justifications at least as plausible as those the Court has approved, such as statutes requiring equal treatment of evolution and creationism in public education (teaching children all sides of a controversial issue) and display of the Ten Commandments in public school classrooms (informing children of the religious roots of much of contemporary secular law).[15] The account that reconciles these disparate holdings has yet to be written.

In its decisions under the establishment clause, the Court has consistently committed itself to broad principles that it has been unable consistently to apply. By contrast, the Court's free exercise decisions betray uncertainty about what substantive principles of religious freedom are embedded in the free exercise clause, if indeed the clause protects religious freedom at all. For years, the Court insisted that government action could burden religious practice only on a showing of a compelling regulatory interest implemented in the least intrusive manner.[16] Although this test appeared highly protective of religion, the fact is that most free exercise plaintiffs (and virtually all non-Christians) who came before the Court while this test was in force were denied relief.[17] Controversial though it was, the Court's decision in *Employment Division v. Smith*[18] merely confirmed what should have been clear for some time—that the Court has only the weakest commitment to freedom of religious exercise in the United States.[19] As Douglas Laycock has pointed out, with *Smith* the Supreme Court explicitly abandoned what was thought to be one of the principal functions of judicial review under the free exercise clause, that of protecting "religious expression from hostile or indifferent consequences of the political process."[20]

The contradictions and inconsistencies in the Court's religion clause doctrine are not just a challenge for academics. While the majority of Americans support the general principle of separation of church and state, most strongly disagree with the strictness and vigor with which the Supreme Court has located and policed the boundary.[21] The inability of most of the American populace to understand why the Constitution requires the doctrine that the Court has formulated has made its religion clause decisions among the most hotly disputed and widely disregarded in grassroots America.[22]

While criticism of Supreme Court decisions is hardly a new phenomenon, attacks on the Court's religion clause jurisprudence stand out as a special case. Since the Court abandoned close review of economic due process rights in 1937,[23] few areas of constitutional doctrine have succeeded like religion clause jurisprudence in simultaneously maintaining internal inconsistency, ridicule by commentators, and lack of popular support over such a long period of time. Some of the most respected Justices to serve on the Court—Felix Frankfurter, Hugo Black, John Harlan, William Brennan, and Lewis Powell, among others—served during this period, and as a group the Justices have always represented some of the most capable practitioners and judges in the profession. How has such a bright and qualified group managed to create such a mess, and why have they been unable to clean it up?

I believe that the Court's tangled web of decisions in this area is traceable to a relatively recent phenomenon—the displacement of a religiously informed communitarian discourse on public morality and politics by a secular, neutral, individualist discourse on such matters. Donald Giannella once observed that "doctrinal formulations designed to achieve certain ends may achieve different or perverse results when the assumptions on which they rest change."[24] This is precisely what has occurred in the Court's religion clause decisions. I will argue that the three doctrinal failures of the Court's religion clause jurisprudence—the inability to supply adequate accounts of neutrality, secular justification, and religious freedom—have their roots in a failure to appreciate the meaning and significance for religion clause jurisprudence of the replacement of public piety with public secularism.

In the Supreme Court's religion clause decisions, the public religious discourse of the nineteenth century is not so much displaced as erased; it is as if the American nineteenth century had never happened. The decisions present the discourse of secular neutrality as the modern culmination of an historically continuous process of secularization and privatization that began with the eighteenth-century European Enlightenment before being exported to the colonies.[25] The general absence in the majority opinions of any recognition of the long and vibrant tradition of religious discourse in American public life, and the legal and social practices that generated it, marks the violence that is always present where one account of the world overcomes and overwhelms another. As Walter Benjamin observed, history is written by the winners of these conflicts.[26]

In this particular case, however, the losing discourse, while unmistakably defeated, was not wholly vanquished. It is as if public religious discourse were driven into the mountains by public secularism, which then decided that it was not worth the trouble to complete the messy task of total eradication. As a result, religious discourse now makes periodic, guerilla-like forays into the public domain of secular neutrality. Those advocating public religious discourse draw power and support from the fact that the Court's decisions that are informed by secular neutrality enjoy minimal public support. The continuing vitality of groups that advocate public religious discourse manifests itself as political pressure for alignments of government and religion not unlike those that were common during the nineteenth century in the United States, such as religion as a subject of study and even worship in public education, equal access to public facilities and benefits for religious individuals and organizations, public funding of private religious education, public (and typically Christian) prayer, and the appropriation or endorsement by government of religious (again, usually Christian) symbols in public and political life. Many of these alignments have been invalidated by the Supreme Court, but a number have been upheld, especially since the 1980s as the cumulative effect of a generation of Republican appointments to the Court shifted its ideological center to the right. Some commentators have seized upon these decisions as evidence of a regression to former days when religion clause doctrine justified persecution of non-Christians and privileges for Protestants.[27] But this criticism is misdirected: such has been the power of the discourse of secular neutrality—and, perhaps as well, the depth of the social and cultural changes in the United States during the last century—that constitutional justifications for alignments of religion and government that are problematic within this discourse have nevertheless been grounded almost wholly within it. Dire predictions to the contrary notwithstanding, the Court has been unable or unwilling to retrieve the religious discourse of the nineteenth century to justify contemporary church-state interactions. One consequence has been a hodgepodge of accommodationist decisions that defend close alignments of church and state with arguments drawn from the very discourse of secular neutrality that was initially used to overthrow such alignments. Under the circumstances, the miracle of contemporary religion clause doctrine is not that it is largely inconsistent and incoherent, but that any consistency or coherence has survived within it at all.

I will begin in chapter 1 with a consideration of the presuppositions, values, and normative principles about church-state relations exemplified by the competing discourses of the nineteenth and twentieth centuries on the constitutionally proper relationship of church and state. The ideology of church and state drawn typified by nineteenth-century discourse I will refer to as "religious communitarianism" and that characteristic of twentieth-century discourse as "secular individualism."[28] Chapter 2 illustrates how contemporary installment of secular individualism as the governing discourse on church-state relations, beginning with *Everson v. Board of Education*, enables "neutrality" to exclude religious belief and action from public life without betraying express hostility toward them.

The next four chapters show how each of the three major flaws in religion clause jurisprudence is a particular and predictable result of the erasure of religious communitarian discourse by secular individualist discourse, even (or, perhaps, especially) when the Court reaches results that coincide with religious communitarian premises. Chapter 3 argues that the Court overtly manipulates the concept of neutrality in order to decide parochial school aid and equal-access cases within the discourse of secular individualism. Chapter 4 argues that the defense of religious communitarian results with arguments from secular individualist discourse leaves the Court no choice but purposefully and consciously to efface the religiosity of practices that it deems permissible under the establishment clause. This phenomenon is clearly evident when the Court must defend in secular individualist terms church-state alignments that do not involve financial aid. Accordingly, I trace in this chapter the development of the Court's establishment clause doctrine principally in this context. The effacement of the religious, however, is evident in other kinds of decisions as well, principally those involving religious tax exemptions and financial aid to religious organizations pursuant to social welfare programs, including assistance programs for religious higher education. Chapter 5 pursues the effacement argument in the context of these other decisions. Finally, chapter 6 shows how effacement has affected free exercise doctrine, and it completes the explanation of doctrinal inconsistency by arguing that the ideology embedded in secular individualist discourse does not permit a coherent theory of free exercise exemptions, providing a justification only for a ban on purposeful religious discrimination.

This book is generally a work of description. My purpose here is not to articulate and defend a particular normative vision of church-state relations. (In fact, many of the doctrinal arguments I criticize have been deployed by the Court to justify results which I support on policy grounds.) Rather, this book is an attempt to understand at a level deeper than doctrine why and how the Supreme Court's religion clause decisions have taken the convoluted form that they have. In the end, however, I hope to have demonstrated that secular individualist discourse is wholly inadequate to account for the Court's religion clause decisions, while also being highly unpopular. I will conclude with the suggestion that it should, therefore, be abandoned.

Chapter 1

. . . . .

Two Discourses of Church and State

. . . . .

The notion that the way a society talks about church and state could affect its normative conclusions about church-state relations is a particular instance of the postmodern insight that human investigation of the world shapes its appearance. I will begin this chapter with a short discussion of this point, and will follow it with a description of the substantive content of religious communitarianism and secular individualism. I will illustrate this content with a brief historical survey of normative conceptions of church and state in the United States, showing how the nineteenth-century understanding of proper church-state relations exemplifies religious communitarian discourse, and how the twentieth-century understanding exemplifies secular individualist discourse. I will close by explaining how the two discourses differ from two comparable constructs of some currency in legal scholarship, republicanism and liberalism.

. . 1 . .

Until recently, truth and knowledge in the Western intellectual tradition had been founded upon a radical distinction between mind and world. Under this view, not only do things exist in the world independent of the human mind, but they are possessed of an essential character that can be discerned by the mind without alteration or distortion.[1] Because these "intelligible essences" were thought to reside in things themselves, the true nature of a thing was never viewed as a function of human perception; to the contrary, the truth of human perception was thought to be a function of the nature of the thing. Thus, within the classical Western tradition, a proposition was true only to the extent that it corresponded to the world "as-it-really-is," and one could know something only by apprehending and experiencing the essential characteristics of this world.[2]

Contemporary philosophers have largely abandoned the classical account of truth and knowledge under the pressure of postmodern arguments that human beings cannot experience the world without simultaneously altering it.[3] In this postmodern view, the world-as-it-is, or "facts," and our understanding of the world, or "theory," are in an antinomial relationship.[4] Facts are not taken to have any essential characteristics or meaning; these are supplied by a theory that orders facts to give them meaning and coherence.[5] Theories are continually evaluated as supplying more or less adequate accounts of the facts they purport to explain. But if facts have no essential characteristics, if their meaning is supplied only by theory, one cannot objectively maintain that one theory describes the world "better" or "worse" than another, since that would be to assume that facts have meaning independent of theory.[6] The antinomy lies in understanding facts to have no meaning independent of a theory that explains them, while simultaneously judging some theories as being better or worse than others on the basis of some pretheoretical meaning these facts are assumed to possess.[7]

The important point is that one's theoretical preconceptions of the world alter his or her intuitive experience of it. Postmodern thinkers have named this phenomenon in various ways, using terms like "mathematical" and "technological" thinking,[8] "horizons" of understanding,[9] "paradigms,"[10] "discourses,"[11] "borders,"[12] and "interpretive communities."[13] What these thinkers all share is the recognition that the knower cannot be separated from the known, that the nature of the object one studies is inextricably bound up with the nature of the subject who studies it. Whatever this phenomenon is called—I will refer to it as "discourse"—it causes us to understand the world in different ways, depending on the theoretical preconceptions that each of us brings to his or her experience. When a human subject holds to a particular conceptualization of the world, that conceptualization participates in the "creation" of this world by predisposing the human subject to a particular interpretation of the phenomena that he or she experiences.

When I refer to "discourses" of church and state, I use the term in this same sense, as a conceptual defining and ordering of the experience of church-state interactions that determines how that experience is to be understood. Each church-state discourse includes a normative conception of how church and state should interact and that therefore determines how these interactions in the phenomenal world are, and are to be, understood.

. . 2 . .

In an important recent study, James Davison Hunter explored the current and controversial participation of certain religious groups and individuals in American politics.[14] Hunter points out that, in contrast to the sectarian divisions that lay at the root of the Reformation Wars, this current conflict is not adequately defined by traditional sectarian boundaries.[15] According to Hunter, on one side of this conflict are the "orthodox," cultural conservatives who are committed to "an external, definable, and transcendent authority"; on the other are "progressivists," liberals with a "libertarian social agenda" whose first instinct is not to reaffirm traditional Judeo-Christian beliefs, but rather to reinterpret them "according to the prevailing assumptions of contemporary life," relying for moral authority on the " 'self-grounded rational discourse' " of " 'Enlightenment rationalism.' "[16] The result is that the conservative wings of theologically diverse religions now often have more in common with each other than they do with their more liberal brothers and sisters within the faith.[17] Other commentators agree that, in contrast to the familiar sectarian lines of earlier conflicts, the fight is now usually between conservative religion and a more—often much more—secular faith.[18]

What I will call "religious communitarian" discourse or "religious communitarianism" incorporates the interdenominational conservative religious beliefs and practices described by Hunter. This discourse presumes a society in which church and state are institutionally but not politically or culturally separated. Religious communitarianism understands religion to be the principal, if not the exclusive, source of certain values and practices that lie at the base of civilized society, such as support for the traditional nuclear family—manifesting itself in opposition to abortion, sex education in public schools, and the feminist and gay rights movements—and public acknowledgement of the preeminence of the biblical God—manifesting itself in general support for public prayer and other public religious observances. In addition, religious communitarian discourse presupposes a faith that relies primarily on tradition and authority, and only secondarily on reason, to articulate and defend these values and practices, as some intellectual historians have suggested that revelation marked the limit on reason prior to the Enlightenment.[19] Finally, while the ideological premises of religious communitarianism require that government refrain from coercing belief and that it tolerate dissenters to some extent, these premises do not require that government remain religiously neutral. Religious communitarianism permits and even demands that government exercise its power to influence citizens to adopt the foundational morality of conservative religion to guide their choices in private life.[20] Under the premises of this discourse, government may act to encourage religious traditions that nurture and reinforce conservative cultural values, and it need protect atheists, agnostics, and dissenters only from the deprivation of classical conceptions of life, liberty and property.[21] In religious communitarian discourse, the lesson of the Reformation Wars is that religious belief cannot be coerced; nevertheless, it remains important that the right kind of beliefs be encouraged, and that religious practices that threaten social order be suppressed.

What I will call "secular individualist" discourse or "secular individualism" incorporates the secularized opposition to the conservative Judeo-Christian tradition in the United States that Hunter identified. On secular individualist premises, knowledge is discovered by the right application of critical reason, and never by simple appeal to religious authority or tradition. Secular individualism considers religion to be an irrational and regressive antisocial force that must be strictly confined to private life in order to avoid social division, violence, and anarchy. Secular individualism requires that government remain neutral between religious sects and between religion and nonreligion generally: religious belief is a choice in private life that is insulated from government influence and control, while public life is the realm of objective, secular discourse protected from the irrationality and subjectivity of faith. In secular individualist discourse, in contrast to religious communitarian discourse, it is never acceptable for government to defend its actions with a religious justification.[22] On the contrary, this is precisely the evil to be avoided. Permitting government to legislate on the basis of religious belief imposes upon public life serious social conflict that cannot be resolved by the application of reason.[23] In the post-Enlightenment West, it is precisely the disconnection of religion from public life that is thought to have pointed Western culture toward individual freedom and political stability and made possible the progress of the last three centuries.[24] Thus, public religion is only acceptable to secular individualism to the extent that it falls within broader secular categories of public life.[25]

Contrasting the two discourses with each other highlights their internal coherence. The privileging of reason over faith and tradition within secular individualist discourse implies the privileging of individuality over community as well, since the processes of reasoning and rationality are primarily individual. Conversely, the preference for faith and tradition over reason within religious communitarian discourse implies the paramount importance of community. Taken a step further, the emphasis on reason and individuality in secular individualist discourse makes it difficult broadly to impose a set of strong values on society. Rather, the emphasis is on preservation of individual choice through value-neutral procedures, so that individuals remain free to act upon the truths they discover in the exercise of their own reason.[26] Secular individualism permits religion to influence government and public life, but only indirectly, as the effect of private choice rather than as the result of direct government encouragement or assistance. By contrast, religious communitarianism's placement of conservative religious values at the heart of community preservation implies a regime of tolerance, not neutrality: when widespread commitment to certain values is essential to the preservation of the good society, government can hardly be indifferent to the task of encouraging these foundational values and discouraging or prohibiting other values that threaten the foundational ones. Within a regime of tolerance, there is nothing remarkable or controversial about giving government aid to corporate and individual exponents of the privileged set of values, while allowing dissenters to believe as they will and prosecuting those whose actions seriously threaten foundational values. Whereas secular individualism finds that religion is oppressive when it is present in public life *as religion,* and thereby co-opts individual choice,[27] religious communitarianism presupposes that a certain kind of religion is not only permitted but required in public life, becoming oppressive only when it coerces belief or punishes behavior that represents no threat to foundational values.

· · 3 · ·

The religious communitarian and secular individualist discourses are not historical, and it is not my purpose to construct an argument that they are the result or residue of history. Still, one can identify certain "moments" in American history that resonate with the substantive content of the discourses as I have defined them. A brief survey of church-state history in the United States will serve to illustrate this content and how it has influenced constitutional adjudication.

. . *a* . .

The evidence bearing on precisely what the First Congress intended to accomplish with the passage of the religion clauses of the First Amendment is ambiguous. At a minimum, the establishment clause was directed at preventing the newly created federal government from granting to any denomination the political and governmental privileges enjoyed in England by the established Anglican Church.[28] On the other hand, it is also clear that the clause was not intended to do away with establishments of Protestant religion then existing among the new American states,[29] and it appears that a least some of the founders thought the clause permitted nondiscriminatory or nonpreferential aid to religion.[30] It is likely that most of the framers meant only to outlaw national religious establishments while leaving the question of state religious establishments to the political judgment of the states themselves.[31]

Similar historical ambiguities exist with respect to the origins of the free exercise clause. Many of the framers hoped that the clause would prevent the governmental persecution of dissenting religions that was permitted in England and many of the colonies under the established religions.[32] Some framers also may have understood the clause to require that religious believers be released from the obligation to obey federal laws that violated their religious consciences.[33] Yet even after enactment of the First Amendment, federal laws were consistently applied to believers without regard to the burden this placed on their religious beliefs and activities, and state governments commonly imposed civil disabilities on non-Protestants and atheists.[34] Again, it is likely that most of the framers intended the free exercise clause to prevent the national government from imposing the most serious civil disabilities on religious dissenters, while still permitting recognition of the preeminent status of Protestant Christianity as the foundation of American cultural and social life.[35]

The formal religious establishments of the states died a natural political death early in the nineteenth century. Even when combined with the establishment clause's prohibition on national establishments, however, the elimination of state establishments did not lead to a separation of religion from public life.[36] Eighteenth- and nineteenth-century Americans understood the Constitution to require separation of church and state only at the institutional level. Thomas Curry, for example, has argued that Americans of the colonial period and the founding era understood "establishment of religion" to refer to the state's funding of and coercing participation in a particular denomination, like the Anglican establishment in England, and not to government aid to religion "in general."[37] Similarly, Gerard Bradley argues that an understanding of Protestantism as the "consummation of religious development" and a preoccupation with producing a "virtuous citizenry" created "an indelible fusion of nondenominational Protestantism and republican government in the early American mind."[38]

This understanding persisted into the nineteenth century. Joseph Story, writing in 1835, described the religion clauses as having been addressed to an America in which "the general, if not universal, sentiment . . . was, that Christianity ought to receive encouragement from the state, so far as it is not incompatible with the private rights of conscience, and the freedom of religious worship."[39] It meant that constitutionally prohibited establishments of religion were understood to have been created when the government coerced funding of or participation in a particular denomination or sect, but it did not require that government or politics be secular.[40] On the contrary, nineteenth-century Americans generally believed that Protestant values formed an important part of the moral foundation on which a free and democratic society is built. Tocqueville observed that nineteenth-century Americans "combine the notions of Christianity and of liberty so intimately in their minds that it is impossible to make them conceive the one without the other."[41] Americans told him, he related, that it was critical "that the new states should be religious, in order that they may permit us to remain free."[42] Justice Story argued that matters of religion "never can be a matter of indifference in any well ordered community," and wondered "how any civilized society can well exist without them," finally concluding that, "it is impossible for those who believe in the truth of Christianity, as a divine revelation, to doubt, that it is the especial duty of government to foster, and encourage it among all the citizens and subjects."[43] During the founding era and throughout most of the nineteenth century, therefore, harm to the community's moral and religious sensibilities counted as a justification for restricting individual autonomy.[44]

Mark De Wolfe Howe described the nineteenth-century relationship between government and Protestant religion as having constituted a "de facto Protestant establishment."[45] Public schools had a distinctly Protestant flavor, with verses from the King James Bible being posted on the schoolroom wall and teachers leading prayers and scriptural readings. Colleges and universities were expected to teach "the ideals of a free, republican, and religious society," and to require "strict morality among the students."[46] Customs like legislative prayer became widespread among the states; Thanksgiving, Christmas, Good Friday, and Easter were officially recognized as holidays; and political rhetoric made frequent reference to the Almighty. Expressions of allegiance and devotion to the Christian God made their appearance on coins, stamps, and government seals and documents. States enforced prohibitions on blasphemy, enforced the Christian Sabbath, and imposed civil disabilities upon non-Protestants and (especially) nonbelievers. The Civil War was an occasion for public acknowledgement of God's vengeful hand in American history. Toward the end of the nineteenth century and into the twentieth, Protestant fundamentalists rallied to invoke government authority to enforce temperance and antievolution laws. As late as 1892, the Supreme Court could safely quote Chancellor Kent to the effect that "we are a Christian people, and the morality of the country is deeply ingrafted upon Christianity," and could cite Justice Story for the proposition that Christianity is part of the common law.[47]

Protestants also were instrumental in building political support for eradication of the Mormon practice of polygamy—after slavery, the other "relic of barbarism." In fact, the twin assumptions of the de facto establishment—that Protestant Christianity is one of the pillars of a well-ordered society, and that government properly may act to encourage belief in this version of Christianity—are unmistakably evident in the Supreme Court's decisions upholding antipolygamy legislation. One finds the Court characterizing polygamy as a barbaric practice that violated natural law and attacked the moral foundation of "civilized society"; indeed, so evil did polygamy appear to the Court that it could not even imagine that it might be motivated by genuine religious belief.[48] Polygamy is described as "a crime against the laws and abhorrent to the sentiments and feelings of the civilized world," a "barbarous practice . . . contrary to the spirit of Christianity and of the civilization which Christianity has produced in the West."[49] By contrast, monogamous marriage—"the union for life of one man and one woman in the holy estate of matrimony"— is described as "the sure foundation of all that is stable and noble in our civilization; the last guaranty of that reverent morality which is the source of all beneficent progress in social and political improvement."[50] By threatening this relationship, "bigamy and polygamy are crimes by the laws of all civilized and Christian countries," tending "to destroy the purity of the marriage relation, to disturb the peace of families, to degrade woman and to debase man."[51] According to the nineteenth-century Court, it was constitutionally proper for government to prohibit and punish even sincerely held religious practices like polygamy when they threatened the "peace, good order, and morals of society."[52]

In summary, the de facto establishment was a curious meld of religion and government not unlike the relationship presupposed by religious communitarian discourse. In the minds of nineteenth-century Americans, the separation of church and state demanded by the establishment clause was merely institutional. They honored that separation not only by refraining from establishing a national church, but also by having abandoned their state religious establishments. Beyond these measures, however, nineteenth-century Americans saw no need to cabin the public influence of religion. On the contrary, they saw that influence as being critical to the creation and maintenance of civilized society. Moreover, notwithstanding their constitutional commitment to religious freedom, they were willing to tolerate religious practices that fell outside the Protestant mainstream, like polygamy, only to the extent that these practices did not threaten the Protestant morality on which civilized society was presumed to rest. As David Smolin has described this era, "an interdenominational Protestantism was both culturally, and in a certain sense, legally, dominant, even as those of other faiths were allowed to practice their faith within the constraints of the civil law."[53]

. . *b* . .

The assumptions of the de facto establishment came under serious pressure early in the twentieth century. Exactly how and why this came about is a complex matter. Edward Purcell identified several influences, including the growth of naturalistic approaches to science spawned by the publication of Darwin's *On the Origin of the Species* in 1859, the professionalization of American higher education, and the rise of legal realism.[54] Purcell describes how under the pressure of these influences, religion in the twentieth century "emerged as the preeminent symbol of everything that was bad in human society," whereas science "was inextricably tied up in the minds of most intellectuals with everything that was best."[55] Similarly, Harold Berman characterizes the radical shift in public philosophy from the nineteenth to the twentieth centuries as being "from a religious to a secular theory of law, from a moral to a political or instrumental theory, and from a communitarian to an individualistic theory."[56] Stephen Monsma argues that although the de facto establishment was culturally dominant in the nineteenth century, it never developed a theoretical justification for its practices and thus was vulnerable to the resurgence of Enlightenment rationality that swept the United States in the early twentieth century.[57] By the 1930s intellectuals in both the United States and Europe were elaborating a "secularization hypothesis." Under this hypothesis, progressive secularization of government and society was seen as an inevitable and positive long-term trend that eventually would end in the elimination of religion as a public influence.[58] Although this hypothesis remains controversial, it can at least be said that since the end of World War II, the creation of a "secular society" in the United States has been understood as a genuine political and social option.[59]

For whatever reasons, the de facto establishment had become problematic by the 1940s. Rather than an indispensable foundation of civilized society, as presupposed by the de facto establishment, religion had come to be seen as a reactionary obstacle to secular progress. This shift in perceptions of religion is evident in the Court's first establishment clause decision in the modern era, *Everson v. Board of Education.*[60] In *Everson* the Supreme Court considered whether a city could pay for the bus transportation of school-aged children to parochial as well as to public schools. Along the way to holding that such funding was constitutionally permissible, the Court summarized the principal force behind the drafting of the establishment clause as the desire of the framers to eliminate the civil disorder and violent persecution that had historically accompanied the establishment of a single sect in Europe:

> The centuries immediately before and contemporaneous with the colonization of America had been filled with turmoil, civil strife, and persecutions, generated in large part by established sects determined to maintain their absolute political and religious supremacy . . . . In efforts to force loyalty to whatever religious group happened to be on top and in league with the government of a particular time and place, men and women had been fined, cast in jail, cruelly tortured, and killed.[61]

Observing that early American colonials had brought with them the European tradition of the established church, the Court stressed the insult and indignity entailed in compelling religious dissenters in America "to pay tithes and taxes to support government sponsored churches whose ministers preached inflammatory sermons designed to strengthen and consolidate the established faith by generating a burning hatred against dissenters."[62] After a review of Virginia's

1785 rejection of general taxation for the support of ministers and churches (in which Madison and Jefferson are somewhat misleadingly portrayed as having played the decisive roles),[63] the Court stated in clear and unequivocal terms that the establishment clause required an absolute neutrality on the part of government, both as between particular religions and as between religion and nonreligion:

> Neither a state nor the Federal government can set up a church. Neither can pass laws which aid one religion, aid all religions, or prefer one religion over another. Neither can force nor influence anyone to go or to remain away from church against his will or force him to profess belief or disbelief in any religion. No person can be punished for entertaining or professing attendance or non-attendance. No tax in any amount, large or small, can be levied to support any religious activities or institutions, whatever they may be called, or whatever form they may adopt to teach or practice religion. Neither a state nor the Federal Government can, openly or secretly, participate in the affairs of any religious organizations or groups, and *vice versa*.[64]

The decision closed with a flourish, quoting the now famous phrase from Jefferson's letter to the Danbury Baptists that the establishment clause "was intended to erect a 'wall of separation' between Church and State."[65]

With *Everson* the Supreme Court clearly signaled that the de facto establishment would be abandoned as a guide to church-state relations in favor of a philosophy like secular individualism. Although governmental neutrality among particular Protestant sects was consistent with the de facto establishment, governmental neutrality between Protestants and non-Protestants and between believers and atheists was antithetical to it. Likewise, although the institutional separation of church and state was consistent with the de facto establishment, the more decisive cultural and political division implied by the "wall of separation" was not.

Perhaps most important, secular neutrality implies a radically dif-

ferent public role for religion, one unconnected to government or to
public life, as prescribed by secular individualist discourse. Whereas
the de facto establishment was built on the premise that religion is
essential to civilized society, secular neutrality's requirement that
government remain detached and neutral with respect to the religious
choices of its citizens suggests that a wholly secular society is possible
and perhaps even preferable. In Professor Smolin's words, "the concept of government neutrality represents a change in the self-identity
of the nation, because it renders the previously dominant concept of a
'Christian America' heretical and repugnant."[66] After *Everson* it was
thought that government can and should remain indifferent about
how religious choice is exercised.

· · 4 · ·

Constitutional scholarship in recent years has been strongly influenced by the intellectual recovery of a "republican" tradition which
contrasts, in some ways sharply, with the more familiar "liberal" tradition of American constitutional history.[67] Certain aspects of these
two traditions resonate to the respective ideologies of religious communitarianism and secular individualism that I have just described.
For example, Morton Horwitz describes the republican tradition as
having emphasized "the growth and development of human personality in active political life. Republicanism proceeded from an objective conception of the public interest and a state that could legitimately promote virtue."[68] By contrast, Horwitz describes the liberal
tradition has having stood for "a subjective theory of value, a conception of individual self-interest as the only legitimate animating force
in society. In addition, liberalism stood for a 'night-watchman' state,
denying any conception of an autonomous public interest independent of the sum of individual interests."[69] Mark Tushnet contrasts
the two traditions in a comparable way, describing republicanism as
having "emphasized the essential social nature of individual being
and examined how individual preferences rest on and constrain social

institutions" and liberalism as having "emphasized the individualism of people acting in society, and examined how social institutions rest on and are constrained by individual preferences."[70] A kind of republicanism is implicit in the ideology of religious communitarianism, and liberalism is implied by secular individualism. Religious communitarian discourse would define the "public interest" as the preservation and encouragement of the conservative cultural values on which society is founded, and would permit government to promote that interest—to "promote virtue," in Horwitz's terms—by using its regulatory power to shape private preferences in accordance with those values. On religious communitarian premises, government properly acts to influence "private" religious behavior because that behavior affects the overall character of social life and thus has an unavoidably "public" dimension as well.[71] The religious aspirations of individuals, rather than constituting public institutions, are to a large extent realized through such institutions.

Secular individualism, on the other hand, would confine religious belief and activity to private life in order to avoid irresolvable conflicts in public life. The public interest with respect to religion, rather than being independent of private religious choice as in religious communitarian discourse, in fact consists of the aggregation of individual religious choices—"individual self-interest"—in private life.[72] Thus, on secular individualist premises government must remain neutral with respect to religion in public life, and indifferent to how religious choice is exercised in private life, so long as it does not harm others. As Tushnet has put it, individual choices in private life are simply "not a subject of political analysis."[73] If the religious character of society in religious communitarian discourse is largely constituted by government and social institutions, as republican theory would suggest, then the dynamic is precisely the opposite in secular individualist discourse: the only time religion may legitimately manifest itself in public life is as the effect of private religious choice.

Despite these similarities, the conceptual territory mapped by the discourses and these related political traditions is not coextensive. On the contrary, there are important differences, especially between religious communitarianism and the republican tradition. Republican theorists are badly split among themselves on the question of how religious communities fit within the new republican vision. Some endorse limited government encouragement and support of religious belief and practice, as in religious communitarian discourse, while others are suspicious of any such government involvement with religion, as one would be in secular individualist discourse.[74] Moreover, republicans generally believe that rational deliberation is the process by which communitarian moral values are chosen, encouraged, and defended by government;[75] there is no place for the transcendent knowledge and deference to authority that form such an important part of religious communitarian discourse, and, even if there were, they would surely not be privileged over rationality, as they are in religious communitarianism. Finally, it is clear that most republican theorists within the legal academy do not themselves share the conservative cultural values that I have located within the ideology of religious communitarianism.[76]

The liberal tradition is much closer to secular individualism than the republican tradition is to religious communitarianism, but here, too, there are complications in assuming that the two are synonymous. For example, some liberals strongly defend the principle that religious practices should be exempted from the incidental burdens of facially neutral laws, while others are strongly opposed to this "accommodation principle."[77] Secular individualism, as I will argue in chapter 6, is generally hostile to *religious* exemptions, although it finds it acceptable for religious individuals to receive relief from oppressive laws when they can fit themselves within an exemption defined in secular terms.

Both the republican and the liberal traditions are historical, whereas the church-state discourses are not. I reiterate that I have not attempted to show that the discourses developed in any meaningful sense from historical antecedents. I have linked the discourses to a general understanding of certain historical periods in American history only as an aid in describing their substantive content. The discourses are ideological constructions for a contemporary purpose—to reorganize and understand more deeply the religion clause jurisprudence of the Supreme Court—and not an attempted reconstruction of the past as it was experienced by those who lived it. The value of the discourses ultimately lies not in their historical but in their rhetorical plausibility—that is, in the extent to which they succeed in organizing contradictory and conflicting decisions of the Supreme Court in a persuasive and satisfying manner.

Chapter 2

. . . . .

Neutrality as Hostility:

The Privatization of Religion

. . . . .

It is tempting to characterize a discourse of church and state as simply a descriptive hypothesis that is continuously adjusted to observations and experiences of how the two interact. This would be mistaken. As Milner Ball has explained, the various ways in which we talk about the world are not "merely rhetorical devices. They are not simply descriptive. They are conceptual, and they are creative of the reality they embody."[1] This "world-creating" character of discourse can be so strong that it may drive out any and all competing conceptions of the world; such a discourse becomes "world-excluding" as well as world-creating.[2] To one in the grasp of such a discourse, alternative worlds disappear, being virtually unimaginable.[3] Thomas Kuhn suggested that geocentric cosmology had such a hold on the medieval mind, preventing most people of that time from taking seriously the heliocentric cosmology based on the Copernican system.[4] In a similar vein, Robin West has described how the pervasive nineteenth-century view that African Americans were morally flawed as a group made the question of what any particular African American had done to merit condemnation "not just *unanswerable*," but "*unaskable*."[5]

The discourses of church and state that I have named and defined do not exert this kind of near-absolute power to order thought. They are more ideological than a classic, Kuhnian paradigm.[6] Holmes Rolston warns against the degeneration of a "good paradigm" into an ideology—"a presuposition with which we view experience, spectacles through which all data will be viewed, with adjustments only in ad hoc hypotheses that are rigged for the sole purpose of saving the theory from refractory facts, and that actually insulate the theory from experience." Thus, "[t]he theory that begins as a synthetic judgment about the world can get subtly transformed into an analytic prejudgment brought to the world, so that variant experience can no longer transform the theory but rather the theory transforms the experience."[7]

What distinguishes the discourses from each other are deeply rooted normative differences about how church and state should interact. No doubt there are secular individualists who literally cannot conceive of a world bounded by religious communitarianism, and vice versa. Most of those inhabiting the world of one church-state discourse, however, understand quite well the world of the other; they simply think the other is wrong. Rather than Kuhnian paradigms, then, the discourses are each closer to what Robert Cover called a *nomos*—a "normative universe" that defines "right and wrong," "lawful and unlawful," "valid and void."[8] These norms are maintained within a discourse by a grammar of "interpretive commitments,"[9] "procedures of exclusion,"[10] or "disciplining rules"[11] that identifies the questions open for discussion and delineates the acceptable forms of argument. In short, the discourses organize disagreement and discussion about church-state interactions by identifying what the "important" questions are, and regulating what can count as an answer to these questions.

Even though those in the world of one church-state discourse generally can understand or imagine the world set up by the other, what counts as an important question or argument in one discourse often does not count at all, or in the same way, in the other. Because the discourses organize and understand discussions of church-state issues differently, adherents to each discourse still see (and fail to see) certain aspects of the world that seem absent (or present) in the experience of adherents to the other discourse.[12] I will argue in this chapter that secular individualist discourse locates the boundary between public and private life in a different conceptual place than does religious communitarian discourse, thereby excluding religion from public life as more properly a matter of private, individual devotion. This exclusion, which clearly appears to the religious communitarian as an unacceptable act of religious discrimination, is defended by the secular individualist as simple neutrality between religion and secularism. This explains why, all too often, religious organizations and individuals experience the Supreme Court's religion clause jurisprudence as oppressive and alienating at the same time that others sincerely believe it to be neutral.

. . 1 . .

Many of those who value religion have contended that American politics and public life are hostile to religion. This, for example, is the premise of Richard Neuhaus's widely read book, *The Naked Public Square*,[13] as well as Stephen Carter's more recent *The Culture of Disbelief*.[14] Others have made similar observations and arguments,[15] especially about the legal academy.[16] As I noted in the introduction,[17] the Supreme Court's religion clause opinions are widely perceived to be hostile to religion, and anecdotes about the antireligious hostility of public life are common.[18] Moreover, studies suggest that some of the principal actors in American public life systematically marginalize religious viewpoints relative to secular ones.[19] Finally, regardless of the evidence, it is clear that many religious people feel excluded and alienated from public life.[20]

Despite this strongly felt perception by some, others are baffled by the suggestion that American public life discriminates against religion. Mark Tushnet, for example, confesses "some puzzlement" at this claim, believing that contemporary American culture is far less hostile to religion than many suggest, even among intellectuals.[21] Others argue that religion is deeply, if controversially, involved in contemporary American politics. Theodore Blumoff, for example, suggests that critics of secularism in public life simply have not been paying attention: "It is as if they had missed the last three decades: the Moral Majority, the Reverends Billy Graham, Martin Luther King, Jesse Jackson, Pat Robertson, Jerry Falwell, Theodore Hesburgh and others . . . . Religion is today and always has been thoroughly admixed in American politics, and this despite the long prevailing liberal ethos."[22] Kathleen Sullivan similarly finds "any picture of rampant secularization difficult to square with numerous indicators of religion's lively role in contemporary American social and political life."[23] Others flatly deny that any hostility to religion exists in American public life, outside of a few isolated instances,[24] and still others suggest that the perception of hostility is the result of misunderstanding.[25] Finally, at least prior to *Employment Division v. Smith*,[26] any disability of religion in American public life seemed justified by the unique benefits conferred upon religion by the free exercise clause.[27]

These conflicting claims are the result of seeing the American experience of church and state through the lenses of different discourses about their proper relationship. Martin Heidegger once noted that Galileo's famous experiment at Pisa not only confirmed Galileo's revolutionary views about the cosmos, but was simultaneously interpreted by his scholastic adversaries as a vindication of Aristotelianism: "[B]oth Galileo and his opponents saw the same 'fact.' But they interpreted the same fact differently and made the same happening visible to themselves in different ways."[28] Similarly, ideological combatants in church-state conflicts experience the same worldly phenomena of church-state relations, but they make these phenomena understandable to themselves in different ways. What divides them is the fundamentally different way in which religious communitarianism and secular individualism each draw the line separating the public from the private: whereas religious belief has important public dimensions in religious communitarian discourse, the privatization of religion presupposed by secular individualist discourse makes it inevitable that religion will be excluded from private life despite (and, indeed, pursuant to) secular individualist claims of religious neutrality.

· · 2 · ·

In the Lockean tradition of natural rights, citizens are thought to have inalienable rights against government that are held independently of the government's existence.[29] This necessitates the conceptual division of human life into mutually exclusive public and private spheres. Under such a political regime, the reach of permissible government action (public life) depends on the boundaries of the inviolable sphere of individual rights (private life).[30]

Conceptually, the boundary between the public and private spheres is marked by the presence or absence of individual free will, mirroring the fundamental division in Western thought between subject and object.[31] In private life, individuals are free to do whatever they please for any reason (or for no reason) without having to account to the government or to other people, so long as they do not harm anyone else.[32] Value choices need not be defended by publicly accessible reasons because private behavior is assumed to be the result of desire, which is beyond rational or empirical analysis.[33] In public life, on the other hand, government and individuals are obliged to serve the collective "public interest" rather than the idiosyncratic tastes and preferences of any individual.[34] Unlike value choices in private life, choices in public life cannot be justified by mere appeal to one's tastes or preferences. Actions in public life must be justified empirically or rationally, by reference to the observable and explainable phenomena of the exterior world.[35]

The border between public and private life is neither peaceful nor stable. For the secular individualist, no less than the contemporary liberal, individual choice is paramount and government imposition of values anathema.[36] The threat of private life is that it will subvert the institutions and actors of public life to some set of idiosyncratic values. The indulgence of individual preference in private life threatens political and social stability if unleashed in public. At the same time, the individual pursuit of values is threatened whenever public life encroaches upon private life.[37] The purpose of the state is to preserve the objectivity of public life from the subjectivity of private life, while nonetheless ensuring that there remains sufficient private space for the continued pursuit of subjective values outside the public sphere.[38] The state accomplishes this by remaining ideologically neutral—that is, by staying aloof from the pursuit of values in private life and acting only on the basis of objective facts rather than subjective values.[39] If individual values are the function of desire, which itself cannot be measured or explained, then no single set of values can be objectively shown to be better than any other set, and government must remain neutral with respect to all sets of values.[40] Thus, when government acts on a particular conception of the good, it arbitrarily deprives individuals of the freedom to choose their own values. Only by staying out of such conflicts can government retain its role as neutral arbiter of social conflict.[41] The most uncontroversial kinds of government actions in a liberal democracy are based on objective facts, and the most problematic actions on subjective values.

For example, this preference for objectivity is a possible explanation for the Supreme Court's reluctance to ban nonobscene pornography, notwithstanding its intuition that such speech is of little individual or social value. In the absence of conclusive empirical ("objective") data showing a link between criminal behavior and consumption of pornography, banning pornography appears as a subjective value preference that arbitrarily privileges one among a number of competing views of human sexuality. Thus, while the Court will allow considerable regulation of the distribution of pornography, it has consistently overturned government efforts to prohibit it outright.[42]

Although at one time the fear was that the objectivity of public life would co-opt individual liberty by invading private life, the contemporary concern now seems more the opposite, that a particularist set of values will capture public life and exclude competing conceptions of the good from participation. One of the key tasks of contemporary liberal politics is to police the boundary between public and private life by distinguishing value from fact and desire from reason. Beliefs or values that reside in private life are suspect as a basis for government action unless they can be relocated in public life on account of their status as facts or reasons. Kent Greenawalt, for example, contrasts rational ways of knowing with what he takes to be less reliable ones, such as "reliance on personal intuition, feeling, commitment, tradition, and authority."[43] On secular individualist premises, only if a belief is confirmed by widely shared human experience, scientific investigation, or reasoning from premises that can be verified by such experience or investigation does it qualify as knowledge upon which government legitimately can act.

Religious belief and practice are forced into private life by the manner in which secular individualist discourse defines the public and the private. Religious belief in the Western tradition is centered on a transcendent force or belief—that is, a force or belief that is beyond the material, phenomenal world. Accordingly, religious beliefs cannot be empirically or rationally validated according to the objectivist conventions of public life.[44] This does not mean, as defenders of a secular public life might claim, that reason and empiricism play no role in religious communitarian discourse, but only that secular ways of knowing are ultimately subordinated to divine authority and religious tradition in this discourse.[45] In secular individualist discourse, by contrast, secularism is the measure of knowledge in public life, and religion by its nature cannot satisfy it.

Keeping religion and religious belief confined to private life enables secular individualism to marginalize religion without having to eliminate it. As Marx argued, "Man emancipates himself *politically* from religion by banishing it from the sphere of public law to that of private law."[46] Explaining the force of this point, Elizabeth Mensch and Alan Freeman observe that by confining religion to private life, rather than abolishing it outright, government reduces religion to "a private whim, an expression of purely subjective individualized values."[47] As such, religion and religious belief need not—and, indeed, cannot—be considered by those who act in public life.[48]

Secular individualism purports to treat religion and religious belief neutrally—as a subjective value preference restricted to private life like all such preferences, rather than as objective knowledge proper to public life.[49] However, this position can be genuinely neutral only if the boundary between the private world of subjective preference and the public world of objective fact is natural, fixed, and inevitable. As I recounted in chapter 1, postmodern criticism has cast serious doubt on the proposition that substantive meaning like "public" or "private" resides in the phenomenal world independent of an act of interpretation.[50] Without a postulate of inherent meaning, however, one cannot be certain that an activity has been "accurately" or "properly" classified as public or private.[51] The public or private character of an activity depends not only on the discovered attributes of the world, but also on the classifier's subjective perception of those attributes.

Far from reflecting the world-as-it-really-is, any particular division of society into public and private life is only a socially contingent way of ascribing meaning to the world-as-we-experience-it.[52] Secularism and "neutrality" do not mark any natural or inevitable distinction between private and public life. The confinement of religion to private life reflects an experience of the world filtered through secular individualist discourse, not the disinterested discovery of essential meaning or preinterpretive reality.

· · 3 · ·

Secular individualism's privileging of secular knowledge as objective and its marginalizing of religious belief as subjective is one of the conceptual foundations of religion clause jurisprudence. Although most of the Supreme Court's religion clause decisions reflect this elevation of the objective/secular over the subjective/religious, two decisions—*Edwards v. Aguillard*,[53] the creation science case decided under the establishment clause, and *Employment Division v. Smith*,[54] the Native American peyote case decided under the free exercise clause—illustrate this phenomenon especially well.

. . *a* . .

In *Edwards* the Supreme Court reviewed a Louisiana law that required public schools to teach creation science whenever evolution was taught. Louisiana officially maintained that the law protected academic freedom and provided for fairness and balance in teaching schoolchildren about the origin of human life. During the enactment process, however, the sponsor of the law and several other legislators had rather indiscreetly stated that they supported the law because creation science coincided with their religious beliefs, and evolution contradicted those beliefs.[55] Relying heavily on a prior decision, *Epperson v. Arkansas*,[56] the Court held the law invalid under the establishment clause for lack of a secular purpose.[57] It found that the legislative purposes officially articulated by the state were shams, and that the real purpose of the law was to advance fundamentalist beliefs about divine creation by making the teaching of evolution more difficult.[58]

The text of *Edwards* suggested that evolution is a matter of objective fact, whereas creationism is a matter of subjective belief. The more general subtext was that science is rational and real, whereas religion is irrational and imaginary. Throughout the opinion, the majority described creationism as "mere belief," while it consistently presented evolution as indisputably "real."

For example, the Court quoted with approval expert testimony to the effect that " 'any *scientific* concept that's based on *established fact* can be included in [the public school] curriculum.' "[59] Similarly, it criticized the law under review for having given "persuasive advantage to a particular religious doctrine which rejects the *factual* basis of evolution in its entirety."[60] The objectivity of evolution assumed by the Court gives that theory a decisive intellectual advantage over creationism, such that placing creationism alongside evolution as an equal or even a superior conception of human origin appears indefensible. The language of science, with its rational proofs and mathematical certainties, differs from the languages of other disciplines and contexts in that it is a "prestige discourse" associated with "the presentation of truth," against which the validity of other languages is measured.[61] Giving credence to creationism becomes like the seventeenth-century church's stubborn adherence to geocentricity despite Galileo's decisive confirmations of the Copernican system. Accordingly, the Court dismissed without argument testimony about the empirical basis of creationism.[62] It quoted with approval the determination in *Epperson* that a decision not to teach any theory of human origin is designed to *"suppress"* evolution,[63] and characterized the Louisiana law as "advanc[ing] a religious doctrine by requiring . . . the *banishment* of the theory of evolution from public school classrooms."[64] By summarily rejecting the possibility that creationism might be empirically plausible, and using terms like "suppress" and "banish," the Court clearly signaled its view that creationism/religion censors evolution/knowledge in an oppressive untruthful way—through despotic coercion rather than scientific proof.

The equation of creationism with evolution as an explanation for human origin evokes secular individualism's nightmare of particularist religious beliefs subverting public life—the imposition of values by the irrational, passionate, and violent overthrow of rationality, reason, and peace. The nightmare is powerful, of course, because it recalls vivid historical and cultural images in the post-Enlightenment West: religion as superstition that denies Reality and suppresses Truth, together with religion as fanaticism that causes its adherents to erupt into persecution, violence, and war against all with whom they disagree.[65] These general images from European history reinforce a specifically American image of religious fundamentalists as oppressive and reactionary, suppressing all knowledge that conflicts with their narrow and literal reading of the Bible.[66]

Science depends upon the notion of falsifiability for proof of its hypotheses. If a hypothesis is such that there can be no empirical test that might prove it false, the hypothesis has no scientific value. Thus, as Karl Popper argued, "*there can be no ultimate statements in science*: there can be no statements in science that cannot in principle be refuted, by falsifying some of the conclusions that can be deduced from them."[67] Science discounts creationism because, in answer to the tough questions presented by the data, creationists offer God as the ultimate nonfalsifiable explanation.[68] But this dismissive attitude also obscures the bias that science, and positivism generally, bring to the question of human origin: What counts as a "tough question"? For those committed to evolution, a tough question is one that cannot be explained by reasoning within the framework of the neo-Darwinist paradigm. Take, for example, the much discussed "gaps" in the fossil record. Evolutionists maintain that human life evolved by random mutation from less complex forms of life. However, little of what the neo-Darwinist paradigm would lead one to expect in the geological record is actually present there.[69] This fossil gap is a puzzle to be solved, but only because evolutionary assumptions themselves demand some explanation consistent with the general hypothesis.[70] For creationists, however, the gap poses no problem. Rather, the gap is evidence of the validity of a different paradigm, one that assumes a master plan implemented by an omnipotent cosmic creator.[71] The circularity of the argument that evolution is objective is unmistakable: An explanation of the fossil gap that is more or less consistent with the evolutionary paradigm will validate this paradigm, but it is the evolutionary paradigm itself that first defines the gap as a "problem" and then delimits the range of acceptable solutions.

The scientific requirement that statements be falsifiable creates a troublesome epistemological problem in light of the fact-theory antinomy: how can one know whether a negative observation is simply a minor aberration to be accounted for by a subsidiary hypothesis, or whether it falsifies the principle theory itself?[72] The raw empirical data about the origin of human life—the "facts," so-called—have no meaning in and of themselves. This is a consequence of the postmodern contention that things in the world have no self-declaring, intelligible essence. It is only by imposing some order on the data by use of the neo-Darwinist paradigm that the data come to have meaning; the different meaning that might come from imposing the creationist paradigm on the same data is rejected because evolution explains the data "better." Yet, if the data have no intrinsic meaning independent of the paradigm imposed on them, how can one discern the greater explanatory power of neo-Darwinism over creationism or some other paradigm? Ruth Anna Putnam describes the conundrum well:

Every experimenter when he turns to construct a theory to fit his data discards some of the latter as erroneous; often he can identify a cause (or a likely cause) of the error, but there are times when data are rejected simply because they do not fit . . . . At which point does this sort of thing turn into "the theory justifies the data," thereby undermining the very integrity of science? At what point do facts which are to be the foundation of science turn into fictions?[73]

Phillip Johnson repeatedly demonstrates that this is precisely the dilemma confronting evolutionists, and that they uniformly resolve it in favor of defending neo-Darwinism.[74] The allocation of creationism to the marginalized world of subjectivity, and evolution to the privileged world of objectivity, seems natural within the framework of secular individualist discourse, but appears biased and contingent when seen through the lens of religious communitarianism. The plausibility of assertions of "neutrality" here depends on the discourse within which one is operating.[75] Evolution is epistemologically preferred in secular individualist discourse because it purports to appeal to rationality and observation (thereby presenting itself as objective knowledge) rather than to a nonfalsifiable cause like God (which is subjective belief). Nevertheless, the bias against such explanations is arbitrary in its rejection of the transcendent as a source of knowledge, as Paul Davies pointed out:

The religious person, who is comfortable with the notion of God's work all around him every day, finds nothing incongruous about miraculous events because they are simply another facet of God's action in the world. In contrast the scientist, who prefers to think of the world as operating according to natural laws, would regard a miracle as a "misbehaviour," a pathological event which mars the elegance and beauty of nature. Miracles are something that most scientists would rather do without.[76]

There is no objective justification for privileging evolution over creationism. Evolution owes its status as the only "factual" account of the origin of human and other life, not to objective reasoning and empirical observation, but rather to rules of scientific discourse that govern what does, and does not, count as valid argument and proper evidence. These rules are constituted by a drawing of the boundary between public and private that places science in the privileged public realm while relegating religion to marginalized private life. In this scheme, creationist positions are out of order because they rely on belief.[77] Only manipulation of the boundary drawn between public knowledge and private belief enables the Supreme Court in *Edwards* to invest evolution as the only valid account of human origin.

. . *b* . .

In *Employment Division v. Smith*,[78] two Native American drug counselors who had been fired by the clinic where they worked for religious use of peyote were denied unemployment compensation. The state of Oregon maintained that because use of peyote constituted criminal conduct under the state penal code, use of the drug for any reason constituted misconduct for which unemployment benefits could be denied. The counselors, on the other hand, argued that the free exercise clause precluded the state from denying them compensation because the act for which they were dismissed constituted an element of their religious worship. Abandoning a generation of precedent,[79] the Supreme Court held in an opinion by Justice Scalia that the free exercise clause does not require that government exempt religious believers from complying with generally applicable law that unintentionally penalizes religious worship, even when the government's regulatory interest is not very important.[80] The Court suggested that such exemptions are not only unworkable but threatening to political order in a religiously plural society, declaring that government in the United States "cannot afford the luxury of deeming presumptively invalid, as applied to a religious objector, every regulation of conduct that does not protect an interest of the highest order."[81] According to the Court, the hardships that minority religions suffer under generally applicable laws are simply an "un-avoidable consequence of democratic government."[82]

As in *Edwards*, the specter of social chaos made a crucial early appearance in *Smith*. The Court began its analysis by quoting with approval language from a World War II decision, *Board of Education v. Gobitis*, which suggested that compliance with the law reflects a value higher than obedience to religious conscience.[83] The Court then quoted language from *Reynolds v. United States* to the effect that permitting religious exemptions would lead to anarchy[84] and drew exactly that conclusion for the contemporary United States.[85]

These dire warnings of the dangers of free exercise exemptions are curious, because life under the exemption doctrine abandoned by *Smith* had hardly been chaotic. On the contrary, surprisingly few exemption cases reached the Supreme Court, and religious objectors lost virtually all of them.[86] These predictions of chaos, then, may have been based upon a fear of the consequences that would likely ensue if the exemption doctrine were to be rigorously applied—far too many people would qualify for exemptions, effectively subverting many legislative and regulatory schemes.[87] As I discuss in more detail in chapter 6, the exemption doctrine was not generally understood to encompass the situation in which government action burdened the religious practices of large numbers of people. In that event the prospective beneficiaries of such an exemption, by virtue of their numbers, would have an effective remedy in the legislature and thus would have no need for judicial protection of their religious practices.[88] Thus, a constitutional policy of exemptions could represent a threat to political order only if one assumes that exemptions would be sought by numerous nonbelievers on the basis of false claims of religious belief that the Court would be unable to detect. In this light, the Court's fear of political chaos suggests that religion is a taste or preference that people will affect in order to take advantage of an exemption from general law. The picture of religion that emerges is that of a cynical, disintegrating force bent on subverting the dreadful majesty of "Law."

Milner Ball has observed that a fear that too many people will claim the protection of constitutional rights is increasingly animating the Court's opinions in free exercise jurisprudence as well as other doctrinal areas.[89] Professor Ball deplores this as a fear of " 'too much justice.' "[90] Given Justice Scalia's oft-expressed distaste for judicial balancing, however, he may well see even a small number of dissenters seeking exemption or excuse from complying with generally applicable laws as putting too much discretion in the hands of federal courts at the expense of the democratically elected Congress and state legislatures that enact such laws.[91] From this point of view, exemptions may be problematic even if not sought by large numbers of people, although it still seems unlikely that they would result in "chaos."

This image of social disintegration is the likely explanation for the Court's fixation with the criminal character of peyote use despite its irrelevance to the question whether persons fired for such use should receive unemployment benefits under state law. The counselors in *Smith* were not seeking an exemption to escape prosecution, but only to receive benefits. Moreover, the state supreme court had determined that the purpose of the "misconduct" provision was not to reinforce the criminal law, but merely to protect the financial integrity of the unemployment compensation fund. If the counselors were denied benefits to protect the fund, then the fact that their dismissal was for prohibited criminal conduct rather than nonprohibited but civilly actionable conduct is irrelevant, as the state court concluded.[92] The relevant consideration is whether the counselors' conduct was so widespread as to threaten depletion of the fund if benefits were paid to them and others similarly situated.[93]

"Law and order" is not a self-defining concept. Absolute order, or something close to it, can be maintained over short periods of time by eliminating civil liberties. Presumably the Court does not intend to gut the entire Bill of Rights. Short of that, what does "absolute order" mean? Absence of crime? Of political dissent? Of antigovernment agitation? Of "social diseases" like alcoholism, drug addiction, or

AIDS? The Court has chosen one stopping point on an artificial continuum between anarchy and order and denied religious exemptions because they appear to threaten one particular conception of order. There are, of course, conceptions of order that religious exemptions do not threaten. For example, one can conceive of a society in which the religious beliefs of its citizens are taken into account in assessing guilt or innocence under the criminal law.[94] One can even conceive of order as demanding the opposite of the Court's holding in *Smith*—that is, one in which religious people are excused from complying with generally applicable laws that contradict their religious beliefs, and are further insulated from civil and social penalties for such noncompliance. Formally, at least, this is the regime under which the United States lived from 1963 to 1990—without anarchy.

Without exemptions, some religious groups will simply be crushed by the weight of majoritarian law and culture. These groups, at least, pose no threat to order. However, majoritarian dominance could radicalize some believers into destabilizing, antisocial activity, including violence.[95] Thus, preserving order by refusing to protect religiously conscientious acts from penalties imposed by generally applicable law potentially undermines the very order that such a no-exemption scheme purports to preserve. In the long run, one can conceive of religious exemptions as preserving order as easily as subverting it.

The Court's conception of order appears most arbitrary in its resurrection of the belief-action distinction which first appeared in *Reynolds*: "Laws are made for the government of actions, and while they cannot interfere with mere religious belief and opinions, they may with practices."[96] A plausible difference between beliefs and actions can be maintained only if one limits belief to purely mental activity. But the Court does not draw the line here, nor could it have: a right that protects only belief is not a right.[97] Instead, the Court stated that "government may not compel *affirmation* of religious belief [or] punish the *expression* of religious doctrines it believes to be false."[98] So, even the Court concedes that the free exercise clause protects "pure" religious speech, including the right not to speak. However, the act of speaking—or of not speaking, for that matter—is still one that impacts the world outside of the mind. Why is the Court willing to protect the act of speaking but not other acts, like the sacramental smoking of peyote in the Native American Church?

A well-developed, if somewhat unevenly applied, First Amendment doctrine extends protection to acts with a significant expressive or communicative dimension—so-called hybrid speech.[99] Smoking peyote, as the central sacrament of the Native American Church, might be characterized as a positive "expression" of Smith's religious beliefs, not unlike how burning—or, for that matter, displaying—the flag expresses negative (or positive) political views about the United States.[100] A variety of arguments have been advanced in favor of outlawing flag desecration, but no one has (yet) suggested that flagburning is unprotected under the First Amendment because it constitutes action rather than belief.

Why, then, is the *Smith* Court's conception of order preferable? Indeed, why is it so clearly preferable that the Court felt confident in asserting it virtually without argument? The Court invoked necessity—that is, the argument that political order in the United States will disintegrate without the elimination of religious exemptions. For example, the Court maintained that it would be impossible to distinguish those who might deserve exemptions, such as the Amish in *Yoder*, from those who do not. Thus, exemptions cannot be granted to anyone if order is to be maintained. Note that the Court did not suggest that the Amish and other religious objectors are not deserving, but only that we cannot tell them apart from the insincere who the Court apparently feared would rush to take advantage of religious exemptions.

It has never been shown that false claims of religious belief are a serious enforcement problem, despite the Court's refusal to examine the reasonableness of particular beliefs.[101] In many areas the Court has eliminated or diluted the potential for false claims by imposing an alternative burden on those granted exemptions which is equal to or more onerous than the one required by law. As Morris Clark sensibly observed, "When it is equally burdensome or more burdensome to claim a religious exemption than not to claim it, there is no motive for fraudulent claims or claims by those with very minor conscientious scruples."[102] Even in the area of tax law, where claims for exemption coincide with financial self-interest, neither the IRS nor the Court seems to have been unduly hindered by free exercise considerations.[103] But granting the premise that the deserving cannot be distinguished from the undeserving, it does not follow that we should penalize the deserving by indiscriminately denying exemptions to everyone. One could argue with equal plausibility that we should grant exemptions even to the undeserving. Constitutional law is full of overly inclusive rules whose articulation and application protect the undeserving as well as the deserving. Requiring proof of "actual malice" in libel cases protects *The National Enquirer* as well as *The New York Times*;[104] the various exclusionary rules that protect interests under the Fourth and Fifth Amendments probably set free more guilty people than innocent ones;[105] and freedom of speech protects pornography as well as political speech.[106]

These kinds of overly broad constitutional rules presume that the values the rules protect are so important that it is worth the risk of protecting some undeserving people precisely to ensure that deserving people are *never* denied constitutional protection.[107] There is a cost to this, to be sure, but it is not the breakdown of political order into violence and chaos. Indeed, the choice is not between order and chaos, but between different conceptions of order. The *Smith* Court had a strong preference for the interests of the modern regulatory state—one that is shared, ironically, with some liberals.[108] The Court avoided explaining why one should prefer its conception of order over the many possible alternatives by falsely presenting it as the only viable alternative to chaos.

· · 4 · ·

The installation of secular individualism as the discourse governing church-state relations in the United States did not simply grant it a privilege over religious communitarianism; it caused religious communitarian discourse to disappear as a realistic and coherent alternative. The Supreme Court's attempts to justify even religious communitarian results with secular individualist arguments, which I will discuss in the following chapters, can be explained by the apparent naturalness and inevitability of secular individualist ideology: to decide church-state controversies with another normative conception of church-state relations rooted in an opposing conceptual world seems absurd and, therefore, indefensible, even when the Court disagrees with the constitutional result indicated by secular individualist discourse. This same naturalness and inevitability make it difficult to formulate persuasive criticisms of the Court's decisions, especially those that are fully consistent with secular individualism; one does not, after all, *criticize* Nature. As Stanley Fish has observed, "It is here that the real power resides, in whatever vocabulary has so permeated the culture that it seems simply descriptive of independent realities."[109]

Few indictments of government policy are more powerful in the contemporary United States than a demonstration that policy discriminates unfairly. The privatization of religion by secular individualist discourse is an act of power that can plausibly be defended as religiously neutral only if religion is presented as a "naturally" private activity, excluded from public life like all value preferences. Within religious communitarian discourse, by contrast, where religion has important public dimensions, privatization constitutes bald—and unwise—religious persecution. Subverting the natural appearance of privileging secular individualist discourse over religious communitarian discourse opens a critical distance from the Court's religion clause jurisprudence which enables analysis and criticism of it from a perspective outside of secular individualism.[110]

Chapter 3

. . . . .

Neutrality as Manipulation:

Parochial School Aid and Equal Access

. . . . .

For over twenty years after *Everson v. Board of Education*,[1] the Supreme Court measured the constitutionality of governmental action under the establishment clause by analyzing whether such action was secular in its purpose and primary impact.[2] The Court later added a third consideration, whether governmental action required or implied a constitutionally dangerous relationship between religion and government.[3] In *Lemon v. Kurtzman* the Court synthesized its prior decisions into a three-pronged test centered on the idea of neutrality first articulated in *Everson:* To escape constitutional invalidation under the establishment clause, governmental action must (1) have a secular purpose that neither endorses nor disapproves of religion, (2) have a primary effect that neither advances nor inhibits religion, and (3) avoid creating a relationship between religion and government that threatens to entangle either in the affairs of the other.[4]

The Court has been widely criticized for its establishment clause decisions under *Lemon*, especially those involving financial aid to private religious schools.[5] These criticisms are misdirected, since they presuppose that *Lemon's* doctrinal formulation of neutrality is the source of these contradictory decisions. This is an unlikely assumption. Any use of language, no matter how specific and constrained, can always be made to appear sufficiently ambiguous to permit plausible arguments leading to mutually inconsistent interpretations.[6] Constitutional interpretation exemplifies this thesis of linguistic indeterminacy, and no amount of doctrinal refinement is likely to reduce the indeterminacy of any constitutional test.[7] In fact, most of the Court's recent decisions that do not rely on *Lemon* have not yielded results different from what one would have expected had the test been applied.[8] If one wishes to discover what is generating the results in the Court's financial aid decisions, one must look beyond *Lemon* and any other doctrinal test.

I will argue in this chapter that the Supreme Court possesses two opposing conceptions of neutrality between which it oscillates in financial aid cases, all the while applying the same doctrinal test. The apparent inconsistency of results in the Court's financial aid cases stems from the Court's alternating use of these competing conceptions from one case to the next. I will argue further that what drives the choice of one conception of neutrality over the other in the financial aid decisions is an analytic preference for secular individualism. Both the results and the rationales of the Court's decisions regarding financial aid to private religious elementary and secondary schools fit well within secular individualist discourse. For these decisions to be defensible in terms of neutrality, however, it must be the case that government aid to public education is insignificant. This implausible assumption is implicit in the Court's decisions in this area, robbing them of most of their persuasive power.

. . 1 . .

Since direct financial support of churches by government was emblematic of the Anglican establishment, government grants of financial or other tangible aid to religious groups have always been among the most suspect of government actions under the establishment clause. In modern establishment clause jurisprudence, direct financial aid by government to religion has most often come before the Supreme Court in the form of state grants to religious schools, especially Roman Catholic parochial schools. The state can always articulate plausible social welfare purposes for such grants, such as promotion of " 'educational programs which are important to our national defense and the general welfare of the state,' " or "furtherance of the educational opportunities available to the young."[9] Variations of these legislative purposes have been found to satisfy the secular purpose test in virtually every financial aid case reviewed by the Court, and the Court routinely accepts the secular purpose that the legislature articulates for private school aid programs even when it finds these programs to violate the establishment clause on other grounds.[10] Accordingly, litigation of the constitutionality of such programs under the establishment clause has centered on whether their primary effect is one that advances religion, and on whether they create an entangling relationship between the government grantor and the religious recipient. Predictably, the Court has developed two separate arguments against financial aid to religious schools, one based on each remaining prong of the *Lemon* test.

. . *a* . .

The premise of the primary effect argument is that private religious elementary and secondary schools—which for brevity I will refer to as "parochial" even though many sponsors of such schools are not Roman Catholic—exist principally to inculcate their students with the religious beliefs and values of the sponsoring religion.[11] In the view of the Court, such schools are so "pervasively sectarian," to use the language of the decisions, that direct aid to them necessarily constitutes direct aid to the schools' efforts to teach religious values to their students.[12] For example, in *Hunt v. McNair*, the Court stated that "aid normally may be thought to have a primary effect of advancing religion when it flows to an institution in which religion is so pervasive that a substantial portion of its functions are subsumed in the religious mission."[13] Thus, financial aid that flows directly to parochial schools advances religion in violation of the primary effect prong of *Lemon*.

The cases suggest that financial aid programs designed to benefit parochial schools are constitutional under the establishment clause only if the aid is given to parochial school students or their parents, rather than to the school itself.[14] The importance of this distinction was evident in *Board of Education v. Allen*, in which the Court reviewed a textbook loan program pursuant to which the state supplied secular books free of charge to students in both public and private schools.[15] A divided Court upheld the program under the establishment clause, but both the majority and the dissenters agreed that the crucial determination was whether the aid was properly characterized as flowing to the students or to the parochial schools. The majority emphasized that "books are furnished at the request of the pupil and ownership remains, at least technically, in the State. Thus no funds or books are furnished to parochial schools, and the financial benefit is to parents and children, not to schools."[16] By contrast, the dissenters characterized the program as supplying for the benefit of the parochial school particular textbooks that the school approved and requested, presumably on the basis of sectarian considerations.[17]

In the years since *Allen*, the Court has repeatedly affirmed the importance of the individual-institutional distinction to the constitutionality of parochial school aid programs.[18] In only two decisions, *Committee for Public Education v. Regan* and *Wolman v. Walter*, has the Court found direct aid to parochial schools constitutional under the establishment clause,[19] and then only because the Justices were convinced that the aid could not under any circumstances be diverted to the schools' religious mission. In these decisions, which involved the preparation, administration, and scoring of state-mandated standardized tests, the Court determined that the parochial schools' lack of control over the preparation of the tests guaranteed that religious beliefs would not be tested.[20] Although the *Regan* program provided for grading of some of the exams by parochial school teachers, as well as for cash reimbursements to the schools for expenses incurred in administering the tests, the Court found that the standardized, objective nature of the test questions ensured that religious considerations would not influence the grades;[21] it further found that a required state

audit of the reimbursement funds required by the program was sufficient to verify that the funds were not used for religious purposes.[22]
In *Wolman* these issues did not arise because the testing program was
wholly administered by the state.[23]

One corollary to the requirement that parochial school aid be channeled to students rather than to schools is that the class of individuals
benefited by the aid program must be broadly and secularly defined.
For example, the Court distinguished the aid programs struck down
in *Committee for Public Education v. Nyquist* from those upheld in
Everson and *Allen* by emphasizing that in the latter cases, the aid
was supplied "in common to all citizens," so that "the class of beneficiaries included *all* schoolchildren, those in public as well as private
school," whereas the programs in *Nyquist* were by their terms available only to parochial school students and their parents.[24] Similarly,
in upholding a personal tax deduction for certain expenses of public
and private education in *Mueller v. Allen*, the Court emphasized that
the deduction was available to "*all* parents," regardless of where their
children went to school.[25] By contrast, the Court generally strikes
down aid programs that define the beneficiaries narrowly in terms of
attendance at parochial or private schools. Most aid programs upheld
by the Court have merely included parochial school students with
public school students in a secularly defined class of beneficiaries.[26]

The reason for this requirement seems to be the Court's recognition that parochial schools benefit substantially, if indirectly, even
when aid flows to students or their parents rather than to the schools
themselves. In *Wolman*, for example, the Court stated that "a meaningful distinction cannot be drawn between equipment used on a collective basis and that used individually. All materials and equipment
must be used to supplement courses, and their value derives from the
support they provide to the collective educational enterprise."[27] Aid
to a beneficiary class defined in terms of parochial school attendance
is aid to parochial schools in both effect and intent and, therefore, aid
to the schools' religious mission.[28] Michael McConnell and Richard
Posner explain that a payment to parents or students, even when it is
for a clearly secular service like bus transportation,

lowers the full price to the student and his parents of attending parochial school, and thereby increases their willingness to pay for the tuition component. The school may therefore be able to raise tuition without losing students, and if it uses the additional tuition to reduce the subsidy needed from the church or to increase expenditures on religious activities, it will have appropriated for religious uses some or all of the benefit of the transportation subsidy.[29]

On the other hand, aid to a broad, secularly defined beneficiary class is thought to benefit the schools only incidentally, pursuant to the provision of social welfare benefits available to all on a religiously neutral basis.[30] Accordingly, aid under programs with religiously defined beneficiary classes has been held by the Court to violate the establishment clause even though the aid is directed to students and their parents.[31] Requiring that the beneficiary class be defined by secular rather than religious criteria, and that it include many indi‑viduals besides those associated with parochial schools, ensures that the prohibition on direct institutional aid cannot be evaded by the formal expedient of routing the aid through students or their parents. As the Court observed in *Wolman*, allowing states to avoid establishment clause prohibitions merely by channeling aid through parochial school students and their parents "would exalt form over substance."[32]

The only exceptions to the requirement of broad, secularly defined beneficiary classes have come when the aid has extended specific services to parochial school students that were already being provided to public school students.[33] The nature of such programs obviously requires that their beneficiaries be described in terms of attendance at private schools. Nevertheless, even though it upheld such programs, the Court insisted that if the services provided by the state are not merely ministerial,[34] they must be administratively and physically separated from the parochial school.[35] This enables the services to be described as delivered directly to the students rather than to the schools. Services that are integrated either administratively or physically into parochial schools continue to be struck down by the Court.[36]

The individual-institutional distinction explains many of the seemingly inconsistent holdings of the parochial school aid cases.[37] The busing and loan programs of *Everson* and *Allen* directed aid to a broad, secularly defined beneficiary class that included both public and parochial school students. By contrast, the busing and loan programs with which *Everson* and *Allen* are typically compared directed aid to a narrow beneficiary class that consisted mostly of parochial schools. From this standpoint, then, it is unremarkable that the former were upheld and the latter struck down under the establishment clause, despite the similarity of the aid granted in both situations. When religious people receive government assistance that is generally available to anyone irrespective of religious belief, "the chain of unconstitutionality is broken by the intervention of individual choice."[38]

. . *b* . .

When the Court began to develop its financial aid jurisprudence in the 1960s, it was not immediately clear that channeling aid directly to religious institutions was the sine qua non of constitutionality under the establishment clause. Accordingly, in response to the Supreme Court's early decisions developing the primary effect argument, many states continued to enact programs that granted aid directly to parochial schools, but tailored those programs so that the aid could be used only for specific educational purposes— usually to fund state-mandated materials and services—unrelated to the school's mission of teaching religious values. Two such programs, for example, sought to supplement by direct cash grants or reimbursements the salaries of parochial school teachers who taught secular subjects.[39] Another program sought to provide state-mandated educational materials and services free of charge to parochial schools.[40] These programs typically contained detailed restrictions and conditions on receipt and use of the aid.[41]

The Court might have held these second-order aid programs unconstitutional on the same ground as the first-order ones, as financial aid to pervasively sectarian organizations. Without the aid, religious schools would have had to pay for the government-funded services with privately raised funds. With government grants, more private funds were available for parochial schools to pursue directly their religious mission.[42] Justice Douglas succinctly summarized this "fungibility" argument in a concurring opinion in Lemon: "The [parochial] school is an organism living on one budget. What the taxpayers give for salaries of those who teach only the humanities or science without any trace of proselytizing enables the school to use all of its own funds for religious training."[43] Thus, it can be argued that even narrowly tailored aid programs free funds for sectarian education that otherwise would be used to pay for state-mandated services, thereby causing a primary effect of advancing religion.

The Court, however, chose a different tack. It observed that the usual effect of the spending controls built into these second-order aid programs was to impede the religious recipients' ability to carry out their primary religious mission, as well as to require secular state authorities regularly to monitor and to audit how such schools spend their funds and implement their religious mission on a day-to-day basis.[44] The Court has held that this is an unacceptable entanglement of the state in the affairs of the parochial school.[45]

The Court's application of the entanglement prong of Lemon ensnares parochial schools in a constitutional catch-22 with respect to financial aid programs. If the aid comes without a means of ensuring that it will not be used to advance the religious mission of the parochial school, it will not run afoul of the entanglement prong, but the Court will almost certainly find the aid unconstitutional under the primary effect prong. For example, in Grand Rapids School District v. Ball, enrichment and extracurricular courses taught in parochial school classrooms by public school employees were found to violate the establishment clause because, inter alia, the courses were not monitored for religious content.[46] If, on the other hand, a means is provided that guarantees the aid will not be used directly to advance the religious mission of the school, the Court will almost certainly find the aid unconstitutional under the entanglement prong. Thus, in Aguilar v. Felton, a companion case to Grand Rapids School District, the Court held it an excessive entanglement with religion for the state to monitor employees who were providing remedial help to parochial school students to ensure that they did not teach religion.[47] Although the Court has held that programs designed to aid parochial schools do not violate the establishment clause when it can be shown that the aid does not directly support the religious mission of such schools, the entanglement prong ensures that in most cases this very showing will result in a violation of the establishment clause. Indeed, in only one parochial school aid decision has the Court held that a monitoring device that sought to guarantee that aid would not advance religion did not also result in a finding of excessive entanglement.[48]

. . 2 . .

Secular individualist discourse assumes that, although individuals may choose to be religious in private life, there is no public role for religion beyond the effect of private choice. Government and other social institutions are constituted by private preferences, not vice versa. Accordingly, attempts by government to influence preferences in private life are illegitimate, unless the exercise of these preferences generates actionable harm to others.

The Supreme Court's decisions holding that parochial aid programs are constitutional only when the aid is channeled to individuals pursuant to a broad, secularly defined beneficiary class are perfectly consonant with secular individualist ideology. So are the analogous equal-access decisions holding that religious activities and organizations are entitled to the same kind of access to public school facilities as is given to other (secular) extracurricular activities or off-campus organizations.[49] Such a rule ensures that whatever religious institutions exist in American society exist as the consequence of the undistorted private choices of religious Americans. As McConnell and Posner observed, "neutrality reduces (and in theory eliminates) the impact that government action has upon individual choice with respect to religion."[50] Donald Gianella agreed, arguing that only if the government is neutral with respect to religion can society be sure "that the capacity of religious ideas to shape our culture depends on society's free and informed response to them rather than on the failure of the state to grant them equality of treatment with competing ideas."[51]

This private choice analysis is explicit in *Mueller v. Allen.* Conceding that a tax deduction to the parents of parochial school students "ultimately has an economic effect comparable to that of aid given directly to the schools attended by their children,"[52] the Court nevertheless held that the deduction did not violate the establishment clause. Because the deduction was available to the parents of public as well as parochial school students, it did not skew parental choice in favor of parochial schools. Thus, whatever financial assistance parochial schools received from the deduction can be considered the result of private rather than governmental choice: "The historic purposes of the Clause simply do not encompass the sort of attenuated financial benefit, ultimately controlled by the private choices of individual parents, that eventually flows to parochial schools from the neutrally available tax benefit at issue in this case."[53]

The Court relied on a virtually identical analysis in *Witters v. Department of Services for the Blind.*[54] *Witters* involved review of vocational rehabilitation assistance by the state of Washington to a visually handicapped student studying for the ministry at a Bible college, rather than aid to parochial school students or parents. However, since the college was apparently sectarian—it was named "Inland Empire School of the Bible" and the Court referred to it several times as a "Christian college"[55]—the decision is analytically identical to the parochial school aid cases. The Court found that "vocational assistance provided under the Washington program is paid directly to the student, who transmits it to the educational institution of his or her choice. Any aid provided under Washington's program that ultimately flows to religious institutions does so only as a result of the genuinely independent and private choices of aid recipients."[56] Accordingly, the Court held on these facts that it was inappropriate to view the financial benefit ultimately received by the Bible college from the individual rehabilitation grant as "resulting from a *state* action sponsoring or subsidizing religion."[57] To the contrary, such financial aid funds the private choices of individuals (including religious individuals), and only incidentally the educational institutions (including religious colleges) that are the beneficiaries of these choices.[58]

In still another case, *Zobrist v. Catalina Foothills School District*, the Court considered whether supplying a statutorily mandated sign-language interpreter to a deaf student at a Roman Catholic high school violated the establishment clause.[59] Noting that these interpreters are supplied pursuant to "a general government program that distributes benefits neutrally . . . without regard to the 'sectarian-nonsectarian, or public-nonpublic nature' of the school the child attends," and that any such interpreter "will be present in a sectarian school only as a result of the private decision of individual parents," the Court held that furnishing interpreters to otherwise qualified parochial school students did not violate the establishment clause.[60]

A similar analysis is evident in the equal-access decisions. Although the Court has confirmed that religious groups and individuals are entitled to the same after-hours access to and use of public education facilities as secular groups and individuals, the Court has been careful to emphasize the same touchstone of private choice that it relies on in financial aid cases. So long as religious groups are only one of many different groups permitted to use the facilities, the Court deems any benefit accruing to religion as "incidental," the result of private rather than public action. In *Widmar v. Vincent*, for example, the Court considered a challenge to a university policy that made its facilities available to all registered student groups except religious ones.[61] The university defended the rule on the theory that allowing religious groups to use its facilities would have had a primary effect of advancing religion in violation of the establishment clause.[62] The Court rejected this argument, observing that "an open forum in a public university does not confer any imprimatur of state approval on religious sects or practices," so long as "the forum is available to a broad class of nonreligious as well as religious speakers."[63] The Court pointed out that, in contrast to situations in which religious groups are the only ones allowed on government property, granting access to a public forum on a viewpoint-neutral basis communicates no government endorsement of the ideas aired in the forum.[64] Justice O'Connor made the same response to the same argument for a plurality of the Court in *Westside Community Board of Education v. Mergens*, which held that a school district's refusal to permit high school students to form a Bible study and prayer group as an extracurricular club violated the Equal Access Act: "There is a crucial difference between *government* speech endorsing religion, which the Establishment Clause forbids, and *private* speech endorsing religion, which the Free Speech and Free Exercise Clauses protect."[65] Noting the "broad spectrum of officially recognized student clubs" at the high school, as well as student freedom "to initiate and organize additional student clubs," the plurality determined that permitting a religious club to meet after school just like any other club "does not convey a message of state approval or endorsement of the particular religion."[66] *Lamb's Chapel v. Center Moriches School District* similarly held that the showing of a Christian-oriented film series at a public high school would not constitute government endorsement so long as the school was generally open for use by secular as well as religious groups, and the showing was after school hours and open to the general public.[67]

The cases in which the Court has found financial aid unconstitutional under the establishment clause all rely on secular individualist discourse to justify their decisions. For example, aid to individuals pursuant to narrow, religiously defined beneficiary classes, which the Court has generally struck down, is inconsistent with secular individualist discourse. Such aid skews individual choice toward parochial schools by providing financial incentives to parochial school attendance that do not exist for public school attendance. The number and vitality of parochial schools under such circumstances are not arguably the result of private choice, but rather of some combination of private choice and the distorting effects of government aid. Likewise, channeling aid to parochial schools directly, which the Court has also refused to permit, bypasses individual choice and presents the possibility that parochial schools receive more government aid than they would if the aid were first given to individuals who could then choose between parochial schools, secular private schools, and public schools.

Again, the popularity of parochial schools under such circumstances cannot be argued to be the result of private choice, but rather the consequence of government aid. Similarly, although the Court has not considered any "unequal access" cases, there is little doubt that granting access only to religious groups would violate the establishment clause.[68] Allowing such access could not be justified with secular individualist discourse, since one could not be confident that individual citizen choice to participate in the favored religious groups would be unaffected by the privileged access to public education facilities.

The Court has extended this argument to the distorting effects of mere government association with religion in some institutional aid cases, although it uniformly rejects it in equal-access cases. In *Grand Rapids School District*, for example, the Court found that institutional aid violated the establishment clause, not because it bypassed individual choice, but in part because the direct financial assistance of parochial schools by government would be widely perceived as a government "endorsement" or "encouragement" of parochial schools.[69] Thus, even if the financial distortions exerted on individual choice by an aid program are otherwise insignificant, the Court has determined that the alignment of government power for or against religion that is implied by direct aid to parochial schools is itself a distortion of such choice and, as such, violates the primary effect prong of *Lemon*.[70]

The problem with the parochial school aid and the equal access cases, then, is not ideological inconsistency. They coincide in almost every respect with the norms of secular individualism. The difficulty with these cases is rhetorical incredibility. Although the Court insists that its decisions in this area are "neutral" as between religion and nonreligion,[71] it is impossible to demonstrate the neutrality of the Court's holdings except by making implausible assumptions about the proper role and behavior of contemporary government.

· · 3 · ·

The parochial school aid and equal-access cases provide a particular example of a general problem that haunts the Supreme Court's decisions under the establishment clause: How does one identify the baseline measure of religious neutrality? Or, as McConnell and Posner have succinctly summarized the point, "To determine whether religion has been 'aided' or 'penalized' . . . one needs a baseline: 'aid' or 'penalty' as compared to what?"[72] To measure whether government has violated the neutrality principle, one must have a starting point that defines neutrality; departure from this point would therefore constitute a violation of the principle.[73]

With respect to direct financial aid, Professor Gianella suggested that in a world in which no individuals or nongovernmental organizations receive any governmental aid whatsoever, any aid to religion, whether to religious individuals or to religious organizations, would depart from the baseline of no-aid and violate *Everson's* neutrality principle.[74] By contrast, the neutrality principle would require a wholly collectivized state that subscribed to the principle of religious liberty to extend to religious organizations aid comparable to that generally given to nonreligious organizations, "in order that they might have appropriate and substantially equal opportunities for self-development."[75] In the modern welfare state that the contemporary United States has become, government aid to both individuals and organizations is widespread and pervasive. Since in the United States most persons and entities are entitled to some kind of government aid, religious neutrality would generally seem to require that this aid not be denied to otherwise qualified recipients simply because they are religious. Indeed, to deny aid to such persons and entities constitutes a tax on religious exercise which skews private choice *away* from religion.[76]

An analogous interpretation is available for cases that present the problem of religious access to the facilities of public education. If one were to imagine a world of minimalist government in which secular public schools did not exist, then government action mandating religious instruction or participation in religious education would violate neutrality. If, on the other hand, all children were wards of the state, with government providing for literally all of their needs, then the neutrality principle would require that opportunities for participation in religious worship and instruction be provided by the government for those who request it.[77] This argument is used to defend government-employed and -compensated chaplains in the military: because members of the military are subject to substantial restrictions on their activities, the government may compensate for these restrictions by providing convenient access to religious counseling and worship.[78] As Professor Galanter generalized the point, "when government exercises total control, it may be required to provide opportunities for religious expression."[79] While children in the contemporary United States are hardly in the situation of wards of the state or even that of members of the armed forces, the state's control over children through secular public education and social welfare bureaucracies is still substantial. To the extent that this nonreligious influence is not balanced in some way, one can argue that the neutrality principle is violated.[80]

The parochial school aid cases, at least, suggest that the Court does not consistently use the same baseline when it measures the religious neutrality of parochial school aid under the *Lemon* test. It generally uses a baseline of pervasive aid when it measures the neutrality of financial aid to religious individuals, which leads easily to the conclusion that such individuals must be granted access to such aid if religious neutrality is to be maintained. When measuring direct financial aid to parochial schools, however, the Court generally reasons from a baseline of no-aid, which leads just as easily in the opposite direction, to the conclusion that religious schools must be denied access to preserve religious neutrality.

The problem is that the no-aid baseline is implausible in the late twentieth century as a measure of the neutrality of government action. Stephen Carter accurately describes our world as one "in which regulation is everywhere" and derides as a "fantasy" the suggestion that careful religious citizens can avoid government regulations.[81] This is especially true of financial aid to elementary and secondary education. Public schools are supported by local tax dollars supplemented, in most cases substantially, by state and federal grants. Parents of parochial school students are not permitted to opt out of paying these taxes, and in very few states are they entitled to any tax relief despite the fact that they save local, state, and federal governments thousands of dollars by educating their children privately.[82] If one focuses on the entire educational system, including parochial as well as public schools, aid to the former can be understood as an attempt to equalize the tax burden of education costs between those parents who desire a secular education for their children and those who wish a religious education.[83] By this argument, neutrality between parochial schools and public schools clearly requires that parochial schools be apportioned a share of these tax dollars; if most schools receive government aid, then religiously neutral funding requires that parochial schools be eligible to receive it, too.[84]

Analysis of the equal-access cases is more complicated, because access can be understood as a financial benefit, a government response to indications of individual religious preference, or a compensation to those under government control for the skewing of values in a secular direction. The Court has relied only on the first two of these arguments. Viewing access purely as a financial benefit, the Court in *Lamb's Chapel* used a pervasive aid baseline in determining the after-hours use of public educational facilities by off-campus religious organizations, allowing such organizations access whenever secular organizations had access. Similarly, viewing access as a response to indications of religious preference by students, the Court in both *Widmar* and *Mergens* adopted a baseline that treated the expression of religious preferences in the same manner as the expression of nonreligious preferences.

However, viewing access as a kind of ideological compensation, one can argue that the Court violates the neutrality principle by refusing to allow public education to supply religious instruction or to give off-campus religious groups access to the public educational curriculum to supply such instruction.[85] In the United States, children are required to surrender thirty to thirty-five hours per week to formal instruction in secular public schools. They are required to spend additional hours completing secular educational assignments at home. Given the tremendous extent to which government is permitted to shape the preferences of children through secular public education, one could argue that neutrality requires some compensating or balancing action by religious groups in the form of access to the same value-shaping mechanism. As Alan Schwarz pointed out,

> The broad scope of the public school curriculum, the intense effect that curriculum has and is intended to have upon the value structure of all public school children, and the rigidly secular viewpoint there emphasized, provide some support to the contention that a secular religionism or antireligionism is being taught there, thus working a discrimination against at least all deistic religions.[86]

Under this analysis, release-time programs are not merely permissible, as the Court held in *Zorach v. Clauson*,[87] but required by the neutrality principle whenever students are released from school attendance for any purpose. More provocatively, the analysis suggests that neutrality can even be argued to require that religious instruction be made available to those students who desire it as part of the formal curriculum,[88] something the Court held unconstitutional in *McCollum v. Board of Education*.[89] For example, it is not difficult to construct a plausible neutrality baseline that permits a religious values approach to sex education in public schools, so long as secular approaches are available as well, and students are permitted to choose between them.

Let me emphasize that I am not making a normative policy argument here. I do not suggest either that parochial schools "ought" to receive public tax dollars to fund their operations, or that religious groups "ought" to receive privileged—or, indeed, any—access to public school facilities or curricula. These are controversial and complicated questions that I do not attempt to address here. My argument is merely that when parochial schools are denied tax dollars, or religious groups are denied access to the public school curriculum, it must be for a reason other than *Everson's* requirement of neutrality between religion and nonreligion. Not only does religious neutrality fail to justify the constitutional denial of direct government aid or compensating religious access under the establishment clause: it can be used to suggest the opposite result. Denying government aid to parochial schools is neutral only if one assumes that government funding of elementary and secondary education is insignificant. Similarly, denying religious groups access to the facilities or curriculum of public education under the establishment clause is neutral only if one assumes that public education itself plays an insignificant role in shaping the values of schoolchildren. Neither has been the situation in the United States for many years.

Chapter 4

. . . . .

The Religious as Secular:

Government Appropriation of Religion

. . . . .

"We are a religious people whose institutions presuppose a Supreme Being." So declared Justice Douglas in *Zorach v. Clauson* in a statement reminiscent of the de facto Protestant establishment. "When the state encourages religious instruction or cooperates with religious authorities by adjusting the schedule of public events to sectarian needs, it follows the best of our traditions. For it then respects the religious nature of our people and accommodates the public service to their spiritual needs."[1]

Against the ideal of neutrality trumpeted by *Everson*, Douglas's rhetoric sounded a discordant note. As it happens, *Zorach* was one of the last cases to rely openly on religious communitarian discourse to justify its decision. Within a decade, the Court began dismantling the de facto establishment. It began with public education, declaring in consecutive terms that prayer in public schools is unconstitutional.[2]

The Court later held that restricting the teaching of evolution in deference to religious sensibilities violated the establishment clause.[3] As we saw in chapter 3, it was shortly after this period that the Court began seriously to scrutinize financial aid to parochial schools and other religious educational institutions, declaring most of them unconstitutional.[4] By the early 1970s, public schools had been largely cleansed of overtly religious influences, parochial schools had been almost completely cut off from government aid, and secular individualism was firmly installed as the reigning discourse of establishment clause jurisprudence.

Although the Court has consistently adhered to these early holdings in subsequent decisions,[5] outside of the public school context the Court has not wholly abandoned the de facto establishment. It has confirmed the constitutionality of practices like Sunday closing laws,[6] legislative prayer,[7] and religious holiday displays.[8] The Court also has upheld certain kinds of direct financial aid to religious colleges and social service auxiliaries,[9] as well as religious property tax exemptions.[10] Each of these decisions is consistent with the noncoercive encouragement of majoritarian religious belief and practice that forms the ideological of religious communitarian discourse. After *Zorach*, however, the Court has generally defended these practices by reference to the secular individualist value of neutrality between religion and nonreligion rather than the religious communitarian value of encouraging socially valuable religion.

In other words, many of the Supreme Court's establishment clause decisions after *Zorach* defend results that are possible only within religious communitarian discourse with arguments that can be made only with secular individualist discourse. The only way one can defend with secular individualist discourse practices that clearly and disproportionately benefit religion is to argue that these practices are not really religious. This forces the Court into the awkward position of arguing the secularity of activities that seem indisputably religious, such as Sunday closing laws and the public display of religious symbols. These vestigial remains of the de facto establishment, understood by nineteenth-century Americans to encourage and reinforce the Protestant religious beliefs and practices on which society is founded, have been recharacterized by the contemporary Supreme Court as having essentially secular motivations and effects. Similarly, when the Court defends financial aid and tax exemptions for religious entities, as I will show in chapter 5, it feels the need to deny or to discount the spiritual motivations and character of the beneficiaries. The confusion in these decisions is the result of the Court's simultaneous reliance on two normative conceptions of church-state relations that are fundamentally irreconcilable.

. . 1 . .

"Separation of church and state" is now firmly established in American political consciousness, but there has always been controversy about precisely what this "separation" requires.[11] Although *Everson* identified neutrality as the defining value of the establishment clause, it was actually separation that drew the attention of the Court in its early establishment clause decisions.

Barely a year after *Everson*, the Supreme Court ruled on a released-time program of religious instruction in *McCollum v. Board of Education*.[12] Under this program, priests, ministers, and rabbis were authorized to come into public school classrooms each week to give religious instruction to students affiliated with their congregations. Students participating in the instruction remained in their classrooms; those choosing not to participate were required to leave their classrooms and go to some other location within the school to continue their secular studies.[13] The Court found this program unconstitutional under the establishment clause, emphasizing that the use of public school buildings for religious instruction and the reliance on compulsory attendance laws and truancy discipline to assure attendance at such instruction was "not separation of Church and State."[14]

Just four years after *McCollum*, the Court seemed to reverse its field in *Zorach*. In this case, students were excused from classes for an hour once each week to travel to religious instruction held off the public school campus, while nonparticipating students attended their normal classes.[15] The churches administering these classes were required to report any of those released for religious instruction who did not actually attend it.[16] In upholding the program, the Court reasoned that although the establishment clause prevented government financing of religion, it did not require opposition to efforts designed to enhance religious influence.[17] Since the *Zorach* program entailed only government cooperation with religion, without financial aid, the Court found it acceptable under the establishment clause.[18]

One obvious distinction between *McCollum* and *Zorach* is the uncompensated use of government buildings by religious groups in the former, but not in the latter. However, this distinction does not account for the fact that in both cases compulsory attendance laws reinforced released-time instruction by ensuring that students were released from their secular studies only if they engaged in religious studies.[19] Critics of *Zorach* accused the Court of abandoning *McCollum*, arguing that the mere removal of religious instruction to off-campus facilities should not have made a difference in the constitutionality of the program when substantial state assistance remained in the form of compulsory attendance laws.[20]

McCollum and *Zorach* illustrate the subtlety of establishment clause disputes that do not involve tangible financial aid to religion. In one sense, *McCollum* was an easy case because even if the released-time program in that case had not relied upon compulsory attendance laws, the substantial financial benefit represented by the participating religions' uncompensated use of public buildings open to no other group was probably sufficient by itself to cause an establishment clause violation. Financial assistance to religion was, after all, the hallmark of the Anglican establishment against which the religion clauses were principally directed. When the financial benefit was removed in *Zorach*, however, the situation became less clear. Substantial nonfinancial assistance to religion remained in the form of the compulsory attendance laws, which, as Justice Black argued, seemed to violate *Everson*'s neutrality principle:

> It is only by wholly isolating the state from the religious sphere and compelling it to be completely neutral, that the freedom of each and every denomination and of all nonbelievers can be maintained. It is this neutrality the Court abandons today when it treats New York's coercive system as a program which *merely* "encourages religious instruction or cooperates with religious authorities."[21]

On the other hand, to prohibit the cooperation of government in making it possible for churches to offer released-time and other such programs seemed, in the majority's words, "to find in the Constitution a requirement that the government show a callous indifference to religious groups. That would be preferring those who believe in no religion over those who do believe."[22] What makes the nonfinancial aid decisions so difficult and controversial is that the choices in these cases so often seem to be between government actions that support religion and alternatives that undermine it. As the Court later observed in ruling on public school prayer, "it is insisted that unless these religious exercises are permitted a 'religion of secularism' is established in the schools."[23]

. . 2 . .

After *Zorach* the Court did not review another establishment clause decision for nearly a decade. In the early 1960s, however, the Court issued establishment clause decisions in three consecutive terms, upholding Sunday closing laws in *McGowan v. Maryland*[24] and striking down public school prayer and Bible reading in *Engel v. Vitale*[25] and *School District v. Schempp.*[26] These three decisions laid the foundation of contemporary establishment clause doctrine by holding that government action must be undertaken for secular rather than religious reasons, and that it must be "neutral" with respect to religion by having a "primary effect" that neither advances nor inhibits it.

. . *a* . .

McGowan involved a challenge to Maryland's Sunday closing laws, which generally prohibited business, commercial, and leisure activities on Sunday.[27] Those challenging the laws argued that the purpose of the laws was to encourage attendance at Sunday worship services conducted by Christian denominations and otherwise to create a social and cultural atmosphere consistent with observance of the Christian sabbath.[28] Although the Court conceded at the outset that the laws were originally motivated by sectarian concerns,[29] it nevertheless concluded after an exhaustive historical review of the laws that the original religious motivations for them had attenuated to the point of constitutional insignificance.[30] In the view of the Court, the laws' "present purpose and effect is not to aid religion, but to set aside a day of rest and recreation."[31] Accordingly, the Court held that the laws did not violate the establishment clause.[32]

The lengths to which the *McGowan* Court went to demonstrate the secular purpose of Sunday closing laws signaled the doctrinal change effected by the decision. Under *Zorach*, government did not violate the establishment clause by cooperating with religion to extend the latter's influence so long as such cooperation did not entail financial aid to religion or coercion of religious belief or practice.[33] Thus, the Court attempted no secular justification of the released-time program it upheld in *Zorach*, ignoring as irrelevant the dissenters' charge that the purpose of the program was to encourage religious instruction.[34] Under this analysis, *McGowan* should have been an easier case than *Zorach* itself: Sunday closing laws did not free citizens from work and other commercial obligations on Sunday only on condition that they attend worship services; those excused from secular obligations were excused unconditionally and left free to decide how to spend the extra time. This was a state of affairs that should have satisfied even the *Zorach* dissenters[35] (and, in fact, those who were still on the Court voted to uphold the validity of Sunday closing laws in *McGowan*).[36]

What complicated *McGowan* was the Court's assumption—absent in *Zorach*—that government action must have a secular purpose: "There is no dispute that the original laws which dealt with Sunday labor were motivated by religious forces. But what we must decide is whether present Sunday legislation, having undergone extensive changes from the earliest forms, still retains its religious character."[37] Since the Sunday closing laws entailed no financial subsidy to religion and no coercion of religious belief or practice, the possibility that the closing laws had the purpose of encouraging religious worship should have been irrelevant, as it was under *Zorach*. The Court was required to decide this question only if a legislative purpose of assisting religion is a ground for unconstitutionality under the establishment clause. The *McGowan* Court's laborious effort to establish a present secular purpose for Sunday closing laws confirmed that, *contra Zorach,* government action that lacks a plausible, nonreligious purpose violates the establishment clause.

Engel was a challenge to the "Regents' Prayer," a twenty-two-word prayer recommended by the state board of education in New York for daily recitation as part of a program of moral training in local public schools.[38] *Schempp* consolidated separate challenges in Pennsylvania and Maryland to the practice of opening each public school day with formal recitation of passages from the Bible, including the Lord's Prayer.[39] In all three situations, students were excused from participating in or being present at the exercises.[40]

The Court held that all three exercises violated the establishment clause because of their undeniably religious character. "It is no part of the business of government," stated the Court in *Engel,* "to compose official prayers for any group of the American people to recite as part of a religious program carried on by government."[41] Similarly in *Schempp,* the Court succinctly declared that these "are religious exercises."[42] In none of the three situations could the government's action plausibly be characterized as having had a religiously neutral effect—that is, one that neither advanced nor inhibited religious practice and belief. In fact, Maryland's attempt to convince the Court that the effect of Bible-reading was primarily secular—"the promotion of moral values, the contradiction to the materialistic tendencies of our times, the perpetuation of our institutions, and the teaching of literature"[43]—was a decisive failure:

> Surely the place of the Bible as an instrument of religion cannot be gainsaid, and the State's recognition of the pervading religious character of the [Bible-reading] ceremony is evident from the rule's specific permission of the alternative use of the Catholic Douay version as well as the recent amendment permitting nonattendance at the exercises. None of these factors is consistent with the contention that the Bible is here used either as an instrument for nonreligious moral inspiration or as a reference for the teaching of secular subjects.[44]

As it had done in *McGowan*, the Supreme Court in *Engel* and *Schempp* transformed a question of institutional separation into a question of neutrality.

. . *b* . .

Together, *McGowan*, *Engel*, and *Schempp* established that government action must have a secular purpose and a primarily secular effect to escape invalidation under the establishment clause, even when the action does not coerce religious belief or practice or constitute financial aid to religion.[45] The *Schempp* Court summarized the new doctrine as requiring courts to ask,

> What are the purpose and the primary effect of the test? If either is the advancement or inhibition of religion then the enactment exceeds the scope of legislative power as circumscribed by the Constitution. That is to say that to withstand the strictures of the Establishment Clause there must be a secular legislative purpose and a primary effect that neither advances nor inhibits religion.[46]

The purpose effect test, later to be merged with entanglement to create the three-part *Lemon* test,[47] was a major departure from the substantive doctrine of *McCollum* and *Zorach*, one that critically altered the development of establishment clause jurisprudence. By setting up legislative purpose as an independent measure of constitutionality, the Court dramatically increased the scope of prohibited government action under the clause.

First, the interaction of purpose and effect exaggerates the importance of effects that by themselves do not have constitutional significance. Although purpose can be neatly separated from effect in theory, in practice the distinction is illusive. The best evidence of what government intended to accomplish by a particular action is usually the effect of the action itself: the effect of a government action implies its purpose.[48] A legislature, for example, is generally assumed to have intended the reasonably foreseeable consequences of the laws it enacts. Thus, the *McGowan* Court stated that, notwithstanding its upholding the particular laws at issue in that case, a Sunday closing law would violate the establishment clause "if it can be demonstrated that its purpose—evidenced either *on the face of the legislation*, in conjunction with its legislative history, or *in its operative effect*—is to use the State's coercive power to aid religion."[49]

In *Stone v. Graham*, for example, the Court struck down a Kentucky state statute that required the posting of the Ten Commandments in public school classrooms together with an explanation that they are the origin of many Western legal norms.[50] The Court did not argue—nor could it have—that the primary effect of posting the Commandments was religious. Given that many Western norms are indeed traceable to the Old Testament, children who read the Commandments and the explanation simply learned a historical fact; it is doubtful that any of these children, let alone most of them, were spiritually affected by the posting of the Commandments. Instead, the Court identified the ground of unconstitutionality as lack of a secular legislative purpose: "The pre-eminent purpose for posting the Ten Commandments on schoolroom walls is plainly religious in nature. The Ten Commandments are undeniably a sacred text in the Jewish and Christian faiths, and no recitation of a supposed secular purpose can blind us to that fact."[51] Yet, there was no evidence in the record of any illicit religious motivation for the law. Nor was this a case in which no secular purpose could have been imagined. The Court's assertions to the contrary notwithstanding, it seems obvious that posting the Commandments and the explanation served quite well the secular goal of introducing school children to the historical fact that contemporary Western law has religious antecedents.[52] To reach its conclusion that the law lacked a secular purpose, then, the Court inferred an illicit religious motivation from its estimation of the effects of posting the Commandments: "If the posted copies of the Ten Commandments are to have any effect at all, it will be to induce the school children to read, meditate upon, perhaps to venerate and obey, the Commandments. However desirable this may be as a matter of private devotion, it is not a permissible state objective under the establishment clause."[53] The Court, in other words, deduced the existence of an impermissible legislative purpose under the establishment clause from the effects of the statute, yet it was far from clear that these effects were "primarily religious."

Second, the lack of a secular purpose and existence of a primary religious effect may cumulatively support a holding of unconstitutionality when either by itself would seem insufficient to defend the result. For example, in *Epperson v. Arkansas*, which reviewed a statutory prohibition on teaching evolution in public schools or colleges, the Court made much of an "upsurge of 'fundamentalist' religious fervor" at the time of the law was framed, comparing the law to an antiblasphemy statute and quoting religiously explicit campaign literature written in support of the voter initiative by which the law was enacted.[54] By itself, though, the "fundamentalist spirit of the times," however well documented, would have seemed a rather weak reed on which to decide that a law violates the establishment clause. Indeed, except in establishment clause cases, the Court has been generally unreceptive to this kind of analysis.[55] Similarly, had the Court restricted itself to reviewing the effect of the statute, it would have had a more difficult time finding that the statute violated the establishment clause. Although the statute was not easily defended as religiously neutral,[56] decisions about what to teach—and what not to teach—in public schools are nonetheless left largely to the discretion of state and local authorities, as Justice Black pointed out.[57] Failing to teach school children the scientific account of human origin may be bad education policy but does not seem to violate religious neutrality so long as religious accounts are also not taught. As William Marshall noted, "How this law would have any actual effect on the establishment of a religion is far from clear. A student attending a public school in Arkansas would be exposed to nothing religious in nature. The law did not require the teaching of religious tenets and, on its face, did not convey any religious idea."[58] Basing its holding of unconstitutionality on both the purpose and the effect of the statutory prohibition enabled the Court to justify a decision that would have been problematic on either ground alone.

Finally, with secular purpose as an independent test of constitutionality, a law that lacks a secular purpose violates the establishment clause even when it is clear, as it was not in *Epperson,* that its effect is religiously neutral. The Court confirmed this in *Edwards v. Aguillard.*[59] As we saw in chapter 2, the Court in *Edwards* reviewed a state statute that prohibited the teaching of evolution unless accompanied by the teaching of "creation science," a hypothesis of human origin that accommodates the existence of a divine, supernatural creator. *Edwards* differed from *Epperson,* then, in that it did not single out evolution for prohibition, but mandated that when either evolution or creation science was taught, its intellectual competitor must be taught as well.[60] *Epperson* itself implied that such an arrangement did not violate establishment clause neutrality: "Arkansas' law cannot be defended as an act of religious neutrality. Arkansas did not seek to excise from the curricula of its schools and universities all discussion of the origin of man. The law's effort was confined to an attempt to blot out a particular theory because of its supposed conflict with the Biblical account, literally read."[61] Nevertheless, the Court held in *Edwards* that the law violated the establishment clause for lack of a secular purpose, finding that the secular purposes articulated by the state in defense of the statute were shams, and that the real purpose of the law was to advance fundamentalist beliefs about divine human creation by making it more difficult to teach evolution.[62]

The addition of governmental purpose as an independent ground of unconstitutionality meant that much government action could violate the establishment clause even when its actual effect does not threaten establishment clause neutrality. With the great expansion of government regulation during the last half-century, and the correlative multiplication of church-state contacts and interactions, a test that invalidates government action on purpose *or* effects grounds has the potential to paralyze government initiative because even a statute that has a primarily secular effect is nevertheless infirm under the establishment clause if it is motivated by a desire to assist or strengthen religion.[63]

It was in the context of this fear—that the Court's establishment clause jurisprudence had become so strict that church and state could not constitutionally interact at all—that Justice O'Connor suggested a reformulation of the *Lemon* test that would focus it more directly on the core value of neutrality. In two concurring opinions in decisions handed down only a year apart, *Lynch v. Donnelly* [64] and *Wallace v. Jaffree*, [65] O'Connor argued that government unacceptably departs from the political neutrality imposed by the establishment clause whenever it endorses or disapproves a person's religious beliefs or practices: "Endorsement sends a message to nonadherents that they are outsiders, not full members of the political community, and an accompanying message to adherents that they are insiders, favored members of the political community. Disapproval sends the opposite message." [66] She then refashioned the *Lemon* test as a means of identifying governmental endorsements of religion: "The purpose prong of the *Lemon* test asks whether government's actual purpose is to endorse or disapprove of religion. The effect prong asks whether, irrespective of government's actual purpose, the practice under review in fact conveys a message of endorsement or disapproval." [67]

With the endorsement test, O'Connor attempted to clarify what purpose and effect each contribute to constitutional review under the establishment clause. Rather than illuminating fundamentally different aspects of government action, purpose and effect in O'Connor's test are both directed at the same thing—government endorsement or disapproval of religion. "Purpose" is the subjective intent of the governmental actor, while "effect" is the meaning of governmental action to an "objective observer acquainted with the text, legislative history, and implementation" of the action. [68] Government violates the establishment clause whenever (1) it subjectively intends to endorse or disapprove religion by its actions, whether or not those actions in fact are understood to endorse or disapprove religion, or (2) its actions are reasonably understood to endorse or disapprove religion, whether or not government in fact intended that meaning by its actions.

As doctrinal innovations go, the endorsement test has been an unqualified success. O'Connor's announcement of the test was greeted with enthusiastic approval by commentators. [69] Only a year after O'Connor announced it, it was cited with approval by the Court in

Wallace.[70] It subsequently surfaced in several majority opinions.[71] A few years later, it became the doctrine of the Court when it was adopted by a majority of the Justices in *County of Allegheny v. ACLU.*[72]

It is far from clear that the endorsement test deserves the accolades that have been heaped upon it.[73] First, it seems to have made no practical difference in the outcome of cases before the Court. O'Connor herself has never used the test to reach a result different from that reached by members of the Court using a different analysis.[74] Several of these decisions, such as *Lynch*, have been savaged by commentators and, indeed, seem not to be terribly persuasive.[75] In fact, in the hands of commentators, the test seems rather consistently to yield results precisely the opposite of those arrived at by Justice O'Connor.[76] Mark Tushnet, for example, is incredulous that Justice O'Connor could argue that Jews and other non-Christians would not have understood the city-sponsored crèche in *Lynch* as an endorsement of Christianity.[77]

· · 3 · ·

As the Supreme Court was at pains to demonstrate in *McGowan*, Sunday closing laws have a history in the United States that reaches back even before the Revolutionary War. Originally enacted to support the established churches, they had evolved by the nineteenth century into legal supports for Christian religion in general. As such, they were part of the de facto establishment and are easily defended by religious communitarian discourse. Christianity being essential to the preservation of those conservative values on which civilized society depends, it is entirely appropriate on religious communitarian premises for government to encourage attendance at Sunday services by reducing or eliminating secular activities that conflict with them. To be sure, Jews, Adventists, Muslims, and others who observe a sabbath other than Sunday bear disproportionate burdens with respect to the closing laws in that they lose an extra business day, being prevented by conscience from working their own sabbath and by law from working on Sunday.[78] Moreover, the closing laws do not free them from secular conflicts with their worship services the way the laws do Christians. Nevertheless, non-Sunday worshippers are tolerated in that they are not coerced to attend Christian services or otherwise religiously to observe the Christian sabbath, and are left free by the state to worship on other days of the week if they can make arrangements to do so. This effect of the closing laws on non-Sunday worshippers is thus consistent with religious communitarianism's stricture against coercion of belief and its toleration of dissenting views to the extent that they do not threaten fundamental social values.

While Sunday closing laws can be justified by religious communitarian discourse, they do not fit very well within secular individualist discourse. Secular individualism does not permit religious justifications for government action; therefore, the fact that the closing laws provide noncoercive support for Christianity, and, by extension, the foundational social values that it contributes to society, is not available as a justification. Secular individualist discourse justifies government support of religion only to the extent that religion manifests itself as the effect of private choice within broader, secular categories of public life.

This is precisely how the *McGowan* Court defended the closing laws. It first determined that, appearances notwithstanding, the purpose for the closing laws was secular rather than religious, arguing that, despite restrictions on business and commercial activities, the sports, entertainment, and other secular activities permitted by the laws "seem clearly to be fashioned for the purpose of providing a Sunday atmosphere of recreation, cheerfulness, repose, and enjoyment, . . . one of relaxation rather than one of religion."[79] Having identified a secular purpose for requiring most businesses to close one day each week, the Court then concluded that Sunday was the day that most people would choose on their own, observing that "people of all religions and people with no religion regard Sunday as a time for family activity, for visiting friends and relatives, for late sleeping, for passive and active entertainments, for dining out, and the like."[80] It would, therefore, be "unrealistic for enforcement purposes and perhaps detrimental to the general welfare to require a State to choose a common day of rest other than that which most persons would select of their own accord."[81]

By showing that Sunday closing laws had a secular purpose, and that the designation of Sunday as the secular day of rest was merely the public effect of private choice, the Court in *McGowan* was able to make a secular individualist defense of government action that was, in truth, a remnant of the de facto Protestant establishment easily defended by religious communitarian discourse. Because both the historical record and contemporary social practice provided support for this determination, the opinion is not unpersuasive, though certainly many disagree with it. History and society are not always so accommodating. The Court has since made ludicrous defenses of alignments of church and state by ignoring religious purposes and effects that are undeniable. As Tushnet describes it, "where the Justices feel pressure to validate a religious activity, they are likely to respond by treating it as essentially nonreligious."[82] The willingness of the Court to describe as secular what are clearly religious practices evidences its deep commitment to secular individualism as the governing discourse of church-state relations, even when it defends religious communitarian results in its decisions. In order to defend a close alignment of church and state with secular individualism, however, the apparently religious practice at issue must be recharacterized as secular. The Court's two religious symbol cases, *Lynch v. Donnelly* and *County of Allegheny v. ACLU*, are excellent illustrations of this phenomenon.

In *Lynch* the Court considered an establishment clause challenge to inclusion of a nativity scene as part of a larger city-owned and -operated Christmas holiday display near the downtown shopping district. Besides the traditional depiction of the birth of Jesus represented by the crèche, the display also included representations of Santa and his reindeer, carolers, clowns, and animals, together with a Christmas tree, colored lights, and a large "Seasons Greetings" banner.[83] The Court found that the display had a secular purpose, being sponsored by the city "to celebrate the Holiday and to depict the origins of that holiday."[84] It further found that the primary effect of the display was also secular, with any benefit to Christianity from including the crèche being "indirect, remote, and incidental," like the passive display of religious paintings in government art museums.[85] With these determinations of secular purpose and secular effect in hand, the Court had little trouble rejecting the establishment clause challenge.

Allegheny involved a similar challenge to two holiday displays, a crèche set by itself in the lobby of a county courthouse, and a seventeen-foot Chanukah menorah set next to a forty-foot Christmas tree and a sign saluting liberty outside a city-county building.[86] In a complex set of opinions,[87] the Court declared that the display of the crèche violated the establishment clause because, "unlike in *Lynch*, nothing in the context of the display detracts from the crèche's religious message."[88] The display was thus found by the Court to endorse Christianity. By contrast, the presence of the Christmas tree and the sign in the second display obscured and overshadowed the religious nature of the menorah and the Chanukah holiday. For two Justices this neutralized any endorsement of Judaism or religion in general.[89] Four other Justices concurred in this judgment on other grounds.[90]

Lynch and *Allegheny* are generally understood as victories for advocates of greater accommodation of religion in public life, and defeats for proponents of stricter separation of church and state. Yet, in both decisions, it is the separationist opinions that take the crèche and the menorah seriously as *religious* symbols, and the accommodationist opinions that strive to empty them of their spiritual content and replace it with secular meaning. For example, dissenting in *Lynch*, Justice Brennan described the crèche as "a mystical re-creation of an event that lies at the heart of Christian faith," whose symbolic content prompts "a sense of simple awe and wonder appropriate to the contemplation of one of the central elements of Christian dogma— that God sent His Son into the world to be a Messiah."[91] He makes a similar observation about the Chanukah menorah, describing its ritual use in "a celebration that has deep religious significance."[92]

Justice Stevens likewise characterizes the menorah as "unquestionably a religious symbol," and quotes rabbinical testimony from the trial record that the menorah is as sacred a symbol to Jews as the crèche is to Christians.[93]

By contrast, the Court in *Lynch* describes the crèche as merely noting "a significant historical religious event" and commemorating "the historical origins of this traditional event long recognized as a National Holiday," thereby creating "a friendly community spirit of goodwill in keeping with the season."[94] Likewise, Justice O'Connor describes the purpose of the crèche as "celebration of the public holiday through its traditional symbols," which have "cultural" as well as religious significance.[95] In *Allegheny*, Justice Blackmun concedes that the menorah is a symbol of the miracle commemorated by Chanukah, but then asserts that the menorah's meaning is not "exclusively religious" and that Chanukah is an American "cultural tradition" analogous to and contemporaneous with Christmas.[96] He goes on to describe Christmas and Chanukah as secular parts of the same "winter-holiday season," so that "in the shadow of the tree, the menorah is readily understood as simply a recognition that Christmas is not the only traditional way of observing" this season.[97] Justice O'Connor chides Justice Blackmun for failing to acknowledge fully the religious symbolism of the menorah, but nevertheless agrees that the placement of the smaller menorah next to the larger Christmas tree properly "obscures the religious nature of the menorah and the holiday of Chanukah," thereby neutralizing any endorsement of Judaism or religion in general.[98]

Intellectual historian Hans Frei has described how in the eighteenth and nineteenth centuries scholarly understanding of the Bible was transformed from interpreting it as the literal story of the world to taking it as a mere manifestation of the mythic consciousness of its human authors.[99] The latter approach to Biblical interpretation, which Frei calls "mythophilic," saw "the subject matter of biblical narratives neither in the events to which they referred nor in the ideas supposedly stated in them in narrative form, but in the consciousness they represented."[100] In other words, the Bible ceased to be approached as the only record of the events of the world, or even as a reliable account of them, and instead was taken as kind of literary or anthropological evidence of the social, cultural, pseudoscientific, and other beliefs and practices of those who wrote it. This "demythologization" of the Biblical text rendered it susceptible of meaning in an era in which scholars had become deeply skeptical of miracles and the supernatural. For example, mythophilic interpretation permitted an understanding of Jesus's resurrection as a new manifestation of divine consciousness rather than a literal historical event.[101]

Something similar to Biblical demythologization is at work in *Lynch* and *Allegheny*. The accommodationist opinions in these cases transform the crèche and the menorah from religious symbols of deep spiritual significance into cultural artifacts. As the Court succinctly stated in *Allegheny*, "the government may acknowledge Christmas as a cultural phenomenon, but under the First Amendment it may not observe it as a Christian holy day by suggesting that people praise God for the birth of Jesus."[102] Rather than allowing the crèche to be understood authentically, as a representation of the central event and doctrine of Christianity—namely, the incarnation of God to save humanity from death and sin—the opinions consign the crèche "to the role of neutral harbinger of the holiday season, useful for commercial purposes, but devoid of any inherent meaning and incapable of enhancing the religious tenor of a display of which it is an integral part."[103]

The Court's desacralization of the crèche in *Lynch* and the menorah in *Allegheny* is betrayed by the analogy to religious art invoked in *Lynch*.[104] The reason why the presence of such art in government galleries is uncontroversial is that it is so often approached primarily as evidence of the religious and other beliefs and practices of societies safely located in the distant past. Religious art thus has little spiritual or normative force in contemporary society. The Court's analogy of the crèche and the menorah to religious museum art suggests that it, too, believes sacred symbols to have little contemporary spiritual significance.

Encouraging devotion to the established religious traditions at the foundation of society is precisely what religious communitarian ideology requires of government. On religious communitarian premises, *Lynch* was correctly decided, and *Allegheny* would be problematic for its refusal to permit publicly sponsored display of the crèche, not for permitting display of the menorah. It is only within secular individualist discourse that such action by government is problematic. It is not by accident that the accommodationist opinions are vague about the "historical religious events" that the crèche and the menorah commemorate; the logic of both opinions, such as it is, depends upon the "deniability" of the sectarian religious meaning signified by these symbols. The Court denied the religious content of the crèche and the menorah because, once it determined to defend its decision with secular individualist discourse, it had no choice: the only way secular individualism can defend an interaction of government with religion is if the "religious" is redefined as essentially secular. Thus, a depiction of the birth of the Christian savior becomes a symbol of good cheer indistinguishable from Santa and his reindeer, and the symbol of the Jewish "Miracle of the Lights" becomes a good-hearted pluralist alternative to all this secular cheerfulness. Only if the religious can be made secular is a defense available within secular individualism.

Chapter 5

. . . . .

The Religious as Afterthought:

Financial Aid and Tax Exemptions for Religion

. . . . .

As we saw in chapter 3, the Supreme Court's refusal to permit direct financial aid to parochial schools can be defended as religiously neutral only if one measures neutrality from an implausible no-aid baseline. Other Supreme Court decisions, however, suggest that outside of the specific context of parochial schools, the governing neutrality baseline in cases of financial aid to religion is one of pervasive aid even when the assistance in question flows directly to religious institutions rather than to individuals. For example, the Court has upheld several programs involving financial aid given directly to religiously sponsored colleges.[1] (For convenience, I will use the term "religious college" to include all religiously affiliated institutions of higher education.) In doing so, the Court has emphasized that government aid to higher education is pervasive. In *Roemer v. Board of Public Works*, for example, the Court argued that "a system of government that makes itself felt as pervasively as ours could hardly be expected never to cross paths with the church. In fact, our State and Federal Governments impose certain burdens upon, and impart certain benefits to, virtually all our activities, and religious activity is not an exception."[2] Thus, the Court has suggested that preventing religious colleges and universities from receiving such benefits when they otherwise fall within a secularly defined beneficiary class unfairly penalizes them.[3] Similarly, in *Bowen v. Kendrick*, the Court held that the Adolescent Family Life Act does not facially violate the establishment clause despite allowing religious as well as secular social service agencies to receive direct federal grants, and despite the AFLA's requirement that grant recipients affirmatively show, inter alia, how their pregnancy counseling programs will encourage interaction with religious communities that encourage abstinence and sexual responsibility.[4] The Court stressed that "nothing on the face of the Act suggests it is anything but neutral with respect to the grantee's status as a sectarian or purely secular institution."[5] The Court was also careful to point out that it had "never held that religious institutions are disabled by the First Amendment from participating in publicly sponsored social welfare programs."[6] Finally, in *Walz v. Tax Commission*, the Court upheld a property tax exemption for nonprofit organizations, including religiously affiliated ones, arguing that granting the exemption to churches, "along with nonprofit hospitals, art galleries, and libraries receiving the same tax exemption" was no different from giving them police and fire protection.[7]

The Court is able to defend these decisions by reference to a plausible baseline for measuring neutrality, that of pervasive aid. They are not, therefore, problematic for secular individualist discourse. But which discourse one uses to interpret the decisions is still important. For example, the decisions can be understood as presupposing that religious groups have an organic status in public life prior and unrelated to the exercise of individual choice in private life. Religious groups are among those institutions that affect private preference formation, and so they are taken to have a public status. If government wishes to achieve a particular public policy goal—improving the quality of higher education, reducing teenage pregnancies, enhancing the quality of community life—religious communitarian discourse justifies giving financial aid to any and all social groups, including religious ones, that help to achieve that goal. Indeed, it is foolish to exclude religion from the formulation and pursuit of public policy goals, since within religious communitarianism religion is one of the foundations of civilized society.

By contrast, secular individualist discourse cannot defend giving government aid to religion *qua* religion since that skews private religious choice. In order to justify within secular individualist discourse situations in which religious entities receive government assistance directly, rather than as the result of the choices of individuals, the Court is forced into a conundrum similar to that in which it found itself in the Sunday closing and religious symbol cases: it must argue that the religious entities receiving direct aid are not really religious, appearances notwithstanding. In the religious college aid cases and in *Bowen*, this argument takes the form of a questionable empirical distinction that contrasts "pervasively sectarian" parochial schools with religious colleges and other institutions that are found not to be "pervasively sectarian." In the tax exemption cases, direct aid is justified by ignoring the faith motivations of such institutions for providing the benefits they do, and by characterizing these benefits as essentially secular, analogous to benefits provided by secular nonprofit organizations. My argument here is not that these arguments are wholly implausible or unpersuasive, but rather overstated. The Court's need to "secularize" the religious institutions receiving aid, brought on by reliance on secular individualist discourse to justify the aid, results in an exaggerated and caricatured account of the comparative religiosity of parochial schools versus religious colleges and other kinds of religious aid recipients. In the tax exemption cases, this need expresses itself in a predisposition to understand sacred religious duties as motivated by the same concerns as those that stand behind secular nonprofit services.

. . 1 . .

In religious communitarian discourse, the question whether an aid recipient is "pervasively" sectarian or merely sectarian is irrelevant. Since this discourse assumes that all kinds of social institutions may be legitimately involved in politics and public life, from the most secular to the most religious, the relative degrees of religiosity among them are unimportant. In secular individualist discourse, however, this inquiry is crucial. Since religious groups have no public status in secular individualist discourse, direct grants to them cannot be justified. As *Grand Rapids School District* suggests, even if there is no financial distortion of individual choice, there is a psychological distortion: direct grants identify government with religion and constitute an implicit endorsement of religion by government that skews private choice in favor of religion.[8]

On the other hand, direct grants to religious institutions can be made consistent with secular individualist ideology if it can be shown that the putatively "religious" recipients are not "really" religious. This is the use to which the Court puts the pervasive sectarian analysis. Nonpervasive religious groups, although formally religious, are considered functionally secular and thus do not trigger the concerns of secular individualism. Correlatively, parochial schools, as pervasively religious institutions, cannot receive financial aid even though they perform substantial secular functions that relieve the state of a significant burden in financing public education. The Court's use of the pervasively sectarian inquiry shows that it has not abandoned secular individualism in cases in which direct aid to religious institutions is upheld, their religious communitarian results notwithstanding. Rather, once again, the Court attempts to justify results that are possible only within one discourse with arguments that are coherent only within the other. The problem with the religious college aid cases and *Bowen* is not that they are rhetorically implausible uses of neutrality, like those employed by the Court in the parochial school aid cases; to the contrary, the Court's use of a realistic pervasive-aid baseline to justify aid to religious groups on the same basis as aid to similarly situated secular groups makes the appeal to neutrality in these decisions highly persuasive. The problem is that "pervasive sectarianism" is not a convincing justification for differential constitutional treatment of aid to parochial schools and aid to other kinds of religious groups.

In the religious college aid cases, the Court determined that in such colleges the secular goal of teaching critical thinking by secular academic methods eclipses the religious goal of inculcating sectarian beliefs and practices.[9] It also accepted the argument that the relative age and maturity of college students compared to elementary and secondary school students made it unlikely that college students would be coerced or manipulated into adopting particular religious beliefs and practices encouraged by a religious college.[10] For both of these reasons, the Court concluded that, in contrast to parochial schools, religious colleges are generally not "pervasively sectarian."[11] Likewise in *Bowen,* the Court concluded that because only a small portion of the eligible religious grant recipients under the AFLA were likely to be "pervasively sectarian," the Act did not facially violate the establishment clause by permitting grants to such religious groups.[12]

Finding that a religious group is "pervasively sectarian" effectively raises the Court's standard of review. Monitoring and audit controls, deemed necessary by the Court to ensure that government aid to parochial schools does not advance religion, are not considered important in nonpervasive contexts.[13] In nonpervasive contexts, "secular activities, for the most part, can be taken at face value . . . . The need for close surveillance of purportedly secular activities is correspondingly reduced."[14] Similarly, in contrast to the strictness with which the Court assesses potential church-state entanglements in parochial schools, it applies the entanglement analysis to nonpervasive sectarian groups only superficially.[15] Finally, whereas in pervasive contexts the Court has insisted that even state employees cannot be trusted to avoid transmitting religious values to their students, in nonpervasive contexts the Court assumes that employees are not significantly influenced by the beliefs and practices of even a sectarian employer.[16]

Obviously, then, whether a religious group is classified as "pervasively sectarian" is critical to the subsequent determination whether direct aid to the group violates the establishment clause. Unfortunately, the distinction cannot bear the analytic weight the Court places upon it. Although there clearly are differences between parochial schools and other religious groups, there is little empirical support for the dramatically different way in which the Court tests the constitutionality of direct aid to each class of entity. First, the Court exaggerates the extent and strength of the sectarian influence at many parochial schools. This is not to suggest that sectarian influence at parochial schools is nonexistent or trivial. Nevertheless, nonmembers of the sponsoring religion make up a significant percentage of the students in parochial schools,[17] especially in those serving minority populations.[18] The faculty at these schools are typically composed of lay members of the sponsoring church rather than ministers or members of religious orders.[19] At some parochial schools significant numbers of nonmembers are on the teaching faculty.[20]

In *Hunt v. McNair*, the Court decided that because a religious college imposed no religious qualifications for faculty hiring, and because the percentage of its students belonging to the sponsoring religion did not exceed that religion's membership in the surrounding area, the college provided an essentially secular education:

> What little there is in the record concerning the College establishes that there are no religious qualifications for faculty membership or student admission, and that only 60% of the College student body is Baptist, a percentage roughly equivalent to the percentage of Baptists in that area of South Carolina. On the record in this case there is no basis to conclude that the College's operations are oriented significantly towards sectarian rather than secular education.[21]

By this test, the education at many parochial schools is not pervasively sectarian either, if it is sectarian at all.

To the same extent that the Court exaggerates the religious influence of parochial schools, it underestimates such influence at religious colleges. Many religious colleges are not "pervasively sectarian" by the Court's criteria, but they remain very religious places. It is hardly self-evident that the typical educational experience at a nonpervasive religious college is better described as "secular" rather than "sectarian." For example, at the University of Notre Dame, which is not considered a pervasively sectarian institution, 93 percent of the student body is Roman Catholic, and over 80 percent of the students live in on-campus dormitories in which the mass is celebrated daily. Undergraduate students are required to take six credit hours of theology and an additional six hours of philosophy. Most classrooms contain a crucifix, and there are statues of Catholic saints scattered across the campus. The president of the University must be a member of the Order of the Holy Cross, which administered the University until 1967 and which is still headquartered on the Notre Dame campus.[22]

It is simply absurd to presume that the sectarian influence at nonpervasive religious colleges like Notre Dame is insignificant. Indeed, it is likely that the atmosphere at a nonpervasive religious college will often be highly religious, closer to that of a "pervasively sectarian" college than that of an unambiguously secular one.[23] Can there be any doubt that many of the students at a Jewish institution like Yeshiva University would be uncomfortable at a Roman Catholic institution like Notre Dame, and vice versa? The maturity and skepticism of college students will not shield them from feelings of alienation and difference at a college sponsored by a religion that differs significantly from their own. In fact, many students attend such colleges precisely to receive sectarian as well as secular instruction.[24]

Second, the Court's exaggeration of the obvious religious influences that exist at parochial schools ignores the fact that much, maybe even most, of the curriculum at such schools is not taught any differently than it would be at a public school. Many parochial schools have been successful in teaching their students traits that are highly valued in secular society, such as tolerance and cooperation.[25] Moreover, it is hard to imagine how the religious character of a school or teacher would make *any* difference, let alone a constitutionally significant one, in how one would teach subjects like mathematics, spelling, English grammar, foreign languages, or geography.[26] Even in more ideologically sensitive classes, it is evident that secular learning forms a substantial part of the plan of study.[27] Indeed, there is a widespread perception that parochial schools actually provide a more rigorous *secular* education than that delivered by public schools,[28] and the fact that parochial school students (especially racial minorities) often show higher academic achievement than their public school counterparts seems to confirm the accuracy of this perception.[29]

As Jesse Choper has sensibly suggested, it is likely "that some secular subject courses in parochial schools are so 'permeated' [by religion] that they are in reality courses of sectarian indoctrination . . . ; that some courses are completely bona fide secular; that some courses fall between these extremes."[30] Michael McConnell and Richard Posner argue that "the secular component of parochial education is very large," and that "the government could support a sizable fraction of the total costs of parochial school education without subsidizing religion in an economically meaningful sense."[31] Contrary to the impression left by the Court's rhetoric, it is not an impossible task to distinguish the "completely secular" subjects at a parochial school from those combined with sectarian instruction.

The differentiation between pervasive and nonpervasive institutions becomes even more strained when it is used to analyze the situation of nonbelieving adults. Even at those parochial schools and religious colleges that cultivate a pervasively sectarian environment, as the Court defines it, it is doubtful that adults are subject to the kind of religious pressure that the Court fears. In *Grand Rapids School District*, for example, the Court referred to the "unacceptable risk" that state-paid instructional employees would advance religious teachings when working on parochial school grounds.[32] Yet, it is difficult to imagine that sectarian environments are so overwhelming—and human beings so weak-minded—that public school teachers and other state employees rendering secular services at a parochial school are likely to feel compelled to alter their teaching to conform to the religious environment.[33] In neither *Aguilar* nor *Grand Rapids School District* was there any evidence in the record of any sort of religious indoctrination by state instructional employees despite the fact that the challenged programs in these cases had been in existence for many years.[34] Since such employees are paid, supervised, and evaluated by the state, the parochial school is not able to exercise meaningful control over them, notwithstanding the general religious influence of the parochial school campus.[35]

An especially implausible version of this argument is presented by the Court's reliance on the entanglement prong of *Lemon* to strike down aid to parochial schools. As I have related, state aid programs that seek to ensure that aid it is not put to religious uses by, for example, having state supervisors monitor the behavior of state employees performing secular functions at parochial schools entangle the state in religion and for that reason are unconstitutional.[36] As John Garvey has observed, this is a very odd claim. It is akin to arguing that a college subject to Title IX cannot receive federal aid "because, in the process of looking for sex discrimination, Department of Education officials might be captured by chauvinists."[37] The Court's entanglement analysis presupposes not only that state instructional employees working in parochial schools "may be swept up in the sectarian spirit of the enterprise and modify their instruction along religious lines," but also that "administrators who go into the parochial schools to make sure that does not happen will catch the same bug and ignore or approve abuses they see."[38] Both claims are doubtful, to say the least. To the extent that entanglement exists to protect the parochial schools from overzealous state regulators, it seems sufficient, rather than foreclosing parochial school aid altogether, to let the schools themselves decide whether the risks and intrusions of monitoring imposed on them as conditions to receiving aid are worth the trouble. Many schools are likely to conclude that they are.

Finally, the Court often seems to overlook the significance of the fact that "students often attend parochial schools precisely in order to receive instruction in religious values."[39] The very presence of students at a parochial school rather than the assigned public one is a strong indication that these students and their parents either accept or do not object to the sectarian beliefs that supposedly pervade it.[40] It seems most unlikely that the faith (or lack of it) of such students is materially affected by the knowledge that the state pays some of their guidance counselor's or math teacher's salary, assuming that children can even recognize when a parochial school employee is paid from secular rather than religious funds.[41]

In fact, formalism and abstraction mark the pervasively sectarian distinction. The Court conclusively presumes that parochial schools are pervasively sectarian and then takes the position that, because sectarian influence pervades the institution, state assistance even to severable, secular aspects of the educational process advances the religious mission of the school. By contrast, the Court presumes, although not conclusively, that religious colleges are not pervasively sectarian and then takes the position that the secular aspects of the educational process can be severed from the religious aspects of the school because the latter do not pervade the educational environment. In both cases, however, a *religious* institution is aided to the extent of the aid given, as the fungibility argument makes clear.[42] Unless one is willing to assume that religious colleges are genuinely secular, aid to a religious, though not pervasively sectarian, college must advance the interests of the sponsoring religion. Conversely, if secular educational services can be identified and isolated at a nonpervasive religious college, as the Court assumes, then it should be no more difficult to identify and isolate such services at a pervasively sectarian parochial school. While it is certainly possible, for example, to teach mathematics or conduct speech therapy in a sectarian manner, neither activity inevitably acquires a theological character simply because it is engaged in by a sectarian believer. It is hardly a difficult undertaking, the entanglement prong notwithstanding, to verify that such activities are not being used to proselytize.

At times the Court's rote adherence to categorical presumptions constituted by the pervasive sectarianism distinction approaches absurdity. In *Bowen* the Court held that federal grants for teenage pregnancy counseling did not have a primary effect of advancing religion even when distributed to religious social service organizations, because such groups generally are not pervasively sectarian. Regardless of what the formal characteristics of a religious social service agency are, the practical truth is that a pregnancy counselor who shares the beliefs of the sponsoring church is not disposed to give counseling that is inconsistent with those beliefs. Even if she were, the knowledge that her sectarian employer would probably discipline or terminate her for such counseling provides a powerful disincentive to providing it. One can never be sure what the Justices are thinking, but certainly none of the litigants in *Bowen* doubted that the pregnancy counseling provided by religiously affiliated grant recipients was precisely congruent with the beliefs and practices of the sponsoring religions; indeed, that provided the motivation for challenging the statute. If one assumes that the operation of religious social service agencies is motivated by the religious beliefs of the sponsoring agency, how can grants to them not advance those beliefs?

The point here is not that there are no differences between parochial schools and religious colleges and other religious institutions. Rather, "pervasive sectarianism" does not elucidate any differences that should be constitutionally significant under the establishment clause. As a means of persuasively differentiating the constitutional treatment of aid to parochial schools from aid to other kinds of religious groups, "pervasive sectarianism" is a failure. So long as the parochial school recipient avoids using government aid directly to advance religion, it is hard to see how the government has affected the pattern of private choice.[43] The Court clings to this distinction because secular individualism forces it to: secular individualist discourse has no resources to defend the constitutionality of financial aid to religious institutions unless these institutions are recharacterized as secular. So long as the Court remains committed to justifying its institutional aid decisions with the rhetoric of secular individualism, denying that the recipients are "pervasively sectarian" is about all that the discourse allows it to do.

· · 2 · ·

Property tax relief for churches and other religious organizations has a long history in the United States. Churches have been exempt from payment of property taxes since the colonial era, and each of the fifty states continues to excuse churches from this tax obligation.[44] Despite this tradition of religious property tax exemptions, however, the Supreme Court did not pass on their constitutionality under the establishment clause until 1970 in *Walz v. Tax Commission*.[45] The question was not trivial. Exempting churches from property taxes is a substantial financial benefit to religion which government finances by foregoing revenues it might otherwise collect.[46] In this respect, property tax exemptions resemble the prototypical religious establishment of colonial times, the tax-supported Anglican Church, and for that reason seemed constitutionally suspect.[47]

Nevertheless, the *Walz* Court found that property tax exemptions did not violate the establishment clause. The majority opinion focused on two themes, institutional separation and social value. The Court read the religion clauses together as having mandated the institutional separation of church and state.[48] At the same time, however, the Court recognized religion as one of a number of activities that were valuable to society, and found it legitimate for the state to encourage voluntary participation in these activities through incentive mechanisms like tax exemptions.[49] In its analysis, then, *Walz* resembled *Zorach v. Clauson.*[50] Once the Court determined that religious activities are socially valuable, it was a simple matter to find that property tax exemptions do not violate the institutional separation principle:

> The grant of a tax exemption is not sponsorship since the government does not transfer part of its revenue to churches but simply abstains from demanding that the church support the state. No one has ever suggested that the tax exemption has converted libraries, art galleries, or hospitals into arms of the state or put employees "on the public payroll." There is no genuine nexus between tax exemption and establishment of religion.[51]

The Court even suggested that exemptions might be necessary to ensure that government did not persecute religion under cover of tax collection.[52]

The majority opinion in *Walz* can be justified by religious communitarian discourse. Recognizing the importance of religion to society and the consequent legitimacy of state efforts to encourage voluntary participation in religious activity, the Court upheld property tax exemptions as one means of providing that encouragement. As Arvo

Van Alstyne concluded, "[t]he proliferation of tax benefits to churches thus must be regarded in part, at least, as a manifestation of a political consensus that aid to organized religion, in nondiscriminatory form, at least, has a special tendency to enhance (to use John Stuart Mill's phrase) 'The first element of good government . . . to promote the virtue and intelligence of the people themselves.' "[53] Not only did the Court find that such exemptions do not violate the institutional separation principle that is part of the religious communitarian discourse, it decided that tax exemptions for churches and other religious groups present a lesser risk of institutional entanglement than tax collection.[54]

Not all the Justices agreed with the majority's rationale. In an important concurring opinion, Justice Brennan argued that religious organizations should be exempted because they "contribute to the well-being of a community" as much as other private, nonprofit organizations that are exempted from taxation.[55] This sounds very much like the majority's recognition of the social value of religion within religious communitarian discourse. At several points Justice Brennan even appeared to recognize the unique *spiritual* value of religion, arguing, for example, that religious organizations "uniquely contribute to the pluralism of American society by their religious activities. Government may properly include religious institutions among the variety of private, nonprofit groups that receive tax exemptions, for each group contributes to the diversity of association, viewpoint, and enterprise essential to a vigorous, pluralistic society."[56] At other points, however, he appears to emphasize that the social value of religion does not lie in its spirituality: "It is true that each church contributes to the pluralism of our society through its purely religious activities, but the state encourages these activities not because it champions religion *per se* but because it values religion among a variety of private, nonprofit enterprises that contribute to the diversity of the Nation."[57]

With this faintly Madisonian argument, Brennan suggests that religious organizations cannot be valued and encouraged by the state *qua* religion, but rather only to the extent that they achieve *secular* goals the fulfillment of which would otherwise be financed directly by the government. Justice Harlan made a similar point in his opinion:

> The statute . . . has defined a class of nontaxable entities whose common denominator is their nonprofit pursuit of activities devoted to cultural and moral improvement and the doing of "good works" by performing certain social services in the community that might otherwise have to be assumed by government. . . .
>
> To the extent that religious institutions sponsor the secular activities that this legislation is designed to promote, it is consistent with neutrality to grant them an exemption just as other organizations devoting resources to these projects receive exemptions.[58]

If indeed Brennan and Harlan were arguing that churches could be eligible for a tax exemption only if they met *secular* criteria, then their argument is not a religious communitarian one, but rather a secular individualist one. It is secular individualism that requires that religion manifest itself in public only when it is part of a broader secular category, like "nonprofit social service institutions." This enables public religious activity plausibly to be described and dealt with as if it were not religious, thereby preserving the secular character of public life required by the ideological assumptions of secular individualist discourse. This difference was underscored by the *Walz* majority's explicit rejection of the Brennan rationale on the ground that it threatened the institutional separation of church and state:

> We find it unnecessary to justify the tax exemption on the social welfare services or "good works" that some churches perform for parishioners and others . . . . To give emphasis to so variable an aspect of the work of religious bodies would introduce an element of governmental evaluation and standards as to the worth of particular social welfare programs, thus producing a kind of continuing day-to-day relationship which the policy of neutrality seeks to minimize. Hence, the use of a social welfare yardstick as a significant element to qualify for tax exemption

could conceivably give rise to confrontations that could escalate to constitutional dimensions.[59]

For the *Walz* majority, what justified the tax exemption was the protection it afforded the spiritual dimensions of religious practices against government intrusion. Brennan recognizes the protective aspect of the exemption, but also suggests that religious practices are entitled to the benefit of the exemption only to the extent that they serve secular government objectives.

Any doubt about what Justice Brennan intended by his ideologically conflicted opinion in *Walz* was resolved in *Texas Monthly v. Bullock*.[60] Although there was no majority opinion, five members of the Court concluded that a state sales tax exemption for religious literature violated the establishment clause.[61] Writing for a plurality of three, Justice Brennan emphasized that the breadth of the exemption in *Walz*, which was available to "a broad class of property owned by nonprofit, quasi-public corporations,"[62] was what had saved it from constitutional invalidation:

> Every tax exemption constitutes a subsidy that affects nonqualifying taxpayers, forcing them to become "indirect and vicarious 'donors.' " Insofar as that subsidy is conferred upon a wide array of nonsectarian groups as well as religious organizations in pursuit of some legitimate secular end, the fact that religious groups benefit incidentally does not deprive the subsidy of the secular purpose and primary effect mandated by the Establishment Clause.[63]

Because the exemption in *Texas Monthly* was by its terms available only for *religious* literature, it constituted an unconstitutional endorsement of religion.[64]

The breadth of a tax exemption is analytically irrelevant in religious communitarian discourse, since on religious communitarian premises government may act to assist religion regardless of whether such assistance is also rendered to secular organizations, so long as the aid does not threaten institutional separation or coerce belief. On secular individualist premises, however, the breadth of an exemption is highly relevant, as we saw repeatedly confirmed in chapter 3, because it affects the determination whether government tax expenditures should be understood as having skewed private preferences about religion.[65] Like a broad, secularly defined beneficiary class in the parochial school aid cases, a broad, secularly defined exemption is assumed to leave private religious choice unaffected, so that any manifestation of that choice in public life cannot be charged to the government. By contrast, a narrow exemption is seen as a government departure from neutrality, so that resulting manifestations of religious choice in public life can be understood as the result of government encouragement. As Justice Brennan stated in *Texas Monthly*, when the Court has upheld religious tax exemptions in prior cases, it has "emphasized that the benefits derived by religious organizations flowed to a large number of nonreligious groups as well. Indeed, were those benefits confined to religious organizations, they could not have appeared other than as state sponsorship of religion." [66] In other words, the social value of religious orgnizations must be measured by secular and not religious criteria.

With respect to the decisions permitting direct financial aid to religion, I argued that "pervasive sectarianism" does not distinguish in a persuasive way those religious institutions that may receive financial aid from those institutions that may not. The tax exemption cases, at least after *Texas Monthly*, illustrate a comparable phenomenon: the breadth of an exemption, including churches and other religious groups as well as secular nonprofit organizations, does not elucidate any similarities between the two kinds of institutions which persuade that one must be given tax exempt treatment if the other is. What motivates religious social service organizations is not, at bottom, a secular commitment to service, but rather simple faith. As Stephen Monsma has pointed out, "whatever form the living-out of one's faith takes, whether direct acts of help and service or attempts to influence public policy, for deeply religious persons, their faith compels them to take these steps. It is as much a part of their faith as kneeling in prayer or attending religious services." [67] As before, what forces the Court into this argument is an analytic preference for secular individualist discourse. Here the motivations of faith are a mere afterthought to the misleading suggestion that churches and other religious organizations are motivated to their good works by the same considerations that move the members of secular nonprofit organizations.

Chapter 6

. . . . .

The Religious as Irrelevant:

Free Exercise Exemptions

. . . . .

Litigation under the free exercise clause of the First Amendment has been largely centered on whether the clause requires government to excuse a person from complying with laws that contradict his or her religious beliefs. Under the doctrine of the "constitutionally compelled exemption," the free exercise clause mandates that believers be relieved from the obligation of obeying any law that requires them to perform an act that is prohibited by their religious beliefs, or that prohibits them from performing any act that is required by their beliefs, unless there exists an overriding or "compelling" governmental interest that would be frustrated by relieving believers of their obligation to obey the law.

The exemption doctrine appears on its face to favor religion. Not only are religious exemptions protective of religion, they are not neutral between religion and nonreligion—exemptions give to religious beliefs and activities a special protection that generally is not available to shield nonreligiously motivated beliefs and actions from the effects of government action. Nevertheless, although the doctrine appears religion-protective, it was never extended by the Supreme Court beyond the facts of the two cases with which it was most closely associated, *Sherbert v. Verner*[1] and *Wisconsin v. Yoder*.[2] The

Supreme Court's abandonment of the doctrine in *Employment Division v. Smith*[3] only made explicit what has always been the functional law of free exercise: whenever the religious action at issue is significantly out of step with majoritarian values and is not defensible by reference to secular principles of constitutional law, an exemption is not constitutionally required. Similar to the structure of decisions under the establishment clause, *Smith* reaches results that are consistent with religious communitarian discourse, but that are justified with arguments that make sense only within secular individualist discourse.

. . 1 . .

The doctrinal narrative of free exercise jurisprudence is circular. The Court began in the late nineteenth century with the belief-action doctrine, which left religious free exercise largely unprotected. In the 1960s and 1970s it moved to the compelling interest test, which was apparently highly protective of religious exercise but which in practice provided only marginally greater protection for religion than the belief-action doctrine. In 1990 the Court abandoned the compelling interest test and largely returned to the belief-action doctrine, with an added (and largely superfluous) prohibition on purposeful religious discrimination.

. . a . .

More than a century ago in *Reynolds v. United States*, the Supreme Court refused to find a constitutionally compelled exemption from antibigamy laws for Mormon polygamists.[4] The Court determined that, while "Congress was deprived of all legislative power over mere opinion" by the free exercise clause, it was "left free to reach actions which were in violation of social duties or subversive of good order."[5] The Court reasoned that, because laws are enacted precisely to regulate actions, it would be anomolous to excuse illegal actions simply because they are religiously motivated.[6]

Reynold's distinction between belief and action controlled the disposition of free exercise claims through the remainder of the nineteenth and into the twentieth century, ensuring that such claims remained almost completely ineffective in securing relief for individuals who found exercise of their religious beliefs burdened by general laws.[7] When the Supreme Court renewed its interest in the religion clauses in the 1940s, it reaffirmed the distinction. In *Cantwell v. Connecticut,* which incorporated the free exercise clause against the states through the due process clause of the Fourteenth Amendment, the Court interpreted the constitutionally protected freedom of religion to encompass both freedom of belief and freedom of action. However, while the Court found religiously motivated belief to be absolutely protected, it held that religiously motivated conduct, "in the nature of things," was "subject to regulation for the protection of society."[8] Under the belief-action doctrine, the free exercise clause deprived government of any authority to punish a person for his or her religious *beliefs,* but did not affect the authority of government to regulate religiously motivated *actions* so long as there existed a public interest rationale for the regulation. Since the government can always carry this light burden of justification, the belief-action doctrine effectively foreclosed the possibility of constitutionally compelled free exercise exemptions.[9]

Because it excused government from the constitutional obligation to exempt believers from burdensome laws on the thinnest showing of social need, the belief-action doctrine permitted government to disadvantage those whose religious conduct strayed from the cultural baseline of Protestant piety that had been traditionally defined by the de facto establishment. For example, in *Braunfeld v. Brown* an Orthodox Jewish merchant argued that Pennsylvania's Sunday closing laws unfairly penalized him for his religious beliefs: under the closing laws, the merchant could match the six shopping days available to his Christian competitors only by abandoning observance of the Jewish sabbath.[10] Acknowledging that the closing laws imposed a significant and disproportionate economic burden on the Orthodox merchant, the Court nevertheless denied relief under the free exercise clause because granting the merchant an exemption from the laws would have interfered with the state's enforcement of a uniform day of "rest, repose, recreation, and tranquility." [11] Although the merchant was left free by the Court to believe in the sacredness of his sabbath, his actual observance of the sabbath was left unprotected from a substantial economic burden because the state was able to articulate a legitimate, if comparatively unimportant, social welfare objective for the closing laws.

Predictably, the *Braunfeld* dissenters found problematic the majority's subordination of a fundamental right to an insignificant regulatory goal. "What overbalancing need is so weighty in the constitutional scale that it justifies this substantial, though indirect, limitation of appellants' freedom?" asked Justice Brennan.

> It is not the desire to stamp out a practice deeply abhored by society, such as polygamy . . . . Nor is it the State's traditional protection of children . . . . It is not even the interest in seeing that everyone rests one day a week, for appellants' religion requires that they take such a rest. It is the mere convenience of having everyone rest on the same day. It is to defend this interest that the Court holds that a State need not follow the alternative route of granting an exemption for those who in good faith observe a day of rest other than Sunday. [12]

Justice Stewart was even more pointed:

> Pennsylvania has passed a law which compels an Orthodox Jew to choose between his religious faith and his economic survival. That is a cruel choice. It is a choice which I think no State can constitutionally demand. For me this is not something that can be swept under the rug and forgotten in the interest of enforced Sunday togetherness. [13]

. . *b* . .

The belief-action doctrine did not survive long past its citation in *Braunfeld.* Barely two years later, in *Sherbert v. Verner,* the Court ordered a state to pay unemployment benefits to a Seventh-Day Adventist even though she would not make herself available for work on Saturday (her sabbath) as required by the state's unemployment compensation law.[14] The state had argued that protecting the integrity of the unemployment insurance fund against depletion by those who "feign objections to Saturday work" and facilitating the scheduling by employers of necessary Saturday work were sufficient reasons to deny the benefits—as they probably were under the deferential standard of review set up by the belief-action doctrine.[15] In *Sherbert,* however, the Supreme Court announced that government could burden a fundamental right like the free exercise of religion only if it could demonstrate that its action was necessary to a "compelling" regulatory interest that could not be protected in any less intrusive manner.[16] The paradigm of a compelling interest is the protection of children and nonconsenting adults from deprivation of classical conceptions of life, liberty, or property.[17] Preventing the subversion of the criminal law or of an entire regulatory program has also been said to constitute such an interest.[18]

The Court was skeptical that the potential for fraudulent claims asserted by the state was really much of a problem, but the Justices concluded that even if it was, the state had failed to make the necessary showing that "no alternative forms of regulation would combat such abuses without infringing First Amendment rights."[19] The Court further concluded that an exemption for Sabbatarians would not threaten the viability of the unemployment benefit program.[20] It thus held the state's denial of benefits to the plaintiff an unjustified burden on the practice of her religion.[21]

In other areas of constitutional law, the absence of a less restrictive alternative to a challenged law or action has sometimes been interpreted as requiring a showing that no *equally as effective* alternative is available.[22] If this were the case in free exercise jurisprudence, an exemption from a burdensome law could never constitute such an alternative, since an exemption by definition undermines the effectiveness of the law to the extent that it excuses people from complying with it. In *Sherbert* and its progeny, however, the less restrictive alternative requirement has been understood to impose upon government the heavier burden of showing that granting an exemption would *substantially* undermine the government's implementation or protection of its compelling interest, rather than showing merely that an exemption or some other alternative would be less effective to some marginal degree.[23] This version of the requirement is more burdensome for the government because it requires the government to demonstrate that the deprivation of civil liberty caused by its action does not outweigh the state's interest in avoiding a small inefficiency in carrying out a legislative or regulatory purpose.[24] As Morris Clark put the point in the context of free exercise claims, "the importance of a law should be measured not by all the benefits it confers on society, but by the incremental benefit of applying it to those with religious scruples."[25] Given the apparently high place of religious liberty in the hierarchy of constitutional values,[26] a marginal drag on the government's ability to enforce a law or administer a program should not justify burdening the free exercise of religion. "Bureaucratic values," Stephen Pepper has argued, "ought to be viewed with skepticism as justifications for impingement on the constitutional right of religious liberty."[27]

The Court attempted to distinguish *Braunfeld* on the ground that an exemption in that case would have completely frustrated the government's purpose in enacting Sunday closing laws.[28] Even conceding the factual premise of the argument that exemptions would have made the statutory scheme unworkable, *Sherbert* remains hard to square with *Braunfeld*. If an individual suffers a constitutionally significant deprivation of liberty when forced to choose between temporary economic benefits and faithfulness to religious conscience, as *Sherbert* held, then surely the deprivation of liberty is even greater when the cost of faithfulness is loss of a lifetime of financial and human capital invested in a small business,[29] as the plaintiffs claimed in *Braunfeld*.[30] In the balance, even a substantial undermining of the state's interest in providing for a uniform day of rest and relaxation does not seem to outweigh the plaintiffs' loss.

Persuasive or not, the *Sherbert* Court's attempt to reconcile its decision with *Braunfeld* did not disguise its de facto abandonment of the belief-action doctrine in favor of a new test. Less than five years after

Sherbert, Professor Giannella could refer to the doctrine as "generally discredited."[31]

In *Wisconsin v. Yoder*, decided not quite ten years after *Sherbert*, the Court confirmed its assignment of the burden of constitutional justification in *Sherbert*.[32] In *Yoder* the Court held that the free exercise clause excused the Old Order Amish from complying with a state compulsory school attendance law.[33] The Court found that the burden the law imposed on the ability of the Amish to practice their religion and perpetuate their traditions was not constitutionally justified because the state did not show that its compelling interest in preparing children for productive and informed participation in society would have been significantly undermined by granting the Amish an exemption from the attendance laws.[34]

Yoder made explicit the government's burden of justifying any generally applicable law that incidentally burdened the free exercise of religion. In contrast to the law at issue in *Sherbert*, which was justified by regulatory interests of questionable importance, the law in *Yoder* was plausibly defended as regulation in support of a substantial and legitimate state interest. The Amish were excused from complying with the compulsory attendance law even though the law served the state's compelling interest in providing for the education of children, and granting the Amish an exemption at least marginally undermined this interest. Thus, to *Sherbert*'s requirement that government justify by a compelling interest a law that burdens the free exercise of religion, *Yoder* added the requirement that the government justify by a compelling interest any refusal to grant exemptions from the law to religious objectors.[35] The combined effect of the two decisions, or the "*Sherbert-Yoder*" doctrine, as Professor Pepper called it,[36] made clear that a law that burdens the free exercise of religion *and* a state's refusal to exempt religious objectors from such burdens must both be justified by a compelling interest. The Court expressly reaffirmed this doctrine on three subsequent occasions.[37]

. . *c* . .

In deciding in particular cases whether the religious claimant truly holds beliefs which conflict with government action, the Court has always privileged the claimant's interpretation of what his or her beliefs demand over alternative evidentiary sources.[38] In *Thomas v. Review Board*, for example, the Court held that unemployment benefits could not be denied a religious pacifist who quit his job rather than work for a division of a company that had begun making armaments.[39] In reaching this decision, the Court refused to credit either arguments that the pacifist was inconsistent in the application of his antiwar principles, or the fact that another member of the same religion worked for the division and found no conflict between his work and his faith.[40] In a later case, *Frazee v. Illinois Department of Employment Security*, the Court found it irrelevant that the religious claimant belonged to no church or organized religious body.[41] Both holdings are consistent with language in an older case, *United States v. Ballard*, in which the Court foreclosed judicial inquiry into the truth or falsity of religious beliefs: "Men may believe what they cannot prove. They may not be put to the proof of their religious doctrines or beliefs. Religious experiences which are as real as life to some may be incomprehensible to others."[42]

The extraordinary protection of religious exercise at least formally granted by the *Sherbert-Yoder* doctrine, combined with the Court's deference to the claimant's understanding of what his or her religion requires, created a potentially serious law enforcement dilemma. In light of *Ballard*, *Thomas*, and *Frazee*, the *Sherbert-Yoder* doctrine apparently created a broad constitutional exemption from compliance with any law, an exemption that seemed to be available merely for the asking to any person who represented him- or herself as a religious objector.[43] While the sincerity with which an objector adhered to a belief or tenet formally remained a legitimate inquiry, the Court's hostility to investigation of the reasonableness of a claimant's religious beliefs and its willingness to credit the claimant's own interpretation of the behavioral requirements of those beliefs in fact made any inquiry into sincerity problematic.

The broad mandate of free exercise exemptions that seemed to follow from the *Sherbert-Yoder* doctrine did not pose a serious difficulty when the benefit to be gained from exemption was something few people would actually want, like receipt of unemployment benefits despite being unavailable for work on one's sabbath, or freedom from prosecution under compulsory school attendance laws.[44] As the Court sardonically observed in *Frazee*, granting benefits to a Christian who refused to accept Sunday work was unlikely to lead to a mass labor movement opposing Sunday employment,[45] and it was equally unlikely that teenagers (or their parents) would be motivated to relocate to Amish communities and go to work on the farm in order to avoid attending high school. In *United States v. Lee*, however, the Amish asked the Court to grant them a free exercise exemption from paying social security taxes.[46] Perhaps fearing a tidal wave of exemption requests by people claiming that their religious beliefs prevented them from paying any kind of tax at all, the Court found the government's interest in denying the Amish an exemption to be compelling.[47]

Although considerations of administration and governmental convenience normally carry little weight when balanced against burdens on important civil liberties like the free exercise of religion, such considerations often indicate denial of an exemption when religious belief overlaps with secular—and especially financial—self-interest.[48] This may be because sincerity is difficult to judge in such cases, although in practice it does not seem to have been difficult for the Court to distinguish posers from true believers; if anything, the Court has erred on the side of the state in making these determinations.[49] More important is the fact that, when action required by religious belief coincides with secular (including financial) self-interest, the number of potential claimants if an exemption for such action is created increases dramatically in comparison to situations in which religious belief requires action inconsistent with secular self-interest.[50] The number of people who might claim an exemption is thus relevant both to the need to safeguard the overall effectiveness of the government's program by applying it to most of the people at whom it was aimed, and to the need to avoid situations in which the government is unable to administer fairly or effectively the exemption because of the large numbers claiming it.[51]

As the number of potential claimants rises, the need for judicial action to create free exercise exemptions correspondingly declines. When large numbers of potential claimants for a religious exemption exist, their very numbers are likely to afford them sufficient influence on the legislative process to obtain an exemption from religiously burdensome laws without resort to the courts, even if those numbers fall short of an outright majority of the voters.[52] In such circumstances, there is no need to protect *judicially* religious minorities from majority oppression; protection is likely available through the political process. Thus, when a proposed exemption is likely to have many potential claimants, the minority-protection theory that has long animated interpretations of the free exercise clause provides a justification for refusing to supply the exemption by judicial rather than legislative action.[53]

Whatever the Court's reasons for denying an exemption in *Lee*, that decision marked the beginning of the end of the *Sherbert-Yoder* doctrine. After *Lee* the Court denied free exercise relief to, inter alia, an Orthodox Jew who sought to wear a yarmulke in violation of Air Force uniform regulations in *Goldman v. Weinberger*,[54] a Native American tribe that sought to prevent construction of a highway that would prevent its members from worshiping in *Lyng v. Northwest Indian Cemetery Protective Association*,[55] and a televangelist who objected to state taxation of religious literature in *Jimmy Swaggart Ministries v. Board of Equalization*.[56] The outright elimination of judicially created exemptions was suggested in *Bowen v. Roy* in a plurality opinion by three members of the Court, who stated that "absent proof of an intent to discriminate against particular religious beliefs or religion in general, the Government meets its burden when it demonstrates that a challenged requirement for governmental benefits, neutral and uniform in its application, is a reasonable means of promoting a legitimate public interest."[57] Surveying these decisions, Mark Tushnet concluded that the Court was willing to protect religious exercise only when doing so either was relatively inexpensive or was otherwise consistent with secular constitutional norms like freedom of expression or due process of law.[58]

In *Employment Division v. Smith,* the Court brought free exercise jurisprudence full circle by ressurecting the belief-action doctrine of *Reynolds.*[59] In *Smith,* as I discussed in chapter 2, a state denied two Native Americans unemployment compensation after they were dismissed from their jobs as private drug counselors for smoking peyote as part of tribal religious rituals. Because use of peyote was a criminal offense under state law, the state ruled that the Native Americans had been dismissed for "work-related misconduct" which permitted benefits to be withheld. The Native Americans sued for the benefits, arguing that the free exercise clause prevented the state from applying the misconduct provision to them.[60]

The Court in *Smith* effectively abandoned the *Sherbert-Yoder* doctrine. Noting that denial of unemployment compensation in *Sherbert* was not based on the plaintiff's commission of an illegal act, the Court held in *Smith* that the state's interest in ensuring the integrity of the unemployment insurance fund was sufficiently important to justify its refusal to pay benefits to claimants who were guilty of unlawful conduct.[61] The majority opinion by Justice Scalia strictly confined *Sherbert* and its progeny to their facts,[62] and recast *Yoder* from a free exercise opinion that protected freedom of religion into a substantive due process opinion that protected parental authority and family autonomy.[63] The opinion suggested that the only independent protection offered by the free exercise clause lay in its prohibition of laws motivated by a desire to disadvantage religion, on the theory that such laws impose on religious exercise an intentional burden, rather than a merely incidental one.[64] However, even this protection is redundant of other parts of the Constitution, since the Court had already held in *Larson v. Valente* that legislation enacted with the demonstrable purpose of disadvantaging particular religious denominations violates the establishment clause.[65] Accordingly, *Smith* left the free exercise clause with little independent content or effect, effectively repealing it.[66] On the other hand, the Court's tepid application of the *Sherbert-Yoder* doctrine during its existence suggests that perhaps little was lost.[67]

. . 2 . .

In one sense, the *Sherbert-Yoder* doctrine seems perfectly consistent with secular individualist discourse. Indeed, Gerard Bradley suggests that the doctrine is simply "one aspect of the post–World War II takeover of our civil liberties corpus by the political morality of liberal individualism."[68] Whereas the belief-action doctrine of *Reynolds* clearly assumes that society is more important than the individual, the *Sherbert-Yoder* doctrine reflects the view that individual rights are prior to any claims society as a whole may make on individual conduct. In nineteenth-century America, for example, the de facto establishment posited traditional Protestant values as the basis of society. Those who refused to conform to these values, like polygamous Mormons, were challenging the very foundations on which society was thought to be organized and thus did not deserve any relief from laws that burdened their subversive religious practices.[69] By contrast, a regime of neutrality within secular individualist discourse purports to remain aloof from the choices that religious Americans make in their private lives. In this view, the government has no business telling people how to live their moral and religious lives. Accordingly, even idiosyncratic religious practices that would have been considered subversive under the assumptions of the de facto establishment may properly be protected by neutrality unless they threaten important state interests, such as protection of the rights or property of others.[70] In the absence of a threat of such damage, the coercive imposition of a particular morality upon consenting adults distorts individual religious choice and is therefore inconsistent with secular individualist premises.

In the contemporary United States, purposeful discrimination by the government on the basis of religion is rare. When it does occur, the Court has not hesitated to strike it down.[71] In most situations in which government action burdens religious belief and practice, government has not undertaken to prohibit or to penalize conduct *because* it is religious. Rather, the federal government pursuant to constitutionally delegated powers, or a state or local government pursuant to the police power, has taken action to protect the health, safety, and welfare of those within its jursidiction, religious and nonreligious alike, and as an incident to such action some people are burdened in the practice of their religion. For example, government-imposed vaccination requirements have clear and demonstrable public health benefits; although submitting to vaccinations conflicts with the beliefs of certain religious groups, it is difficult to maintain that those who enacted vaccination requirements intended to persecute members of these groups. In this kind of situation, government has not engineered a religious gerrymander or otherwise singled out certain religious groups for adverse treatment, but has simply acted according to its perception of the public interest which has the unfortunate and (usually) unintended side effect of burdening certain religious beliefs and practices.

The difficulty for religious freedom under this analysis is that secular individualism does not provide a basis for relieving burdens on religious practice caused by government action that is facially neutral and fully justified on secular grounds. As I have shown, secular individualist discourse permits religion to manifest itself in public life only as the effect of private choice. For example, under a secular individualist interpretation of the establishment clause, government can maintain a position of neutrality with respect to—and thus avoid constitutional responsibility for—financial aid to religion so long as the aid is funneled to individuals pursuant to broad, secularly defined beneficiary categories. Under these circumstances, the government has not distorted the "natural" pattern of private choice by creating a special benefit available only to religious institutions. The fact that some, or even most, of such aid ultimately ends up in the coffers of religious institutions is not chargeable to the government because the decision to spend the aid to benefit religion is made by the individual recipient and not the government itself.[72]

This private choice analysis has permitted the Court to uphold against establishment clause challenge a variety of government actions that assist religion.[73] But the same analysis that permits aid to religion under the establishment clause cuts in a different direction under the free exercise clause. To excuse religious individuals from compliance with generally applicable law, solely because of religious belief, distorts the pattern of private religious choice by creating an advantage available only to believers.[74] Put another way, if under secular individualist premises the establishment clause does not require that religious individuals be uniquely deprived of public welfare benefits otherwise generally available to all, then under the same premises the free exercise clause does not require that religious individuals be uniquely relieved of legal burdens otherwise generally imposed upon all.[75] This general principle is familiar to other areas of constitutional law. For example, not even so weighty a constitutional principle as freedom of the press justifies exempting news reporters and their institutional employers from generally applicable laws that incidentally burden the process of gathering and disseminating news.[76] As Justice Scalia suggested in *Smith*, "It is no more necessary to retard the collection of a general tax, for example, as 'prohibiting the free exercise [of religion]' by those citizens who believe support of organized government to be sinful, than it is to regard the same tax as 'abridging the freedom . . . of the press' of those publishing companies that must pay the tax as a condition of staying in business."[77]

To the contrary, secular individualist discourse seems to foreclose the possibility of a *religious* exemption from generally applicable laws precisely because such exemptions distort private religious choice.[78] Analogous to situations in which financial aid to religious individuals under the establishment clause is justified by secular individualism, exemptions from the unintended burdens of generally applicable laws can be consistently defended by secular individualist discourse only if they are not defined in terms of religion.[79] In this instance, conduct would be protected (or not) based on whether it fell within the secularly defined boundaries of the exemption, regardless of any religious motivation for the conduct. Thus, decisions like *Wooley v. Maynard*[80] and *West Virginia Board of Education v. Barnett*,[81] which relieve individuals of the obligation to engage in religious speech or expression with which they disagree, are correct on secular individualist premises because the state's effort to compel speech and action violates rights to freedom of speech (secularly defined), and not because the compulsion infringes rights to the free exercise of religion.[82] Similarly, the *Smith* Court's reformulation of *Yoder* as a "hybrid rights" decision is really a thinly disguised judgment that this decision should not have been tied to the free exercise clause in the first place. Parental rights to control the education of their children under the due process clause were a sufficient secular basis for exempting the Amish from compulsory school attendance laws.[83] To say that the free exercise clause mandates exemptions from generally applicable law only when another part of the constitutional text also mandates such an exemption is to say that the free exercise clause does not mandate exemptions.

The problem that religious exemptions pose for secular individualist discourse is exemplified by *Corporation of the Presiding Bishop v. Amos*, in which an employee of the Mormon church was terminated for failing to comply with certain religious standards of conduct that were not related to performance of his job.[84] The employee had no action against the church for religious discrimination because section 702 of the Civil Rights Act of 1964 exempts religious groups from antidiscrimination provisions that burden religious belief and practice.[85] Accordingly, the employee challenged this exemption as an unconstitutional establishment of religion, arguing that it constituted government action that advanced religion. The Supreme Court unanimously agreed that the provision did not violate the establishment clause, although the Justices differed among themselves on the reason.

The majority admitted that religion was advanced as a consequence of the exemption, but maintained that this advancement was attributable to the church's decision to avail itself of the exemption and to discriminate on the basis of religion, and not to any action of the government.[86] This is a distinction that cannot be maintained. As Justice O'Connor pointed out, it proves too much; *any* government benefit to religion, including the direct financial grants to parochial schools which the Court has consistently refused to allow, will advance religion only if the recipient accepts the benefit.[87] Obviously, benefits are made available by government with the full expectation that those eligible will make use of them, and it was precisely the Mormon church's reliance on secion 702 that enabled it to discriminate religiously without violating the Civil Rights Act. It is, therefore, disingenuous to suggest that the government is somehow not responsible for the natural and foreseeable consequences of having enacted the exemption, or, for that matter, of providing any other benefit which assists religion.

Recognizing this, secular individualist discourse absolves government of responsibility for the religious effects of having granted a benefit only when the benefit is made available to a broad, secularly defined beneficiary class, and the religious effect of the benefit is mediated by individual choice. Section 702 fails on both counts. The exemption is worded in terms of religion, so that only religious groups can take advantage of it, and by its terms it is granted directly to religious groups rather than received by them as the result of the choices of religious individuals.[88] Indeed, the majority explicitly admitted that the exemption skews individual religious choice.[89] Under these circumstances, the fact that the immediate cause of the discrimination was the church and not the government is at best insufficient for, and at worst irrelevant to, justification of the decision by secular individualist ideology.[90]

The real ground for the exemption, as Justice Brennan made clear, is the recognition that religious groups make important contributions to individuals and society that might be lost without an exemption. Brennan observed that, under this rationale, a religious group should be able to discriminate only with respect to its *religious* activities. However, he believed that forcing a church to defend itself in litigation by proving that a particular activity is religious would have had an unacceptable chilling effect on the religious group's definition of its own purposes and mission. Accordingly, he determined that a rule that the nonprofit activities of religious groups be considered per se religious would be the better resolution of the conflict.[91] But Justice Brennan's position cannot be justified by secular individualist discourse. Because it characterizes the value of religious groups expressly in terms of their religiosity,[92] Brennan's opinion can only be defended with religious communitarian discourse.

· · 3 · ·

In addition to illustrating the problematic character of religious exemptions in secular individualist discourse, the foregoing analysis of *Amos* makes clear that exemptions do not become justifiable by this discourse merely because they are provided by the legislature rather than imposed by the courts. Just as direct financial aid to religious—or, in the Court's words, "pervasively sectarian"—institutions violates secular individualist premises even though approved by a popularly elected body, so do legislative exemptions excusing religious (but not nonreligious) groups and individuals from complying with general laws. The distortion of individual religious choice is as apparent whether the exemption is legislative or judicial. (Again, I am not arguing here that legislative exemptions are a bad idea, only that they cannot be justified within the parameters set by the secular individualist discourse that the Court relies on for justification of its exemption decisions.)

The Court in *Smith* approved legislative exemptions at the same time that it struck down judicial ones.[93] This is consistent with decisions of the Court (other than *Amos*) that permit Congress and the states voluntarily to provide for exemptions from generally applicable law for religious conduct even though exemptions are not mandated by the free exercise clause, so long as the exemptions are defined in secular terms.[94] Nevertheless, this endorsement of legislative exemptions demonstrates that *Smith* is not fully consistent with the premises of secular individualism. More important, it demonstrates that *Smith*'s elimination of judicially mandated free exercise exemptions, like the Court's doctrine under the establishment clause, relies on secular individualist discourse to reach religious communitarian results.

In a sense, judicial exemptions enhance neutrality, by giving to religious minorities the same protections from burdens on their religious practices that are available to religious majorities by virtue of their numbers. What the majority believes interferes with its religious practices—e.g., mandatory Sunday work—is unlikely to become law; what the majority considers necessary for its religious practices—e.g., sacramental wine—is unlikely to be prohibited by law; and what the majority finds objectionable—e.g., forced sterilization—is not likely to be made a legal obligation.[95] In other words, government is permitted under the establishment clause to accomplish secular objectives in a manner that incidentally assists or accomodates majoritarian religious practices.[96] This being the case, genuine neutrality among religious sects requires that government restore the balance between majority and minority religions by making equivalent accommodations of the minority in the form of exemptions when majority preferences burden the minority.[97]

Although either legislative or judicial exemptions can accomplish this goal, the granting of judicial exemptions is subject to different dynamics than legislative exemptions. Ira Lupu has cataloged a variety of institutional differences between legislatures and courts that affect the decision to create an exemption.[98] Judges are insulated from majoritarian political pressures to a much greater extent than are legislators. Judges must decide disputes that are properly before them, and in doing so they must attempt to justify their decisions in a principled way that plausibly conforms to prior relevant decisions.[99] (This as much as anything else may account for the controversy over *Smith*: it is simply not a persuasive account of the free exercise precedents.) Finally, judicial decisions on exemptions are limited in scope: they usually apply only to the litigant before the court and others similarly situated, and rarely involve class claims. These institutional differences suggest that religious minorities will in most cases find exemptions easier to obtain from courts than from legislatures.[100] Indeed, the decision to seek judicial rather than legislative relief will itself often indicate that the claimant and others in his or her situation lack the numbers that would enable them to obtain a legislative exemption.

Of course, courts are not themselves immune from majoritarian bias. No Jewish, Muslim, or Native American plaintiff has ever prevailed on a free exercise claim before the Supreme Court.[101] Fundamentalist Christians and sects outside so-called mainline Protestantism have had only mixed success in seeking exemptions.[102] Of course, the fact that these groups were compelled to seek *judicial* relief underscores the point that legislatures tend not to create exemptions for adherents to unusual or idiosyncratic religions.[103]

Nevertheless, although prior to *Smith* claimants for religious exemptions were not particularly successful in litigation before the Supreme Court, in a number of cases they still succeeded in obtaining judicially what had been denied them legislatively or administratively.[104] The Court's elimination of judicial but not legislative exemptions not only permits religious majorities to tailor generally applicable law to avoid conflicts with their own religious practices, it also leaves exemptions for minority religions wholly subject to majoritarian preference. Experience teaches that legislatures are unlikely to create exemptions from general law for minority religions whose beliefs and practices deviate substantially from the majoritarian baseline of cultural acceptability.[105]

This result coincides with the premises of religious communitarian discourse: government may—and, in fact, should—reinforce those religious practices thought to be important to a well-ordered society, and needs to tolerate religious dissenters only to the extent that their practices do not threaten majoritarian religious values. Consistent with the pattern we have seen under the establishment clause, the Court in *Smith* uses a secular individualist analysis to justify what is a religious communitarian result.

Conclusion

. . . .

Death of a Discourse?

. . . . .

The Supreme Court's religion clause jurisprudence is limited and controlled by the rhetorical resources of secular individualist discourse. By confining religion to private life, secular individualism can subordinate religion to secularism in public life, or exclude it altogether. Secular individualist ideology prevents religious institutions from participating in social welfare programs on the same basis as secular private and public institutions, and religious institutions may benefit indirectly from such programs only if the benefit category is secularly defined and the institution receives it as the result of the religious choices of individuals. Secular individualist discourse requires that when government appropriates for public use a religious symbol or celebration, or grants financial aid directly to a religious institution, the symbol appropriated or the institution aided must be characterized as only nominally religious. Finally, secular individualist discourse cannot justify religiously defined free exercise exemptions, be they legislative or judicial.

As ruled by secular individualist discourse, religion clause jurisprudence is neither plausible nor popular. Take the Court's extreme sensitivity to coercive possibilities in establishment clause controversies, and its virtual ignorance of coercive effects in free exercise

117

contexts. In *Lee v. Weisman*, for example, the Court declared that invocations and benedictions at public school graduation ceremonies violated the establishment clause, citing as its principal rationale the coercion implicit in requiring students and their families to be present and silent during the prayers as a condition to participating in graduation exercises.[1] Yet in *Lyng v. Northwest Cemetery Protective Association*, the Court refused to grant any free exercise relief to members of a Native American tribe who contended that they would be left unable to practice their religion because of governmentally sanctioned logging and road construction on government lands the tribe held sacred.[2] The Court held that, even assuming that the sanctioned activities would "virtually destroy the . . . Indians' ability to practice their religion," the free exercise clause provided no basis for granting relief to the Native Americans.[3] Although *Lyng* was decided two years before *Smith*, it is almost perfectly congruent with *Smith's* holding that religious individuals are not constitutionally entitled to judicially imposed relief from the coercive effects of facially neutral, generally applicable laws.

One need not deny that coercion might exist in the practice of graduation prayer to realize that any such coercion pales beside that assumed and sanctioned by the Court in *Lyng*. How does one explain a jurisprudence that finds it constitutionally unconscionable to require that high school students and their families sit quietly through forty-five seconds of civil religious platitudes as a condition to participating in graduation ceremonies, while simultaneously finding constitutionally unobjectionable the destruction of an entire religious culture for something as mundane as a logging road? On secular individualist premises, this juxtaposition is entirely defensible. For the secular individualist, religion is a matter of private religious choice that government must not influence. This means that public, governmentally sponsored manifestations of religious belief, like graduation prayer, cannot be defended within secular individualist discourse. Relieving the religious but not the secular burdens imposed on individuals by facially neutral, generally applicable government action likewise encourages religious belief and practice by granting a unique benefit to religion, and thus is similarly indefensible by secular individualist ideology.

Unfortunately, while secular individualism may provide an explanation of certain aspects of religion clause jurisprudence, as a general matter its account of the jurisprudence is simply implausible. Secular individualism's confinement of religious belief and action to private life is neutral between religion and nonreligion only if one can demonstrate the undemonstrable—that religion is inherently and intrinsically private. Similarly, secular individualism can defend the parochial school aid decisions as neutral between religion and nonreligion only if one makes the ridiculous assumption that contemporary government aid to public elementary and secondary education is insignificant. Secular individualism can justify the religious symbol, religious college aid, and tax exemption cases only by disingenuously arguing that sacred celebrations and potent symbols of religious faith—the Sabbath, the crèche, the menorah—have little or no religious significance; that religious colleges and social service organizations are not significantly religious; and that churches and other religious organizations look and act like secular nonprofit organizations. Finally, secular individualism can defend legislative, but not judicial, free exercise exemptions only by draining the free exercise clause of substantive content and effect. Thus, for secular individualism to become a plausible account of religion clause jurisprudence, this jurisprudence must abandon the ideal of neutrality between religion and nonreligion in justifying decisions; it must eliminate any kind of direct financial or other assistance, including religiously defined tax exemptions, to religious institutions; and it must refuse to countenance even legislatively approved free exercise exemptions.

For most of the American cultural elite, who have secularized, weak, or nonexistent faith commitments, these changes pose little personal threat. Abandoning neutrality—in favor of, say, an ideal of cultural and political as well as institutional separation of church and state—would make clear what most elites have long thought: that individuals should be shielded from the regressive and superstitious influence of traditional religious beliefs and practices, even if doing so requires that government treat religion less favorably than non-religious belief systems. Eliminating direct financial and other assistance to religious groups, as well as all religiously defined exemptions, would ensure that whatever influence religion is able to exert on political and public life is both the result of individual choice and subordinate to the secular goals of government. Such changes would undoubtedly enhance the possibility of making the "secularization hypothesis" into the reality of the secular society.

Of course, large numbers of Americans reject the desirability of secularization. Although the Christian right and other religious conservatives in the United States who describe their world with religious communitarian discourse are often portrayed as radical fringe elements, as a matter of fact the mainstream of popular American thought is far closer to the religious communitarian ideology espoused by religious conservatives than it is to the secular individualism of cultural elites. For example, the majority of Americans feel the same way as the majority of religious conservatives on such issues as the desirability of traditional morality and family structure, the social threats presented by feminists and gay rights activists, the importance of prayer in public schools, and the relative credibility of creationism versus evolution.[4] For these people, the juxtaposition of *Weisman* with *Lyng* and *Smith*, symptomatic of the Court's religion clause jurisprudence in general, is deeply problematic. As Stephen Carter has pointed out, public school prayer is no more coercive than an educational curriculum that forces a religious conservative school child to learn about evolution or condoms.[5] Why, Americans can ask, is the Court's sensitivity to coercion so high with respect to religious practices that threaten secular programs, and so low with respect to secular practices that threaten religious belief and practice? Indeed, why are the mere *feelings* of atheists, agnostics, and other dissenters entitled to constitutional protection, as *Weisman* held, while essential *practices* of religious groups are left to the uncertain mercies of the political process by *Lyng* and *Smith*?

The answer that secular individualism can give—that religion is a regressive, antisocial force that should be strictly confined to private life and subordinated to secular goals in order to preserve rationality and order in public life—is unacceptable and unpersuasive to most religious Americans. The doctrinal changes necessary to make religion clause jurisprudence a coherent expression of secular individualism would be highly unpopular and controversial with a very large number of Americans, perhaps a majority. The charge that Jefferson Powell has leveled against constitutional theory in general applies equally to theorizing about the religion clauses: "Rather than explicating the coherence of shared American moral commitments, contemporary theorists offer little more than a veiled apologia for rule by a liberal oligarchy." [6] Isolated Supreme Court dicta to the contrary notwithstanding, the view that religious belief and practice are unique evils against which politics and public life must shield themselves is simply not part of the American constitutional tradition—[7] all in all, a curious state of affairs for a country that calls itself democratic.

The fact that secular individualism is persuasive only to a small, if powerful, cultural minority in the United States is important. A constitutional doctrine can be called "successful" if it persuades most people of its correctness so that they will generally abide its principles. Thus, it is obvious that constitutional doctrine will succeed if it is articulated with consistency and coherence, and commands widespread popular support. Even without both, doctrine might succeed if it has one trait or the other. For example, the pre-*Roe* sexual privacy decisions, which prohibit government from restricting adult access to artificial birth control,[8] lack an internally coherent doctrinal account, but have such broad and deep support that this is unimportant. Conversely, the First Amendment decisions that have granted constitutional protection to those who desecrate the American flag as a political protest are highly unpopular. Nevertheless, that this kind of expression falls within what seems to be the "core" of free speech protection in a liberal democracy—political speech that is critical of government [9]—and that the Court has consistently relied on this principle to justify its decisions[10] invest this doctrine with a rhetorical power that allows it to succeed as constitutional law despite the extreme distaste of most Americans for the speech it protects.

While constitutional doctrine might succeed if it lacks either coherence or popular support, it is destined to fail if it lacks both, which is the current dubious state of religion clause jurisprudence. Secular individualist discourse cannot plausibly account for religion clause doctrine, and, while it is the discourse within which most cultural elites make their intellectual home, its assumptions are rejected by large numbers of Americans—too many for even a fully coherent secular individualist doctrine to entertain hope of success. As a result, religion clause doctrine in the 1990s stands in the same position as economic due process stood in the 1930s—a failed jurisprudence ripe for dismantling.

What, then, of religious communitarian discourse? If secular individualism has failed, might not one response be a revitalized religious communitarianism? Religion clause jurisprudence would need radical surgery before religious communitarian discourse could give an account of it that is any more coherent than that of secular individualism. Some of the doctrinal changes that religious communitarianism would probably spawn—for example, private school tuition vouchers and public school prayer—would undoubtedly be popular; others—for example, direct financial grants to majoritarian religious organizations, public school instruction by ministers and priests, and repression of minority religions and others who threaten foundational social values—would be, at the least, controversial. Certainly, the prospect of the Court's explicitly owning religious communitarian discourse as the organizing rhetoric of religion clause doctrine is more than a little frightening. Neither the Supreme Court's recent disposal of free exercise exemptions, which leaves religious minorities vulnerable to the burdens of majoritarian religious preferences, nor the way religious communitarian discourse functioned in the nineteenth century to justify legal persecution of religious, racial, and ethnic minorities is reassuring to those who find themselves outside the religious mainstream in the locality in which they live. Whether all the doctrinal changes implied by religious communitarianism would command sufficient popular support actually to be enacted and effective as law is uncertain; that at least some of them are undesirable is clear. Religious communitarian discourse is not a viable alternative to secular individualism.

At this point, the conventions of legal scholarship require that I propose a third discourse of church and state, one that could weave the threads of religion clause jurisprudence into a coherent whole and attract popular support, which secular individualism has failed to do, and which could also protect a meaningful measure of religious freedom and pluralism, which religious communitarianism would threaten. I know of no such discourse and doubt that one yet exists. At present, secular individualism and religious communitarianism are the only two imaginable alternatives. Virtually every proposal of theoretical or doctrinal reform in religion clause jurisprudence modulates between secular individualism and religious communitarianism. But since each of these discourses is antithetical to the other, efforts to mediate a compromise position between the two are doomed.[11]

For example, Stephen Carter maintains that the hostility of public life to religious belief would be ameliorated if only we could appreciate the value that churches and other religious groups bring to society as intermediate institutions standing between the individual and the state. In the long run, he argues, the Court must protect the independence and autonomy of churches and other religious groups so that this social value is preserved.[12] This suggestion, like many normative proposals in religion clause scholarship, is both rhetorically impossible and practically unlikely. What Carter proposes, in the terms of my argument, is that secular individualist discourse incorporate certain aspects of religious communitarian discourse in its resolution of church-state conflicts. But these two discourses are mutually exclusive: asking secular individualism to incorporate some religious communitarian ideology would be like having asked the intricately ordered and reassuringly fixed medieval cosmos to incorporate a little infinity, or deterministic Newtonian mechanics a little relativity. The Court's actual performance in religious clause cases is the best evidence of the futility of this kind of effort; it inevitably leads to the implausibilities and incoherences that now characterize the jurisprudence.

Even granting the dubious assumption that a coherent (if unholy) combination of secular individualism and religious communitarianism is rhetorically possible, championing this amalgamated discourse is likely to have little practical effect. Based on periodic hints in religion clause decisions, legal scholars—myself included—have regularly argued for the development of a constitutional doctrine of religious group rights.[13] Despite this scholarly advocacy, hints in isolated opinions are still all that this "doctrine" amounts to, and almost certainly what it will remain so long as secular individualism is the dominant discourse of church and state. A Court that is so captured by secular individualist discourse that it is willing to make the implausible and unpersuasive arguments that now characterize religion clause jurisprudence is not likely to embrace even in part an account of the religion clauses so at odds with secular individualism.

C. S. Lewis once proposed that, contrary to widespread intellectual belief, the cosmic paradigm of the Middle Ages was not abandoned because it was eventually overwhelmed by contrary empirical observations and other naturalistic reports of the world; to the contrary, these contrary phenomena only appeared because changes in the human mind had already produced a distaste for the existing model and a longing for something new.[14] So, too, for our day. "It is not impossible," Lewis argued,

> that our own Model will die a violent death, ruthlessly smashed by an unprovoked assault of new facts . . . . But I think it is more likely to change when, and because, far-reaching changes in the mental temper of our descendants demand that it should. The new Model will not be set up without evidence, but the evidence will turn up when the inner need for it becomes sufficiently great. It will be true evidence. But nature gives most of her evidence in response to the questions we ask her.[15]

A new discourse of church and state (including a resurrected or revitalized religious communitarianism) will emerge only when those who practice theory begin to look for it, and that will happen only when they become convinced, as it now seems they are not, that secular individualism has wholly failed and something else is needed. The fact that failure is so clearly written in religion clause jurisprudence suggests that this recognition may not be far off.[16] Though we may well do "what comes naturally," what will seem natural to do in the American world of church-state relations will surely depend on how this world is described. It is enough, I hope, to have demonstrated that secular individualist discourse cannot do the work required of contemporary constitutional doctrine, and should be abandoned. Time will tell its replacement.

Notes

. . . . .

Introduction: The Religion Clause
Jurisprudence of the Supreme Court

1. Jesse Choper, "The Religion Clauses of the First Amendment: Reconciling the Conflict," 41 U. Pitt. L. Rev. 673, 680 (1980).

2. Phillip E. Johnson, "Concepts and Compromise in First Amendment Religious Doctrine," 72 Cal. L. Rev. 817, 817 (1984). Johnson later suggests that the Court's sacrifice of conceptual coherence in its religion clause doctrine has preserved that doctrine's palatability to large numbers of people holding disparate religious views. See id. at 839–40, 846. See also Marc Galanter, "Religious Freedom in the United States: A Turning Point?," 1966 Wis. L. Rev. 216, 296 ("In an era when both religion and government are undergoing rapid change, the lack of a single, comprehensive principle for responding to all claims for religious freedoms may not be entirely a disadvantage."); William P. Marshall, " 'We Know It When We See It': The Supreme Court and Establishment," 59 S. Cal. L. Rev. 495, 540 (1986) ("Current case law, while not perfect and undoubtedly debatable, is essentially a moderate position which presents a workable solution.").

3. Mark De Wolfe Howe, *The Garden and the Wilderness* (Chicago: University of Chicago Press, 1965), 156.

4. Michael A. Paulsen, "Religion, Equality, and the Constitution: An Equal Protection Approach to Establishment Clause Adjudication," 61 Notre Dame L. Rev. 311, 317 (1986).

5. Michael W. McConnell & Richard A. Posner, "An Economic Approach to Issues of Religious Freedom," 56 U. Chi. L. Rev. 1, 1 (1989).

6. Steven D. Smith, "Separation and the 'Secular': Reconstructing the Disestablishment Decision," 67 Tex. L. Rev. 955, 956 (1989).

7. 435 U.S. 872 (1990).

8. See, e.g., James D. Gordon III, "Free Exercise on the Mountaintop," 79 Cal. L. Rev. 91 (1991); Douglas Laycock, "The Remnants of Free Exercise," 1990 Sup. Ct. Rev. 1; Michael W. McConnell, "Free Exercise Revisionism and the *Smith* Decision," 57 U. Chi. L. Rev. 1109 (1990); Steven D. Smith, "The Rise and Fall of Religious Freedom in Constitutional Discourse," 140 U. Pa. L. Rev. 149 (1991).

9. See Everson v. Board of Educ., 333 U.S. 1 (1947).

10. Compare Everson v. Board of Educ., 333 U.S. 1 (1947) with Wolman v. Walter, 433 U.S. 229, 252–54 (1977).

11. Compare Wolman v. Walter, 433 U.S. 229, 248–51 (1977) and Meek v. Pittenger, 421 U.S. 349, 362–66 (1975) with Board of Education v. Allen, 392 U.S. 236 (1968).

12. Compare Meek v. Pittenger, 421 U.S. 349, 367–73 (1975) with Wolman v. Walter, 433 U.S. 229, 248 (1977).

13. See School Dist. v. Schempp, 374 U.S. 203 (1963); McGowan v. Maryland, 366 U.S. 420 (1961).

14. See County of Allegheny v. ACLU, 492 U.S. 573 (1989); Lynch v. Donnelly, 465 U.S. 668 (1984); McGowan v. Maryland, 366 U.S. 420 (1966).

15. See Edwards v. Aguillard, 482 U.S. 578 (1987); Stone v. Graham, 449 U.S. 39 (1980).

16. Wisconsin v. Yoder, 406 U.S. 205 (1972); Sherbert v. Verner, 374 U.S. 398 (1963).

17. Compare *Unemployment Compensation Cases,* 489 U.S. 829 (1989); 480 U.S. 136 (1987); 450 U.S. 707 (1981); 374 U.S. 398 (1963) (unemployment benefits cannot be denied a person who leaves or loses employment for reasons of religious conscience); Wisconsin v. Yoder, 406 U.S. 205 (1972) (Amish parents cannot be prosecuted for violation of compulsory school attendance statute) with Swaggart v. Board of Equalization, 493 U.S. 378 (1990) (denying television ministry exemption from general tax on sales of Bibles); Lyng v. Northwest Indian Cemetery Protective Ass'n, 485 U.S. 439 (1988) (free exercise clause does not prevent federal government from implementing land use plan that would destroy Native American religion); O'Lone v. Estate of Shabazz, 482 U.S. 342 (1987) (denying prison inmates exemption from policy that prevented them from attending Muslim worship services); Bowen v. Roy, 476 U.S. 693 (1986) (free exercise clause does not prevent government from assigning and using Social Security number of Native American child in violation of parent's religious beliefs); Goldman v. Weinberger, 475 U.S. 503 (1986) (denying Orthodox Jewish serviceman exemption from uniform regulation which prevented his wearing a yarmulke); Jensen v. Quaring, 472 U.S. 478 (1985) (affirming by equally divided Court denial of exemption from driver's license photograph requirement to person who believed photographs were "graven images" in violation of the Ten Commandments); Tony & Susan Alamo Found. v. Secretary of Labor, 471 U.S. 290 (1985) (denying religious foundation exemption from federal labor regulations); Bob Jones University v. United States, 461 U.S. 574 (1983) (denying religious university exemption from regulation that denies tax exemption to

racially discriminatory educational institutions); and United States v. Lee, 455 U.S. 252 (1982) (denying Amish employer exemption from payment of Social Security taxes). See also Braunfeld v. Brown, 366 U.S. 599 (1961) (denying Orthodox Jewish merchant exemption from Sunday closing law) (decided before *Sherbert*).

18. 494 U.S. 872 (1990).

19. See Milner S. Ball, "The Unfree Exercise of Religion," 20 Cap. U. L. Rev. 39 (1991) (explaining how the Court avoids evaluating religious practices and beliefs by leaving their free exercise at the mercy of the political process); Mark Tushnet, *Red, White, and Blue: A Critical Analysis of Constitutional Law* (Cambridge, Mass.: Harvard University Press, 1988), 264–66 (describing reluctance of Court to protect free exercise of religion when significant state interests are at stake).

20. Laycock, "Remnants," 68.

21. See Herbert McCloskey & Aida Brill, *Dimensions of Tolerance: What Americans Think about Civil Liberties* (New York: Russell Sage Foundation, 1983), 133–35. See also Stephen L. Carter, *The Culture of Disbelief: How American Law and Politics Trivialize Religious Devotion* (New York: Basic Books, 1993), 186–87 ("Even though support has fallen a bit, most Americans since the 1960s have supported the effort to amend the Constitution to overturn the school prayer cases—a movement celebrated quadrennially in the Republican Party's presidential platform.").

22. See Galanter, "Turning Point," 269. See also Philip B. Kurland, "The Religion Clauses and the Burger Court," 34 Cath. U. L. Rev. 1, 8–9 (1984) (noting the "public furor against the Court" resulting from its early establishment clause opinions).

23. See West Coast Hotel v. Parrish, 300 U.S. 379 (1937).

24. Donald A. Giannella, "Religious Liberty, Nonestablishment, and Doctrinal Development—Part I: The Religious Liberty Guarantee," 80 Harv. L. Rev. 1381, 1383 (1967).

25. Compare Everson v. Board of Educ., 330 U.S. 1 (1947) (arguing that the principal force behind inclusion of the establishment clause in the Bill of Rights was the desire to eliminate the civil disorder and persecution that was associated with established churches in Europe) with David M. Smolin, "The Judeo-Christian Tradition and Self-Censorship in Legal Discourse," 13 U. Dayton L. Rev. 345, 379–80 (1988) ("America was at its outset a Protestant or Reformed Christian nation, rather than an Enlightenment nation; one must journey to France to find an example of a contemporary revolution truly dominated by the ideas of philosophers.").

26. Walter Benjamin, "Theses on the Philosophy of History" in *Illuminations: Essays and Reflections*, ed. Hannah Arendt, trans. Harry Zahn (New York: Schocken, 1968), 256.

27. See, e.g., Kurland, "Religion Clauses," 15–17; William Van Alstyne, "Trends in the Supreme Court: Mr. Jefferson's Crumbling Wall—A Comment on *Lynch v. Donnelly*," 1984 Duke L.J. 770, 785–87.

28. A number of commentators have cataloged normative conceptions of church-state relations. See, e.g., Carl Esbeck, "Five Views of Church-State Relations in Contemporary America," 1986 B.Y.U. L. Rev. 371; Michael W. McConnell, "You Can't Tell the Players in Church-State Disputes without a Scorecard," 10 Harv. J.L. & Pub. Pol'y 27 (1986); John Witte Jr., "The Theology and Politics of the First Amendment Religion Clauses: A Bicentennial Essay," 40 Emory L.J. 489 (1991). None of these prior works has linked the normative conceptions they identify to the doctrine of the Court in the comprehensive and systematic way that I argue in this work opting instead simply to note their apparent influence in various cases.

Chapter 1. Two Discourses of Church and State

1. Roberto Unger, *Knowledge and Politics*, 2d ed. (New York: Free Press, 1984), 31–32, 79–80.

2. For descriptions of the correspondence theory of truth, see Dorothy Grover, "Truth and Language-World Connections," 87 J. Phil. 671, 671–72 (1990); Garth Hallett, *Language and Truth* (New Haven: Yale University Press, 1988), 5–16; Michael J. Perry, *Morality, Politics and Law: A Bicentennial Essay* (New York: Oxford University Press, 1988), 40–42.

3. See, e.g., Grover, "Truth," 672, 686–87; Hallett, *Language*, 17–30. For an account of this abandonment, see Allen Thiher, *Words in Reflection: Modern Language Theory and Postmodern Fiction* (Chicago: University of Chicago Press, 1984).

4. Holmes Rolston III, *Science and Religion: A Critical Survey* (Philadelphia: Temple University Press, 1987), 2–5; Unger, *Knowledge*, 31–36.

5. 1 Emilio Betti, "Prolegomena," § 8-*b* to *Teoria generale della interpretazione*, ed. Giuliano Crifò, corrected and expanded ed. (Milan: Giuffrè, 1990), 46 (author's translation): "We possess facts, we succeed, that is, in having them in our power in clear and precise form, only to the extent that we succeed in translating them into the language of our representing and idealizing, of our judgments and concepts, into the fluid and flexible instrument of our conceptualizing and dialectizing, that continually sustains itself in the communicative process." See also 1 id. at 47 (author's translation): "[Facts]

cannot remain unchanged from the moment that, in the act of conceiving and representing them, we situate them and order them in genetic links and nexes which are not clearly 'intrinsic' to the facts themselves considered abstractly in a kind of bare objectivity, but instead they come to be established, recognized, and rendered explicit in our mode of conceiving and understanding them, by virtue of that apperceptive and reconstructed synthetic energy, thanks to which we are in a position to grasp and dominate them."

6. Cf. Stanley Fish, *Doing What Comes Naturally: Change, Rhetoric, and the Practice of Theory in Literary and Legal Studies* (Durham, N.C.: Duke University Press, 1989), 174 ("The intrinsic . . . is a political rather than an essential category, and as such it will always reflect the interests—wholly legitimate because without interest there would be no value—of those who have had a hand in fashioning it.").

7. Cf. id. at 11 (emphasis in original): "All preferences are principled, that is, they are intelligible and doable only by virtue of some principled articulation of the world and its possibilities; but by the same token all principles are preferences, because every principle is an extension of a particular and *contestable* articulation of the world and none proceeds from a universal perspective."

8. Martin Heidegger, "Modern Science, Metaphysics, and Mathematics," trans. W. B. Barton & Vera Deutsch, and "The Question Concerning Technology," trans. William Lovitt, in *Basic Writings*, ed. David Farrell Krell, rev. and expanded ed. (New York: HarperCollins, 1993), 267, 307.

9. Hans-Georg Gadamer, *Truth and Method*, rev. trans. Joel Winesheimer & Donald G. Marshall, 2d rev. ed. (New York: Continuum, 1993).

10. Thomas Kuhn, *The Structure of Scientific Revolutions*, 2d ed. (Chicago: University of Chicago Press, 1970).

11. Michel Foucault, *L'ordre du discours* (Paris: Gallimard, 1971). See also Jacques Derrida, "The Other Heading: Memories, Responses, and Responsibilities" in *The Other Heading: Reflections on Today's Europe*, trans. Pascale-Anne Brault & Michael B. Naas (Bloomington: Indiana University Press, 1992), 3, 54–56 (observing how the "discursive norm" of free speech in Western Europe shapes the content of public political discussion in both positive and negative ways).

12. Jacques Derrida, *Aporias*, trans. Thomas Dutoit (Stanford, Cal.: Stanford University Press, 1993).

13. Stanley Fish, *Is There a Text in This Class?* (Cambridge, Mass.: Harvard University Press, 1980).

14. James Davison Hunter, *Culture Wars: The Struggle to Define America* (New York: Basic Books, 1991).

15. Id. at 34–39.

16. Id. at 44–45, 46, 124–25 (quoting Presidential Biblical Scoreboard, "The American Paradox: Christian Majority—Christians *can* Regain Control from the Liberal Minority" [Spring 1988], 6).

17. Id. at 47, 96.

18. See, e.g., W. Cole Durham & Alexander Dushku, "Traditionalism, Secularism, and the Transformative Dimension of Religious Institutions," 1993 B.Y.U. L. Rev. 421, 425 ("Increasingly, it is the divide between traditionalists and secularists that constitutes the fundamental challenge for pluralism in contemporary society."); David M. Smolin, Book Review, "Regulating Religious and Cultural Conflict in a Postmodern America: A Response to Professor Perry," 76 Iowa L. Rev. 1067, 1073 (1991) (describing the contemporary religious conflict as one between "secularized" and "modernist" Protestants on the one hand, and Roman Catholics and "fundamentalist" and "evangelical" Protestants on the other); id. at 1091 ("This conflict . . . is not so much between those of different religions . . . , but rather primarily is between those whose religious and moral views reflect a modernist commitment to individual autonomy, and those whose religious and moral views reflect traditional theistic, or other traditionalist communitarian values.").

19. See, e.g., Ernst Cassirer, *The Philosophy of the Enlightenment* (Princeton: Princeton University Press, 1951), 158–59, 167–77; Peter Gay, *The Enlightenment: An Interpretation—The Rise of Modern Paganism* (New York: W. W. Norton, 1966), 237, 254, 330, 376–77.

20. Cf. Steven D. Smith, *Foreordained Failure: The Quest for a Constitutional Principle of Religious Freedom* (New York: Oxford University Press, 1995), 104 (describing the "civic virtue rationale" for government support of religious institutions) ("If a particular institution is essential to society, it seems to follow that government should use its powers to foster or promote that institution, instead of simply leaving the institution to fend for itself (much less excluding it from benefits, such as public subsidies, for which other institutions *are* eligible).") (emphasis in original).

21. Cf. id. at 66 (from a communitarian standpoint, "the dissenter's obnoxious views may not immediately threaten the property or bodily integrity of others, but they surely do influence the nature of the community that the citizens share").

22. Cf. Robert Audi, "The Separation of Church and State and the Obligations of Citizenship," 18 Phil. & Pub. Aff. 259 (1989) (arguing that religious citizens must have secular motivations for their political views and actions).

23. Cf. Philip B. Kurland, "The Religion Clauses and the Burger Court,"

34 Cath. U. L. Rev. 1, 3 (1984) ("[T]he alliance between religion and government had always resulted in bloody divisiveness within a nation and bloody wars between nations."). See also John Rawls, "The Idea of an Overlapping Consensus," 7 Oxford J. Leg. Studies 1, 4 (1987) (the social and historical conditions, including the "Wars of Religion," which gave birth to modern liberal democracy, suggest that any conception of justice "must allow for a diversity of general and comprehensive doctrines, and for the plurality of conflicting, and indeed incommensurable, conceptions of the meaning, value, and purpose of human life").

24. See, e.g., Richard Rorty, "The Priority of Democracy to Philosophy" in *The Virginia Statute for Religious Freedom: Its Evaluation and Consequences in American History,* ed. Merrill D. Peterson & Robert C. Vaughn (New Brunswick, N.J.: Transaction, 1988), 257. See also Durham & Dushku, "Traditionalism," 428 (describing Maine's view that religion is "an important co-founder of law . . . but one whose contribution can be dispensed with once a more advanced stage of civilization is attained"); Henry F. May, *The Enlightenment in America* (Oxford: Oxford University Press, 1976), 361–62 (one of the differences between the European Enlightenment and the elaboration of its principles in the United States was the latter's association of Enlightenment principles with democracy); John Witte, Jr., "The Theology and Politics of the First Amendment Religion Clauses: A Bicentennial Essay," 40 Emory L.J. 489, 495 (1991) (for "enlightenment separationists," only by removing religion from politics "could society achieve a properly focused and properly restricted political process").

25. Cf. Phillip B. Kurland, *Religion and the Law: Of Church and State and the Supreme Court* (Chicago: University of Chicago Press, 1961) (arguing that religion should not be used as a basis for government classifications); William P. Marshall, "Solving the Free Exercise Dilemma: Free Exercise as Expression," 67 Minn. L. Rev. 545 (1983) (arguing that religious expression should receive constitutional protection under the free exercise clause only if analogous secular expression would be protected by the speech clause).

26. Cf. Durham & Dushku, "Traditionalism," 432 ("Rawlsian liberalism is skewed toward atomizing individualism from the beginning and cannot adequately account for the significance of religion and tradition in social life.").

27. Cf. id. at 440: "Some with attitudes that trace back to the secular Enlightenment exhibit open hostility toward organized religion, viewing it as a pillar of the *ancien régime* and its traditionalist heirs or, at a minimum, as a source of disintegration and separatism in contemporary society. Their

attacks on religion often focus on the despotic role they perceive religion to have played in preventing people from enjoying their natural rights and using their rational minds."

28. Michael J. Malbin, *Religion and Politics: The Intentions of the Authors of the First Amendment* (Washington, D.C.: American Enterprise Institute, 1978), 14.

29. Id. at 15.

30. Compare id. at 7, 14 (arguing that the founders understood the establishment clause only to prohibit government aid to a particular sect) and Gerard V. Bradley, "Imagining the Past and Remembering the Future: The Supreme Court's History of the Establishment Clause," 18 Conn. L. Rev. 827, 833–34 (1986) (same) with Douglas Laycock, " 'Nonpreferential' Aid to Religion: A False Claim about Original Intent," 27 Wm. & Mary L. Rev. 875 (1986) (arguing that the founders intended the clause to prohibit nonpreferential aid to religion). See generally Arlin M. Adams & Charles J. Emmerich, *A Nation Dedicated to Religious Liberty: The Constitutional Heritage of the Religion Clauses* (Philadelphia: University of Pennsylvania Press, 1990), 19.

31. See, e.g., Malbin, *Religion*, 16; Stephen Pepper, "A Brief for the Free Exercise Clause," 7 J.L. & Relig. 323, 329 (1989).

32. See Pepper, "A Brief," 330–31.

33. Compare Michael W. McConnell, "The Origins and Historical Understanding of Free Exercise of Religion," 103 Harv. L. Rev. 1409, 1511–12 (1990) (founders were familiar with both legislative and judicial exemptions for believers from general laws that burdened religious belief or practice, although the latter were not common) with Gerard V. Bradley, "Beguiled: Free Exercise Exemptions and the Siren Song of Liberalism," 20 Hofstra L. Rev. 245, 261–306 (1991) (original understanding of the free exercise clause did not contemplate judicial exemptions from general laws) and Malbin, *Religion*, 39 (founders favored exemptions but did not consider them a matter of constitutional right). See also J. Morris Clark, "Guidelines for the Free Exercise Clause," 83 Harv. L. Rev. 327, 327 (1969) ("Historically it is by no means certain that all or even most of the men who voted for the first amendment believed that government could exercise full control over the actions of religious men.").

34. See generally McConnell, "Origins," 1503–11.

35. See Witte, "Theology and Politics," 497. Compare U.S. Const. art. VI (prohibiting religious tests for federal office) with Torcaso v. Watkins, 367 U.S. 488, 495 (1961) (declaring unconstitutional a state religious test for position of notary public which had been in existence since the founding

era). See also Donald A. Giannella, "Religious Liberty, Nonestablishment, and Doctrinal Development—Part I: The Religious Liberty Guarantee," 80 Harv. L. Rev. 1381, 1386 (1967) (the two historical evils of religious establishment, "direct restraints on belief and worship" and "civil disabilities," were eliminated and liberty of religious conscience secured against the federal government "by simply placing matters of religion beyond the competence of the central government"). Steven Smith has recently argued that the free exercise clause as well as the establishment clause is a purely structural federalism provision without any substantive content. See Smith, *Foreordained Failure*, 35–43.

36. Harold S. Berman, *Faith and Order: The Reconciliation of Law and Religion* (Atlanta: Scholars Press, 1993), 223; Steven D. Smith, "Separation and the 'Secular': Reconstructing the Disestablishment Decision," 67 Tex. L. Rev. 955, 966–67 (1989); Witte, "Theology and Politics," 497, 499.

37. Thomas Curry, *The First Freedoms: Church and State in America to the Passage of the First Amendment* (New York: Oxford University Press, 1986), 133–172 passim, 191–92.

38. Bradley, "Imagining the Past," 834–35.

39. Joseph Story, *Commentaries on the Constitution of the United States*, § 988, ed. Ronald D. Rotunda & John E. Nowak (Durham, N.C.: Carolina Academic Press, 1987), 700.

40. Philip B. Kurland, "The Origins of the Religion Clauses of the Constitution," 27 Wm. & Mary L. Rev. 839, 856 (1986); e.g., Story, *Commentaries*, § 987 at 699 (distinguishing aid "to religion in general" from aid "to an ecclesiastical establishment").

41. 1 Alexis de Tocqueville, *Democracy in America*, ed. Phillips Bradley (New York: Vintage, 1990), 306.

42. 1 id. at 307.

43. Story, *Commentaries*, § 986 at 699. See also id. at 698–99 ("[T]he right of a society or government to interfere in matters of religion will hardly be contested by any persons, who believe that piety, religion, and morality are intimately connected with the well being of the state, and indispensable to the administration of civil justice.").

44. Gerard V. Bradley, "The No Religious Test Clause and the Constitution of Religious Liberty: A Machine That Has Gone of Itself," 37 Case Res. L. Rev. 674, 684–85 (1987). See also Berman, *Faith and Order*, 223 ("Religion was understood to be not only a matter of personal faith and personal morality but also a matter of collective responsibility and collective identity."); McConnell, "Origins," 1496 ("Not until the second third of the nineteenth century did the notion that the opinions of individuals

have precedence over the decisions of civil society gain currency in American thought.").

45. Mark De Wolfe Howe, *The Garden and the Wilderness* (Chicago: University of Chicago Press, 1965), 11–15, 31, 98.

46. May, *Enlightenment in America*, 347.

47. Holy Trinity Church v. United States, 143 U.S. 457 (1892) (quoting People v. Ruggles, 8 Johns. 290, 295 [N.Y. 1811] and citing Vidal v. Girard's Executors, 98 U.S. [2 How.] 127, 198 [1844]). For summaries of the mutual reinforcement and extensive interactions of government authority and Protestant religion during this period, see Berman, *Faith and Order*, 211–14, 225–30; Laycock, " 'Nonpreferential' Aid," 914–18; David M. Smolin, "The Judeo-Christian Tradition and Self-Censorship in Legal Discourse," 13 U. Dayton L. Rev, 345, 380–85 (1988); Witte, "Theology and Politics," 497–99.

48. Marc Galanter, "Religious Freedom in the United States: A Turning Point?," 1966 Wis. L. Rev. 216, 256.

49. Late Corp. of the Church of Jesus Christ of Latter-Day Saints v. United States, 136 U.S. 1, 48, 49 (1890).

50. Murphy v. Ramsey, 114 U.S. 15, 45 (1885).

51. Davis v. Beason, 133 U.S. 333, 341 (1890).

52. Id. at 50; accord Late Corp. of the Church of Jesus Christ of Latter-Day Saints v. United States, 136 U.S. 1, 50 (1890); Murphy v. Ramsey, 114 U.S. 15, 45 (1885); Reynolds v. United States, 98 U.S. 145, 164 (1878).

53. Smolin, "Cultural Conflict," 1070–71. See also Ferdinand F. Fernandez, "The Free Exercise of Religion," 36 S. Cal. L. Rev. 546, 565 (1963): "[T]he government fosters Christianity by incorporating its moral and philosophical concepts into the very fabric of our law. This does not mean that Christianity is the established religion in a heinous sense; it does mean that . . . no person can in his actions deviate too far from its concepts without running afoul of the law itself."

54. See generally Edward Purcell Jr., *The Crisis of Democratic Theory: Scientific Naturalism and the Problem of Value* (Lexington: University Press of Kentucky, 1973).

55. Id. at 61.

56. Berman, *Faith and Order*, 214.

57. Stephen V. Monsma, *Positive Neutrality: Letting Religious Freedom Ring* (Westport, Conn.: Greenwood, 1993), 126–29.

58. See Frederick Mark Gedicks & Roger Hendrix, *Choosing the Dream: The Future of Religion in American Public Life* (Westport, Conn.: Greenwood, 1991), 48–49.

59. Smith, "Separation and the 'Secular,'" 978.

60. 330 U.S. 1 (1947).

61. Id. at 8–9.

62. Id. at 10; accord id. at 40, 53–54 (Rutledge, J., dissenting) ("Public money devoted to payment of religious costs, educational or other, brings the quest for more. It brings too the struggle of sect against sect for the larger share . . . . The dominating group will achieve the dominant benefit; or all will embroil the state in their dissensions.").

63. See id. at 11–13; id. at 33–41 (Rutledge, J., dissenting).

64. Id. at 15–16. Justice Rutledge, writing in dissent for four Justices, seemed to go even further, arguing that the purpose of the establishment clause "was broader than separating church and state in this narrow sense [i.e., of prohibiting established churches]. It was to create a complete and permanent separation of the spheres of religious activity and civil authority by comprehensively forbidding every form of public aid or support for religion." Id. at 31–32 (Rutledge, J., dissenting).

65. Id. at 16.

66. Smolin, "Cultural Conflict," 1072. See also Witte, "Theology and Politics," 501 ("In determining the intent of the framers [in *Everson* and other early establishment clause cases], the Justices turned principally to the writings of the enlightenment political separatists . . . and largely ignored the equally prominent writings of the evangelical theological separationists.").

67. See, e.g., Steven G. Gey, "The Unfortunate Revival of Civic Republicanism," 141 U. Pa. L. Rev. 801 (1993); Morton J. Horwitz, "Republicanism and Liberalism in American Constitutional Thought," 29 Wm. & Mary L. Rev. 57 (1987); Frank I. Michelman, "The Supreme Court, 1985 Term—Foreword: Traces of Self-Government," 100 Harv. L. Rev. 4 (1986); Suzanna Sherry, "Civic Virtue and the Feminine Voice in Constitutional Adjudication," 72 Va. L. Rev. 543 (1986); Cass R. Sunstein, "Interest Groups in American Public Law," 38 Stan. L. Rev. 29 (1985); Symposium, "The Republican Civic Tradition," 97 Yale L.J. 1493 (1988); Mark Tushnet, *Red, White, and Blue: A Critical Analysis of Constitutional Law* (Cambridge, Mass.: Harvard University Press, 1988). See generally Gordon Wood, "Classical Republicanism and the American Revolution," 66 Chi.-Kent L. Rev. 13 (1990).

68. Horwitz, "Republicanism and Liberalism," 66–67; accord Sherry, "Civic Virtue," 552 ("In the republican vision, the primary function of government is to order values and to define virtue, and thereby educate its citizenry to be virtuous.").

69. Horwitz, "Republicanism and Liberalism," 66–67.

70. Tushnet, *Red, White and Blue,* 4–5.

71. Cf. Witte, "Theology and Politics," 495 ("Evangelical separation-ism . . . was based on the belief that persons were fundamentally communal beings . . . ."). See generally Horwitz, "Republicanism and Liberalism," 73 (the republican tradition understood law "as constitutive of culture"); Tush-net, *Red, White and Blue*, 10 ("The republican tradition insisted that people are social beings who draw their understandings of themselves and the mean-ing of their lives from their participation with others in a social world that they actively and jointly create.").

72. Cf. Witte, "Theology and Politics," 495 ("Enlightenment separation-ism . . . was based on the belief that a person is fundamentally an individual being and that religion is primarily a matter of private reason and conscience and only secondarily a matter of communal association and corporate con-fession."). See generally Horwitz, "Republicanism and Liberalism," 68–69 ("The republican tradition promotes the concept of an autonomous pub-lic interest, whereas the liberal ideal holds that the public interest is either simply procedural or the sum of private interests.").

73. Tushnet, *Red, White and Blue*, 271.

74. Compare Cass R. Sunstein, "Beyond the Republican Revival," 97 Yale L.J. 1539, 1578 & n.214 (1988) (arguing that interpretations of the estab-lishment clause "should recognize the role of religious organizations in the cultivation of republican virtues" by permitting those public accommoda-tions of religious belief and practice necessary to preserve neutrality) with Tushnet, *Red, White and Blue*, 274–76 (arguing that establishment clause con-troversies would be better decided by "mutual forbearance" than by formally authorizing or prohibiting government sponsorship of the disputed religious practices) and Sherry, "Civic Virtue," 593–95 (arguing that the establishment clause should bar public accommodation of religious belief and practice when it communicates to nonadherents a "message of exclusion" from the political community). See also H. Jefferson Powell, *The Moral Tradition of Ameri-can Constitutionalism: A Theological Interpretation* (Durham, N.C.: Duke University Press, 1993), 69 n.83 (noting that the relationship between "En-lightenment liberalism, the 'Machiavellian' revival of an essentially pagan notion of civic virtue, and Christian and Aristotelian thought is extremely complicated," and expressing skepticism that contemporary republicans have accurately captured this relationship); Steven D. Smith, *Foreordained Failure*, 104 ("[E]arly proponents of the civic virtue rationale used it to argue for a conclusion just opposite that typically favored by current proponents [of the rationale—i.e., republicans]. Religion is essential for the inculcation of civic virtue, it was argued, and therefore government ought to support religion in various ways, many of which involved the use of coercion.").

75. See, e.g., Sunstein, "Republican Revival," 1548–49. See also Powell, *American Constitutionalism*, 92 ("Republican constitutional thought was a quintessential product of Enlightenment liberalism in its modes of reasoning as well as in its substantive account of political society.").

76. See, e.g., Frank Michelman, "Law's Republic," 97 Yale L.J. 1493 (1988) (developing a republican critique of Supreme Court refusals to extend constitutional rights to marginal members of the national political community like gays); Sunstein, "Republican Revival," 1580 (suggesting that republicanism might "provide a basis for understanding that the role of constitutionalism in countering classifications in such areas as race, gender, sexual orientation, and poverty").

77. Compare Douglas Laycock, "The Remnants of Free Exercise," 1990 Sup. Ct. Rev. 1 (strongly criticizing the Supreme Court's abandonment of the accommodation principal) with Steven G. Gey, "Why Is Religion Special?: Reconsidering the Accommodation of Religion under the Religion Clauses of the First Amendment," 52 U. Pitt. L. Rev. 75 (1990) (criticizing the accommodation principle).

Chapter 2. Neutrality as Hostility:
The Privatization of Religion

1. Milner Ball, *Lying Down Together: Law, Metaphor, and Theology* (Madison: University of Wisconsin Press, 1985), 8–9.

2. See, e.g., Hans-Georg Gadamer, *Truth and Method*, rev. trans. Joel Winesheimer & Donald G. Marshall, 2d rev. ed. (New York: Continuum, 1993), 476 ("[S]cience attempts to become certain about entities by methodically organizing its knowledge of the world. Consequently it condemns as heresy all knowledge that does not allow of this kind of certainty and that therefore cannot serve the growing domination of being."); Martin Heidegger, "The Question concerning Technology," trans. William Lovitt, in *Basic Writings*, ed. David Farrell Krell, rev. and exp. ed. (New York: Harper-Collins, 1993), 307, 332 ("technological" thinking "banishes man into the kind of revealing that is an ordering. Where this ordering holds sway, it drives out every other possibility of revealing").

3. See, e.g., Michel Foucault, *L'ordre du discours* (Paris: Gallimard, 1971), 36–37 (describing how Mendel's accurate criticisms of nineteenth-century biology were ignored because they were inconsistent with then-dominant conceptions of plant life); Martin Heidegger, "Modern Science, Metaphysics, and Mathematics," trans. W. B. Barton & Vera Deutsch, in *Basic Writings*, 267, 280 (observing that although Newton's First Law of

Motion was anticipated in various ways by Galileo, Baliani, Descartes, and Leibniz, prior to Newton this "law" was nevertheless inconceivable).

4. See Thomas Kuhn, *The Copernican Revolution* (New York: Vintage, 1959), 43–44, 91–118 passim, 189–95. See also C. S. Lewis, *The Discarded Image* (Cambridge: Cambridge University Press, 1967) (arguing that the medieval conception of the cosmos, of which geocentricity was only a small if integral part, exerted such extraordinary power because the fixed and finite order that it imposed on the world enabled a complete, certain, and satisfying understanding of each person's place in the world).

5. Robin West, *Narrative, Authority, and Law* (Ann Arbor: University of Michigan Press, 1993), 128–29 (emphasis in original).

6. Cf. Terry Eagleton, *Literary Theory: An Introduction* (Minneapolis: University of Minnesota Press, 1983), 14 (defining "ideology" as "[t]he largely concealed structure of values which informs and underlies our factual statements," and "the ways in which what we say and believe connects with the power-structure and power-relations of the society we live in").

7. Holmes Rolston III, *Science and Religion: A Critical Survey* (Philadelphia: Temple University Press, 1987), 10.

8. Robert Cover, "The Supreme Court, 1982 Term—Foreword: *Nomos* and Narrative," 97 Harv. L. Rev. 4, 4 (1983).

9. Id. at 7.

10. Foucault, *L'ordre du discours*, 11.

11. Owen Fiss, "Objectivity and Interpretation," 34 Stan. L. Rev. 739, 744 (1982).

12. Cf. Rolston, *Science and Religion*, 8 (describing a "paradigm" as an "established pattern of expectation" or "a controlled patterned seeing" that organizes and orders one's understanding of the world).

13. Richard John Neuhaus, *The Naked Public Square: Religion and Democracy in America*, 2d ed. (Grand Rapids, Mich.: Eerdmans, 1986).

14. Stephen L. Carter, *The Culture of Disbelief: How American Law and Politics Trivialize Religious Devotion* (New York: Basic Books, 1993).

15. See, e.g., Peter Berger, "Religion in Post-Protestant America," 81 Commentary 41 (May 1986); Gerard V. Bradley, "Dogmatomachy—A 'Privatization' Theory of the Religion Clause Cases," 30 St. Louis L.J. 275 (1986); David M. Smolin, "The Judeo-Christian Tradition and Self-Censorship in Legal Discourse," 13 U. Dayton L. Rev. 345 (1988).

16. See, e.g., Roger C. Cramton, "Beyond the Ordinary Religion," 37 J. Legal Educ. 509 (1987); W. Cole Durham & Alexander Dushku, "Traditionalism, Secularism, and the Transformative Dimension of Religious Institutions," 1993 B.Y.U. L. Rev. 421, 427; Kent Greenawalt, *Religious Convic-*

tions and Political Choice (New York: Oxford, 1988), 5–6; Michael J. Perry, *Morality, Politics and Law: A Bicentennial Essay* (New York: Oxford, 1988), 10, 211 n.10; Steven D. Smith, Book Review, 8 Const. Comm. 227, 228–29 (1991).

17. See introduction, text at nn.16–22.

18. See, e.g., John Dart, "The Religion Beat" in *The Religion Beat* (New York: Rockefeller Foundation, 1981), 19, 20–21 (observing that the religion editor of a typical urban newspaper is a nonbeliever); Mark Edmundson, "A Will to Cultural Power: Deconstructing the De Man Scandal," *Harper's* (July 1988), 67, 69–70 (observing that English faculty at elite universities generally believe that literature has replaced religion as the principal source of moral values); Kent Greenawalt, "Religious Convictions and Political Choice: Some Further Thoughts," 39 DePaul L. Rev. 1019, 1035 (1990) (noting the marginalization of religion in public media and intellectual life); Neuhaus, *Naked Public Square*, 97–98 (describing how the news media ignored the religious dimension of Martin Luther King's political activism).

19. See, e.g., Peter Benson & Dorothy Williams, *Religion on Capitol Hill: Myths and Realities* (New York: Oxford University Press, 1986) (arguing that national media do not report on the religious beliefs of Congress or the religious dimensions of political activity in Congress despite the fact that members of Congress are as religious as the general population); Ellis Sandoz, *A Government of Laws: Political Theory, Religion, and the American Founding* (Baton Rouge: Louisiana State University Press, 1990) (arguing that scholars of the American revolution emphasize the influence of political philosophy on the founders at the expense of religious and theological influences); Paul Vitz, *Religion and Traditional Values in Public School Textbooks* (Washington, D.C.: U.S. Department of Education, 1985) (arguing that American public school textbooks ignore the influence of Christianity and Judaism in history).

20. See Frederick Mark Gedicks & Roger Hendrix, *Choosing the Dream: The Future of Religion in American Public Life* (Westport, Conn.: Greenwood, 1991), 29–32, 82–84.

21. Mark Tushnet, "Religion in Politics" (Book Review), 89 Colum. L. Rev. 1131, 1134 (1989) (reviewing Greenawalt, *Religious Convictions*).

22. Theodore Y. Blumoff, "Disdain for the Lessons of History: Comments on *Love and Power*," 20 Cap. U. L. Rev. 159, 186–87 (1991). See also Tushnet, "Religion in Politics," 1135 n.17: "Public debate on abortion seems to me another example of an area where people are not terribly suspicious of the religious motivations that lie behind the opposition many people have to relatively unregulated systems of obtaining abortions. That is, supporters of such systems do not appear to object substantially to the fact that as a

result of their religious beliefs, Catholics and certain Christian fundamentalists are prominent in the opposition, although they do object to the substance of the religiously motivated positions and, sometimes, to what they regard as the fact that religious institutions are abusing their tax exempt status by lobbying for restrictions on the availability of abortions."

23. Kathleen Sullivan, "Religion and Liberal Democracy," 59 U. Chi. L. Rev. 195, 195–96 (1992).

24. See, e.g., William P. Marshall, "The Case against the Constitutionally Compelled Free Exercise Exemption," 40 Case Res. L. Rev. 357, 408–11 (1990); Oliver Thomas, "Comments on Papers by Milner Ball and Fred Gedicks," 4 Notre Dame J.L. Ethics & Pub. Pol'y 451, 453 (1990).

25. See, e.g., Marshall, "Constitutionally Compelled," 407, 409; David A. J. Richards, *Toleration and the Constitution* (New York: Oxford University Press, 1986), 141; Ellis West, "The Case against a Right to Religion-based Exemptions," 4 Notre Dame J.L. Ethics & Pub. Pol'y 591, 636 (1990).

26. 494 U.S. 872 (1990).

27. See Marc Galanter, "Religious Freedom in the United States: A Turning Point?," 1966 Wis. L. Rev. 216, 292; Tushnet, "Religion in Politics," 1134–35; West, "Religion-based Exemptions," 616–17. Whatever might have been made of this argument during the erosion of free exercise rights in the 1980s, little seems to remain of it after *Smith*. See generally Abner Green, "The Political Balance of the Religion Clauses," 102 Yale L.J. 1611 (1993).

28. Heidegger, "Modern Science," 289–90.

29. See John Locke, "An Essay concerning the True Original Extent and End of Civil Government," §§ 135–38 in *Treatise of Civil Government and a Letter Concerning Toleration,* ed. Charles L. Sherman (New York: Irvington, 1979), 3, 89–94.

30. Elizabeth Mensch, "The History of Mainstream Legal Thought" in *The Politics of Law,* ed. David Kairys, rev. ed. (New York: Pantheon, 1990), 13, 17.

31. Gary Peller, "The Metaphysics of American Law," 73 Cal. L. Rev. 1151, 1196–99, 1215, 1265 (1985); J. G. Merquior, *Liberalism: Old and New* (Boston: Twayne, 1991), 18–23.

32. Alan Freeman & Elizabeth Mensch, "The Public-Private Distinction in American Life and Law," 36 Buff. L. Rev. 237, 237, 243; Note, "Reinterpreting the Religion Clauses: Constitutional Construction and Conceptions of the Self," 97 Harv. L. Rev. 1468, 1471 (1984).

33. Mark Kelman, *A Guide to Critical Legal Studies* (Cambridge: Harvard University Press, 1987), 61–62, 127; Roberto Unger, *Knowledge and Politics,* 2d ed. (New York: Free Press, 1984), 42–43.

34. Freeman & Mensch, "Public-Private Distinction," 237, 243; cf. H. Jefferson Powell, *The Moral Tradition of American Constitutionalism: A Theological Interpretation* (Durham, N.C.: Duke University Press, 1993), 60 ("Just as the social contract defined the boundary between civil society and the anarchy of the state of nature [within the political tradition of the Enlightenment], so the rule of law marked the limits of reason's control over human conduct.").

35. See Mark Tushnet, *Red, White and Blue: A Critical Analysis of Constitutional Law* (Cambridge, Mass.: Harvard University Press, 1988), 278. See also Stanley Fish, *Doing What Comes Naturally: Change, Rhetoric, and the Practice of Theory in Literary and Legal Studies* (Durham, N.C.: Duke University Press, 1989), 10 (criticizing the conception of the self "in relation to which the ascendancy of force is a disaster" and in which "the self is a quantity of desire that must be constrained by something independent of it so that its actions might have a social or public direction rather than a merely personal one").

36. See chap. 1, text at nn.22–25.

37. Louis Seidman makes these points in the context of a discussion of liberal political theory. See Louis Michael Seidman, "Public Principle and Private Choice: The Uneasy Case for a Boundary Maintenance Theory of Constitutional Law," 96 Yale L.J. 1006, 1007–8 (1987). See also Edward Purcell Jr., *The Crisis of Democratic Theory: Scientific Naturalism and the Problem of Value* (Lexington: University Press of Kentucky, 1973), 244 (describing Reinhold Neibuhr's view that men and women are constantly tempted to proclaim their personal beliefs universally applicable).

38. Cf. Karl Marx, "On the Jewish Question," in 3 Karl Marx & Frederick Engels, *Collected Works* (New York: International, 1975), 146, 163 ("*Security* is the highest social concept of civil society, the concept of *police*, expressing the fact that the whole of society exists only in order to guarantee to each of its members the preservation of his person, his rights, and his property.") (emphasis in original).

39. See Kelman, *Critical Legal Studies*, 66; Joel F. Handler, "Dependent People, the State and the Modern/Postmodern Search for the Dialogic Community," 35 U.C.L.A. L. Rev. 999, 1060–61 (1988).

40. Cf. Bruce Ackerman, *Social Justice and the Liberal State* (New Haven: Yale University Press, 1980), 11 ("While everyone has an opinion about the good life, none can be known to be superior to any other.").

41. Peller, "Metaphysics," 1261; Unger, *Knowledge and Politics*, 73, 89.

42. Compare Young v. American Mini-Theatres, Inc., 427 U.S. 50, 70 (1976) ("[F]ew of us would march our sons and daughters off to war to pre-

serve the citizen's right to see 'Specified Sexual Activities' exhibited in the theatres of our choice.") and Paris Adult Theatre I v. Slaton, 413 U.S. 49, 63 (1973) (lack of conclusive or empirical evidence on the harmfulness of pornography does not preclude a state from adopting harmfulness as a regulatory premise) with Miller v. California, 413 U.S. 15, 30, 33–36 (1973) (pornography may be outlawed as obscene only if [1] it appeals to the "prurient interest," [2] it portrays "specifically defined" sexual conduct in a "patently offensive" way as defined by "community standards," and [3] it lacks "serious" intellectual content when considered "as a whole"). For a defense of pornography against prohibition or regulation, see Ronald Dworkin, "Women and Pornography", N.Y. Rev. (Oct. 21, 1993), 36; Dworkin, "Liberty and Pornography," N.Y. Rev. (Aug. 15, 1991), 12.

43. Greenawalt, *Religious Convictions*, 24.

44. Gedicks & Hendrix, *Choosing the Dream*, 64–71.

45. See chap. 1, text at n.19. Compare Carter, *Culture of Disbelief*, 24–25, 42–43 (observing that liberals often see reason and belief as mutually exclusive) and Steven G. Gey, "Why Is Religion Special?: Reconsidering the Accommodation of Religion under the Religion Clauses of the First Amendment," 52 U. Pitt. L. Rev. 75, 167–79 passim (1990) (asserting that religious belief is not based on logic or reason) with Greenawalt, "Further Thoughts," 1032 (agreeing that rationality is an important component of religious belief); Elizabeth Mensch & Alan Freeman, "The Politics of Virtue: Animals, Theology, and Abortion," 25 Ga. L. Rev. 923, 1042–44 (1991) (describing the rational aspects of Biblical inerrancy); and Richard Myers, "The Supreme Court and the Privatization of Religion," 41 Cath. U. L. Rev. 19, 60–79 (1992) (arguing that secular and religious beliefs with respect to abortion are equally rational). See also Larry Alexander, "Liberalism, Religion, and the Unity of Epistemology," 30 San Diego L. Rev. 763 (1993) (arguing that liberal epistemology is neither superior to nor different from religious epistemology); Rolston, *Science and Religion*, 27–30 (although science often reaches a higher level of objective rationality and empirical testability than religion, religion still entails strong elements of rationality).

46. Marx, "Jewish Question," 155 (emphasis in original).

47. Freeman & Mensch, "Public-Private Distinction," 241; accord Carter, *Culture of Disbelief*, 22 (suggesting that this view considers religion to be "like building model airplanes, just another hobby: something quiet, something private, something trivial—and not really a fit activity for intelligent, public-spirited adults").

48. Cf. Mensch & Freeman, "Politics of Virtue," 1129 (the secular account of freedom renders theological concerns irrelevant to public policy);

Peller, "Metaphysics," 1266 ("[In materialist discourse], belief without veri-
fication is mere subjectivity or empty formalism, since the internal coherence
of propositions may have no relation to the real world.").

49. Cf. Ackerman, *Social Justice*, 364 (neutrality marks "the conceptual
boundary on the secular authority of all those who pretend to be God's
vice-regent on earth").

50. See chap. 1, text at nn.1–13.

51. See Unger, *Knowledge and Politics*, 32.

52. Seidman, "Public Principle," 1006. See also Peller, "Metaphysics,"
1178 (" 'Private' relations are 'private' to the extent that they are represented
as not constituted or influenced by 'absent' or social forces; 'individual will'
is 'individual' to the extent that it is self-present and not dependent on the
practices of others."); Unger, *Knowledge and Politics*, 80 ("Because facts have
no intrinsic identity, everything depends on the names we give them."). This
is one implication of Larry Alexander's argument that religion and secular
political ideologies like liberalism share a common epistemology:

> I come to the conclusion, then, that liberalism and religion are on
> the same epistemological level, and that the knowledge each claims, if
> it be knowledge, has the same pedigree in experience and reason. There
> are not two ways of "knowing," religious and secular/liberal; there are
> not both sectarian and secular/liberal "truths." As a consequence of
> epistemological unity, liberalism must establish its tenets by rejecting
> conflicting religious ones, not by the illusion of "neutrally" banishing
> them to the "private" realm, where they can somehow remain true but
> impotent, but by meeting them head on and showing them to be false or
> unjustified. Liberalism is, as many critics claim it to be, the "religion"
> of secularism. [This means] that both liberalism and antiliberal reli-
> gious views inhabit the same realm and make conflicting claims within
> it. Liberalism is not at a different level, where it can remain neutral
> and impartial with respect to religious controversy that is truth-seeking
> within a restricted domain, but not within the domain of liberalism.

Alexander, "Epistemological Unity," 790. See also id. at 792 ("[G]iven epistemological unity, any line the courts draw between the religious and the nonreligious, the sectarian and the secular—a line on which First Amendment
doctrine largely depends—will prove to be theoretically indefensible.").

53. 482 U.S. 578 (1987).

54. 494 U.S. 872 (1990).

55. See *Edwards*, 482 U.S. at 586, 592.

56. 393 U.S. 97 (1968) (law forbidding teaching of either evolution or cre-

ationism held violation of establishment clause for lack of secular purpose).

57. *Edwards*, 482 U.S. at 594.

58. See id. at 586–87, 590–92. See also id. at 589 (quoting Aguillard v. Treen, 765 F.2d 1251, 1257 [5th Cir. 1985]) ("[T]he Act does not serve to protect academic freedom, but has the distinctly different purpose of discrediting 'evolution by counterbalancing its teaching at every turn with the teaching of creation science.' "). For succinct overviews of the evolution versus creationism conflict in the context of public school curricula, see Carter, *Culture of Disbelief*, 157–62; Mensch & Freeman, "Politics of Virtue," 1034–39.

59. 482 U.S. at 587 (quoting testimony of representative of Louisiana Science Teachers Association) (emphasis added).

60. Id. at 592 (emphasis added).

61. Fish, *What Comes Naturally*, 298; accord Carter, *Culture of Disbelief*, 217 ("[I]n the world of post-Enlightenment liberalism, science deals with *knowledge* about the natural world, whereas religion is simply a system of *belief*, based on faith.") (emphasis in original).

62. 482 U.S. at 591–92. Justice Scalia summarized the considerable evidence in the record supporting creationism in his dissent. See id. at 622–25 & n.4 (Scalia, J., dissenting). For arguments that creationism is science and should be taught as such, see Wendell Bird, Note, "Freedom of Religion and Science Instruction in Public Schools," 87 Yale L.J. 515 (1978); Henry M. Morris & Gary E. Parker, *What Is Creation Science?* (San Diego: Creation-Life, 1982).

63. 482 U.S. at 590 (emphasis added) (quoting 393 U.S. 97, 109 [1968]).

64. 482 U.S. at 596 (emphasis added).

65. See, e.g., William P. Marshall, "The Other Side of Religion," 44 Hastings L.J. 843 (1993) (arguing that the dynamic of religious faith, which causes people to cling passionately to their beliefs and thus has the potential to be a powerfully destruction political force, justifies special constraints on religious participation in public life). See generally Ernst Cassirer, *The Philosophy of the Enlightenment* (Princeton: Princeton University Press, 1951), 160–82 (arguing that, in Enlightenment philosophy, the enemies of knowledge and faith were not skepticism and doubt, but the dogma and superstition of traditional religion); Peter Gay, *The Enlightenment: An Interpretation— The Rise of Modern Paganism* (New York: W. W. Norton, 1966), 168–70 (summarizing the Enlightenment's view that persecution of nonbelievers and dissenters formed part of both the theology and the policy of the medieval church). For works of Enlightenment thinkers espousing these or similar views, see David Hume, "Of Superstition and Enthusiasm" (1742) in 3 *The Philosophical Works*, ed. Thomas Hill Green & Thomas Hodge Grose (Darm-

stadt: Scientia Verlag Aalen, 1964), 144; David Hume, "The History of Natural Religion," §§ 2, 3, 6, 9, 11, 14 (1757) in 4 id. at 309–57 passim; Immanuel Kant, "What Is Enlightenment?" (1784), trans. Catherine Porter in *Philosophical Writings*, ed. Ernst Behler (New York: Continuum, 1986), 263; Voltaire, "The Age of Louis XIV" (1751), trans. Martyn P. Pollack in *Candide and Other Writings*, ed. Haskell M. Block (New York: Random House, 1956), 221; Voltaire, "Philosophical Dictionary" (1764) (entries for "Tolerance," "Freedom of Thought," "Persecution") in id. at 367, 384, 410, 428–29, 449–50.

66. See, e.g., *Epperson*, 393 U.S. at 103 & n.11, 107 & n.15, 108 & n.16, 109 nn.17–18; Daniel O. Conkle, "Different Religions, Different Politics: Evaluating the Role of Competing Religious Traditions in American Politics and Law," 10 J.L. & Relig. 1, 14–15 (1994).

67. Karl Popper, *The Logic of Scientific Discovery*, 2d ed., § 8 (New York: Harper & Row, 1968), 47 (emphasis in original).

68. See, e.g., Phillip E. Johnson, *Darwin on Trial*, 2d ed. (Downers Grove, Ill.: InterVarsity, 1993), 43 ("Materialist scientists are full of scorn for creationists who invoke an invisible creator who employed supernatural powers that cannot be observed operating in our own times."). See also id. at 164 ("To scientific naturalists, recognition of a supernatural reality amounts to superstition, and hence to an abandonment of science."). Carter suggests that ultimate statements are falsifiable if the right kind of evidence—e.g., scripture—is accepted. See Carter, *Culture of Disbelief*, 222–24.

69. Phillip Johnson documents this absence in *Darwin on Trial*, 45–62. He summarizes his reading of the evidence with the observation that, "if evolution means the gradual change of one kind of organism into another kind, the outstanding characteristic of the fossil record is the absence of evidence for evolution." Id. at 50. See also id. at 54 ("The discontinuities between major groups—phyla, classes, orders—are not only pervasive, but in many cases immense."). Gerald R. Schroeder, in a less exhaustive review of the evidence in *Genesis and the Big Bang: The Discovery of Harmony between Modern Science and the Bible* (New York: Bantam, 1990), 134–39, similarly concludes that "an account of the fossil record shows that as far as macroevolution is concerned, *stasis, not change*, is the trend with all species yet formed," id. at 135 (emphasis in original). See also id. at 19 ("[T]here is no *dynamic* pro-Darwinian evidence in the fossil record. Neither the fossils nor the variety of life that surrounds us provides any proof of one species changing into another, or a development of complex forms of life from earlier, more simple forms.") (emphasis in original); id. at 114, 115 ("[T]he fossil record itself cannot be explained by the conventional laws of chemistry and bi-

ology. There is a new awareness in the scientific community that the simple evolutionary approach of inorganic chemistry leading to the biochemical requires modification. *[R]andom events did not do the forming."*) (emphasis in original).

70. The current account is "punctuated equilibrium," which postulates long periods of stasis punctuated by intense periods of evolutionary change. See Niles Eldredge & Stephen Jay Gould, "Punctuated Equilibria: An Alternative to Phyletic Gradualism," appendix to Niles Eldredge, *Time Frames: The Rethinking of Darwinian Evolution and the Theory of Punctuated Equilibria* (New York: Simon & Schuster, 1985), 193. See generally *The Dynamics of Evolution: The Punctuated Equilibrium Debate in the Natural and Social Sciences,* ed. Albert Somit & Steven A. Patterson (Ithaca, N.Y.: Cornell University Press, 1992).

71. See, e.g., Schroeder, *Big Bang,* 140–41, 144–45. Schroeder emphasizes, however, that the fossil gap does not prove the existence of a divine creator, but only discredits neo-Darwinism. See id. at 146. For a review of recent scholarship on the conflict between evolution and creationism, see Stephen Jay Gould, "The Confusion over Evolution," N.Y. Rev. (Nov. 19, 1992), 47.

72. Rolston, *Science and Religion,* 4–5.

73. Ruth Anna Putnam, "Creating Facts and Values," 60 Phil. 187, 195 (1985). See also Johnson, *Darwin on Trial,* 36 ("Are we dealing here with science or with rationalist versions of Kipling's fables?"); Rolston, *Science and Religion,* 6: "Every comprehensive theory has got to argue away some of the evidence it faces. Sometimes we do not believe the theory because it is not confirmed by the facts; but sometimes we do not believe the 'facts' because there is no theory that confirms or predicts them and they go against a well-established theory that we have. We could handle this exception, if we had a little more time to deal with it!"

74. See Johnson, *Darwin on Trial,* 28–29, 68–71, 111, 117, 199n, 210n.

75. Cf. Durham & Dushku, "Traditionalism," 445 ("Whatever else one might think of the controversy [between evolution and creationism], the Court's decision [in *Aguillard*] can scarcely be said to be neutral as between world views.").

76. Paul Davies, *God and the New Physics* (New York: Simon & Schuster, 1983), 197. In fact, science's focus on identifying falsifiable causes, rather than elaborating meaning, may actually obscure important knowledge about the world offered by religion. Cf. Rolston, *Science and Religion,* 31: "Religion is the science of the spirit, where a rationality suited for objects is inadequate. Here the reflective scientist will not say that he comes to nature without

assumptions, despising the theologian as being overcome with them. But he will see that, so far as his selection employs empirical causation as his fishing net, he has a different set of assumptions; and he may even wonder whether just these assumptions might prevent him from receiving the data of religion in an undistorted form."

77. This is Johnson's principal thesis. See Johnson, *Darwin on Trial*, 8, 11–14. For similar arguments, see Alan Freeman & Betty Mensch, "Religion as Science/Science as Religion: Constitutional Law and the Fundamentalist Challenge," Tikkun (Nov./Dec. 1987), 64, 69; Peter Gabel, "Creationism and the Spirit of Nature," Tikkun (Nov./Dec. 1987), 55, 62.

78. 494 U.S. 872 (1990).

79. The Court did not view its opinion as having departed from prior decisions, maintaining that it "ha[d] never held that an individual's religious beliefs excuse him from compliance with an otherwise valid law prohibiting conduct that the State is free to regulate." Id. at 878–79. It distinguished the *Unemployment Compensation Cases* on the absence of criminal conduct on the part of the religious objector in those cases, as well as the presence in those cases of a mechanism for particularized assessment of misconduct. Id. at 876, 884. It distinguished Wisconsin v. Yoder and its antecedents on the coincidence of other constitutional rights with the free exercise claim asserted in those cases. Id. at 881. Commentators found this (re)reading of the precedents highly questionable. See, e.g., James D. Gordon III, "Free Exercise on the Mountaintop," 79 Cal. L. Rev. 91, 94–99 (1991); Douglas Laycock, "The Remnants of Free Exercise," 1990 Sup. Ct. Rev. 1, 2–3; William Marshall, "In Defense of *Smith* and Free Exercise Revisionism," 58 U. Chi. L. Rev. 308, 309 (1991); Steven D. Smith, "The Rise and Fall of Religious Freedom in Constitutional Discourse," 140 U. Pa. L. Rev. 149, 233–34 (1991). But cf. Donald A. Giannella, "Religious Liberty, Nonestablishment, and Doctrinal Development—Part I: The Religious Liberty Guarantee," 80 Harv. L. Rev. 1381, 1410 (1964) (suggesting that because jury duty statutes provide "[n]umerous exemptions for personal reasons, . . . religious liberty could probably be added to the list without noticeable effect").

80. See 494 U.S. at 882.

81. See id. at 888.

82. Id. at 890.

83. Id. at 879 (quoting 310 U.S. 586, 594–95 [1940]). Inexplicably, Justice Scalia did not note that *Gobitis* was overruled by the Court barely three years after it was decided. See Board of Educ. v. Barnette, 319 U.S. 624 (1943). Although one might argue that the proposition is still authoritative since it was not necessary to the Court's holding in *Gobitis*, the fact that it was

written to support a result that was promptly abandoned undercuts its persuasiveness, and should have been noted.

84. 494 U.S. at 879 (quoting Reynolds v. United States, 98 U.S. 145, 166–67 [1878]).

85. Id. at 888.

86. See introduction, text at n.17.

87. See, e.g., 494 U.S. at 888: "If 'compelling interest' really means what it says . . . many laws will not meet the test. Any society adopting such a system would be courting anarchy, but that danger increases in direct proportion to the society's diversity of religious beliefs, and its determination to coerce or suppress none of them."

88. See chap. 6, text at nn.52–53.

89. Milner S. Ball, "The Unfree Exercise of Religion," 20 Cap. U.L. Rev. 39, 53 (citing, as additional examples, Richmond v. J.A. Croson Co., 488 U.S. 469 [1989] [affirmative action under the Fourteenth Amendment]; McClesky v. Kemp, 481 U.S. 279 [1987] [capital punishment under the Eighth Amendment]).

90. Id. at 54 (quoting McClesky v. Kemp, 481 U.S. 279, 339 [1987] [Brennan, J., dissenting]).

91. See, e.g., Barnes v. Glen Theatre, Inc., 501 U.S. 560, 580 (1991) (Scalia, J., concurring separately) ("I think we should avoid whenever possible [a] mode of analysis that requires judicial assessment of the 'importance' of government interests—and especially government interests in various aspects of morality."); Smith, 494 U.S. at 889 n.5 ("It is horrible to contemplate that federal judges will regularly balance against the importance of general laws the significance of religious practice.").

92. See 494 U.S. at 875.

93. See Gordon, "Mountaintop," 94–96.

94. Cf. John Garvey, "Free Exercise and the Values of Religious Liberty," 18 Conn. L. Rev. 779, 798–801 (1986) (arguing that obedience to religious conscience, like insanity, places in question whether believers may be held responsible for violations of law committed while under its influence).

95. Gedicks & Hendrix, *Choosing the Dream*, 82–91. See generally James Davison Hunter, *Before the Shooting Begins: Searching for Democracy in America's Culture War* (New York: Free Press, 1994).

96. 98 U.S. at 166.

97. Cf. Carter, *Culture of Disbelief*, 130 ("The vision of the [free exercise] clause as protecting communicative acts rather than acts of worship or public acts carries with it precisely the message that the separation of church and self entails: you are free to believe as you like, but, for goodness sake,

don't act on it!"); Phillip B. Kurland, *Religion and the Law: Of Church and State and the Supreme Court* (Chicago: University of Chicago Press, 1961), 101–2 (observing that the belief-action distinction "is obviously not a line that can provide real assistance" in resolving church-state conflicts since its consistent application would permit the infringement of unquestioned First Amendment rights).

98. 494 U.S. at 877 (citation omitted) (emphasis added).

99. Compare *Flagburning Cases*, 496 U.S. 310 (1990); 491 U.S. 397 (1989) (burning the American flag as political protest is expression protected by the First Amendment) and Tinker v. Des Moines School Dist., 393 U.S. 503 (1969) (high school student who wore black armband as an antiwar protest was engaged in expression protected by the First Amendment) with Clark v. Community for Creative Non-Violence, 468 U.S. 288 (1984) (refusing to protect sleeping at certain national monuments as constitutionally protected communication of the plight of the homeless) and United States v. O'Brien, 391 U.S. 367 (1968) (refusing to recognize draft-card burning as protected expression protesting the Vietnam war).

100. But see Marshall, "Free Exercise Revisionism," 313 n.25 (stating that the religious conduct at issue in *Smith* was not expressive).

101. See United States v. Ballard, 322 U.S. 78 (1944). See also J. Morris Clark, "Guidelines for the Free Exercise Clause," 83 Harv. L. Rev. 327, 351 (1969) ("It seems unlikely that fact-finding agencies will be misled by claims of conscience from individuals who act primarily from self-interest. If anything, the experience of conscientious objectors to war indicates that the fault will lie in the opposite direction."); Ferdinand F. Fernandez, "The Free Exercise of Religion," 36 S. Cal. L. Rev. 546, 547 (1963) ("[I]t has seldom been claimed that something which is clearly not religiously motivated is a religion or a religious act although there have been some rather close approximations to this . . . .").

102. Clark, "Guidelines," 348–49.

103. See, e.g., Hernandez v. Comm'r, 490 U.S. 680 (1989) (payments made to Church of Scientology for spiritual awareness and training courses under church's "doctrine of exchange" held not deductible as charitable contributions); Bob Jones Univ. v. United States, 461 U.S. 574 (1983) (revocation of tax exemption for discriminatory conduct upheld despite claim that discrimination was required by organization's religious beliefs); Moon v. United States, 718 F.2d 1210 (2d Cir. 1983) (tax fraud conviction of leader of Unification Church on theory that he held assets personally and not in trust for church upheld despite church's belief that any use of funds by leader was ipso facto a religious use), cert. denied, 466 U.S. 971 (1984).

104. E.g., Curtis Pub. Co. v. Butts, 388 U.S. 130 (1967); New York Times v. Sullivan, 376 U.S. 254 (1964).
105. See, e.g., Miranda v. Arizona, 384 U.S. 436 (1966).
106. Miller v. California, 413 U.S. 15 (1973); Paris Adult Theatre I v. Slaton, 413 U.S. 49 (1973); Roth v. United States, 354 U.S. 476 (1957).
107. See Lawrence Sager, "State Courts and the Strategic Space between the Norms and Rules of Constitutional Law," 63 Tex. L. Rev. 959 (1985); Sager, "Fair Measure: The Legal Status of Underenforced Constitutional Norms," 91 Harv. L. Rev. 1212 (1978).
108. See, e.g., Gey, "Reconsidering Accommodation," 78 ("If religion is defined broadly enough to encompass all behavior that is motivated by religion, most activities of the modern regulatory state are thrown into chaos."); Richards, *Toleration*, 143 (federal courts' tepid application of pre-*Smith* exemption doctrine was motivated by a desire to avoid the "explosive" curtailment of state power).
109. Fish, *What Comes Naturally*, 24. See also West, *Narrative*, 128 ("When we accept a state of the world that derives from an act of power as a part of the natural world, we lose sense of how to evaluate that state of the world; it becomes arbitrary in a perfectly benign sense.").
110. Of course, this kind of perspective is no less contingent or situated. See, e.g., Fish, *What Comes Naturally*, 158–59 ("To ask 'what really happened independently of any account or description whatsoever' is to ask for a description that is not a description; it is what no one could ever tell you, not because it remains hidden as the real truth behind all the partial ones, but because there is nothing to tell."); id. at 432 ("Contingency *itself* is never on trial, only those divisions and hierarchies that follow from the institution of some or other contingent plan; and when those divisions and hierarchies have been abandoned or supplanted it will only be because other divisions and hierarchies, themselves no less contingent, have been instituted in their place.") (emphasis in original).

Chapter 3. Neutrality as Manipulation: Parochial School Aid and Equal Access

1. 333 U.S. 1 (1947).
2. See School Dist. v. Schempp, 374 U.S. 203, 222 (1963).
3. See Walz v. Tax Comm'n, 397 U.S. 664, 674 (1970).
4. 403 U.S. 602, 612–13 (1971).
5. See, e.g., Jesse Choper, "The Religion Clauses of the First Amendment: Reconciling the Conflict," 41 U. Pitt. L. Rev. 673 (1980); Michael W.

McConnell & Richard A. Posner, "An Economic Approach to Issues of Religious Freedom," 56 U. Chi. L. Rev. 1 (1989); Michael A. Paulsen, "Religion, Equality, and the Constitution: An Equal Protection Approach to Establishment Clause Adjudication," 61 Notre Dame L. Rev. 311 (1986).

6. See generally Jacques Derrida, "Signature Event Context," trans. Samuel Weber & Jeffrey Mehlman in *Limited Inc* (Evanston, Ill.: Northwestern University Press, 1988), 1; e.g., Stanley Fish, *Doing What Comes Naturally: Change, Rhetoric, and the Practice of Theory in Literary and Legal Studies* (Durham, N.C.: Duke University Press, 1989), 358–59 (showing latent indeterminacy of constitutional provision that U.S. president must be thirty-five years of age).

7. See Frederick Mark Gedicks, "Arrogance Cloaked as Neutrality" (Book Review), 65 St. John's L. Rev. 1235, 1257–64 (1991).

8. See, e.g., Board of Educ. v. Grumet, 114 S. Ct. 2481 (1994) (holding that special creation of a public school district consisting solely of members of a particular religious sect violated the establishment clause); Lee v. Weisman, 112 S. Ct. 2469 (1992) (holding that graduation prayers violated the establishment clause). But see Marsh v. Chambers, 463 U.S. 783 (1983) (holding that nondenominational legislative prayer did not violate the establishment clause).

9. See, e.g., Board of Educ. v. Allen, 392 U.S. 236, 239 (1968) (quoting N.Y. Sess. Laws 1950, c. 239, § 1); 392 U.S. at 243.

10. E.g., Grand Rapids School Dist. v. Ball, 473 U.S. 373, 382 (1985); *Lemon*, 403 U.S. at 613.

11. E.g., Grand Rapids School Dist. v. Ball, 473 U.S. 373, 379 (1985); Meek v. Pittenger, 421 U.S. 349, 366 (1975); *Lemon*, 403 U.S. at 613, 615–16, 620.

12. See Grand Rapids School Dist. v. Ball, 473 U.S. 373, 385 (1985); Committee for Pub. Educ. v. Regan, 444 U.S. 646, 652 (1980); Meek v. Pittenger, 421 U.S. 349, 366 (1975); Committee for Pub. Educ. v. Nyquist, 413 U.S. 756, 779–80 (1973).

13. 413 U.S. 734, 743 (1973); accord Donald A. Gianella, "Religious Liberty, Nonestablishment, and Doctrinal Development—Part II: The Nonestablishment Principle," 81 Harv. L. Rev. 513, 573 (1968) ("[I]t can be persuasively argued that aid to any part of a parochial school's integrated curriculum effectively furthers the institution's central purposes.").

14. Jesse Choper, "The Establishment Clause and Aid to Parochial Schools," 56 Cal. L. Rev. 260, 313 (1968); Gianella, "Nonestablishment Principle," 576.

15. 392 U.S. 236 (1968).

16. Id. at 243–44.

17. Id. at 252 (Black, J., dissenting) (characterizing the law as "using tax-raised funds to buy school books for a religious school"); id. at 254, 265 (Douglas, J., dissenting) ("The statute on its face empowers each parochial school to determine for itself which textbooks will be eligible for loans to its students . . . . The initiative to select and requisition 'the books desired' is with the parochial school."); id. at 270, 271 (Fortas, J., dissenting) ("[D]espite the transparent camouflage that the books are furnished to students, the reality is that they are selected and their use is prescribed by the sectarian authorities . . . for use in their sectarian schools.").

18. See, e.g., Mueller v. Allen, 463 U.S. 388, 399 (1983); Committee for Pub. Educ. v. Nyquist, 413 U.S. 756, 780 (1973); Lemon, 403 U.S. at 621.

19. See Committee for Pub. Educ. v. Regan, 444 U.S. 646 (1980); Wolman v. Walter, 433 U.S. 229 (1977).

20. See 444 U.S. 646, 654–57 (1980); 433 U.S. 229, 240 (1977) (plurality opinion).

21. 444 U.S. at 654–56.

22. Id. at 659–61.

23. See 433 U.S. at 438–39 (plurality opinion).

24. 413 U.S. 756, 781–82 & n.38 (1973) (emphasis in original).

25. 463 U.S. 388, 397, 398 (1983) (emphasis in original).

26. E.g., Mueller, 463 U.S. at 388 (tax deduction for educational expenses); Allen, 392 U.S. at 236 (textbook loan program); Everson, 333 U.S. at 1 (public transportation to and from school).

27. See 433 U.S. at 249 n.16 (citations omitted).

28. Choper, "Parochial Schools," 315.

29. McConnell & Posner, "Economic Approach," 31; accord Paul A. Freund, 82 Harv. L. Rev. 1680, 1691 (1969) ("Public aid to parochial schools . . . would in some measure benefit the religious mission of these faiths, because religion, on our present hypothesis, permeates all their instruction.").

30. Michael W. McConnell, "Accommodation of Religion: An Update and a Response to the Critics," 60 Geo. Wash. L. Rev. 685, 698 (1992); Jonathan Weiss, "Privilege, Posture, and Protection: 'Religion' in the Law," 73 Yale L.J. 593, 617 (1964).

31. E.g., Wolman, 433 U.S. at 229; Meek v. Pittenger, 421 U.S. 349, 353 (1975); Nyquist, 413 U.S. at 756. See also Board of Educ. v. Grumet, 114 S. Ct. 2481, 2491, 2492 (1994) (school district authorized by special state legislation which designated boundaries precisely coincident with those of

religious community violated establishment clause because community "did not receive its new governmental authority simply as one of many communities eligible for equal treatment under a general law" and "the benefit flows only to a single sect").

32. See *Wolman*, 433 U.S. at 250. See also *Nyquist*, 413 U.S. at 785–86 (rejecting argument that the aid recipient was not a "mere conduit").

33. *Regan*, 444 U.S. at 646 (standardized testing); *Wolman*, 433 U.S. at 229 (standardized testing, health care services, and counseling services).

34. See, e.g., *Regan*, 444 U.S. at 646 (provision and scoring of standardized tests); *Wolman*, 433 U.S. at 241–44 (provision, administration, and scoring of standardized tests).

35. See, e.g., *Wolman*, 433 U.S. at 244–48 (counseling services provided by the state in mobile units adjacent to parochial school campuses).

36. E.g., Aguilar v. Felton, 473 U.S. 402 (1985) (remedial instruction supplied by state employees in public school classrooms violated establishment clause); Grand Rapids School Dist. v. Ball, 473 U.S. 373 (1985) (enrichment and extracurricular courses taught in parochial school classrooms by public school employees, some of whom were also parochial school employees, violated establishment clause); Meek v. Pittenger, 421 U.S. 349, 367, 371–72 (1975) (supplementary educational services provided by state employees on parochial school campus violated establishment clause). The Court has permitted states to provide health care services to parochial school students in locations on parochial school campuses, on the theory that such services are clearly severable from the religious mission of the schools and that, as independent contractors acting in accordance with professional standards of ethics, health care professionals are effectively beyond the administrative control of parochial schools. See, e.g., Wolman v. Walter, 433 U.S. 229, 241–44 (1977) (diagnostic speech and hearing services). See also Zobrist v. Catalina Foothills School Dist., 113 S. Ct. 2462 (1993) (sign language interpreter). One wonders if it any longer makes sense to consider health care unrelated to a school's religious mission now that public school health services increasingly include dispensing condoms and providing "safer sex" counseling.

37. See introduction, text at nn.9–15.

38. Marc Galanter, "Religious Freedom in the United States: A Turning Point?," 1966 Wis. L. Rev. 216, 289.

39. *Lemon*, 403 U.S. at 607–8, 609–10.

40. Meek v. Pittenger, 421 U.S. 349, 352–55 (1975).

41. E.g., *Lemon*, 403 U.S. at 619 (recipients of salary supplements "must

teach only those courses that are offered in the public schools and use only those texts and materials that are found in the public schools. In addition the teacher must not engage in teaching any course in religion").

42. Choper, "Parochial Schools," 317, 319, 326. See also Gianella, "Non-establishment Principle," 574 ("Support of any part of [a parochial school's] activities entails some support of the disqualifying religious function of molding the religious personality of the young student.").

43. 403 U.S. at 641 (Douglas, J., concurring). See also McConnell & Posner, "Economic Analysis," 20 ("[S]ince money is fungible, support for one activity of an organization supports every other activity as well.").

44. E.g., Meek v. Pittenger, 421 U.S. 349, 370–72 (1975); Lemon, 403 U.S. at 619–20. See also id. at 621–22: "The government cash grants before us now provide no basis for predicting that comprehensive measures of surveillance and controls will not follow. In particular the government's post-audit power to inspect and evaluate a church-related school's financial records and to determine which expenditures are religious and which are secular creates an intimate and continuing relationship between church and state."

45. E.g., Meek v. Pittenger, 421 U.S. 349, 372 (1975); Lemon, 403 U.S. at 619, 620, 621–22.

46. 473 U.S. 373, 386–87 (1985). See also Leavitt v. Committee for Pub. Educ., 413 U.S. 472, 479–80 (1973) (program of reimbursement for state-mandated achievement tests prepared by parochial school teachers violated establishment clause because program provided no means of ensuring that the tests would be free of religious influence).

47. 473 U.S. 402 (1973).

48. Committee for Pub. Educ. v. Regan, 444 U.S. 646 (1980).

49. Lamb's Chapel v. Center Moriches School Dist., 113 S. Ct. 2141 (1993); Westside Comm. Bd. of Educ. v. Mergens, 496 U.S. 226 (1990); Widmar v. Vincent, 454 U.S. 263 (1981).

50. McConnell & Posner, "Economic Analysis," 11.

51. Gianella, "Nonestablishment Principle," 587. See also Philip B. Kurland, "The Religion Clauses and the Burger Court," 34 Cath. U.L. Rev. 1, 18 (1984) ("Any religion that needs government to succor it, to persuade or compel adherence to religious faith, is not likely to survive, except as a mere tool of government.").

52. 463 U.S. at 399.

53. Id. at 400.

54. 474 U.S. 481 (1986).

55. Id. at 482, 483, 488.

56. Id. at 487.

57. Id. at 488.

58. See Gianella, "Nonestablishment Principle," 585. See also id. at 581 ("If the state directly or indirectly supports [free and open] inquiry [into religion by college students] it is not providing unconstitutional aid to religion; rather the gain of new or renewed interest in religion flows from a secular order characterized by academic freedom."). But see John Garvey, "Another Way of Looking at School Aid," 1985 Sup. Ct. Rev. 61, 72, 85 (arguing that the real justification for *Mueller* is not private choice, but a functional rule that prohibits religious instruction by recipients of government assistance in the same way that Title IX prohibits gender discrimination by recipients of federal funds).

59. 113 S. Ct. 2462 (1993).

60. Id. at 2467, 2469. See also id. at 2466 ("We have consistently held that government programs that neutrally provide benefits to a broad class of citizens defined without reference to religion are not readily subject to an Establishment Clause challenge just because sectarian institutions may also receive an attenuated financial benefit.").

61. 454 U.S. 263 (1981).

62. Id. at 270–72.

63. Id. at 273–74. *Widmar* suggested that if, in fact, religious groups "dominated" the university forum, permitting access to religious groups might constitute a primary effect of advancing religion. See id. at 275. This possibility was apparently ignored by *Mueller*, which found it irrelevant that parochial school parents and children were the predominant beneficiaries of the aid program at issue in that case despite the facial neutrality of the aid classification. 463 U.S. at 400–402.

64. 454 U.S. at 271 n.10.

65. 496 U.S. 226, 250 (1990) (plurality opinion) (deciding the constitutionality of 20 U.S.C. §§ 4071–74 [1984]).

66. Id. at 252.

67. 113 S. Ct. 2141, 2148 (1993).

68. Cf. Stone v. Graham, 449 U.S. 39 (1980) (mandatory posting of Ten Commandments on bulletin boards of public school classrooms violates the establishment clause); McCollum v. Board of Education, 333 U.S. 203 (1948) (allowing religious instruction in public school classrooms for one hour once each week violates the establishment clause).

69. 473 U.S. 373, 389, 392 (1985). See also id. at 390: "An important concern of the effects test is whether the symbolic union of church and state effected by the challenged governmental action is sufficiently likely to be perceived by adherents of the controlling denominations as an endorsement, and

by the nonadherents as a disapproval, of their individual religious choices."
70. See id. at 390–92. Compare *Witters*, 474 U.S. at 493 (O'Connor, J.,
concurring in part and concurring in the judgment) (because financial aid
flowing to sectarian institution is the result of private choice, no inference of
government endorsement of such institution can be drawn) and *Mueller*, 463
U.S. at 399 ("Where, as here, aid to parochial schools is available only as a result of decisions of individual parents, no 'imprimatur of state approval' . . .
can be deemed to have been conferred on any particular religion.") (quoting
Widmar v. Vincent, 454 U.S. 263, 274 [1981]).
71. See, e.g., *Aguilar*, 473 U.S. at 414; *Grand Rapids School District*, 473
U.S. at 382; *Mueller*, 463 U.S. at 397–98.
72. McConnell & Posner, "Economic Analysis," 6.
73. See, e.g., Galanter, "Turning Point," 289 ("Neutrality is in itself an
equivocal standard."); Phillip E. Johnson, "Concepts and Compromise in
First Amendment Religious Doctrine," 72 Cal. L. Rev. 817, 828 (1984) ("The
notion that it is wrong for the legislature to have the purpose or effect of
assisting religion only makes sense in terms of an assumed 'neutral' starting point that defines what advantages or disadvantages religion ought to
have."); Douglas Laycock, "Formal, Substantive, and Disaggregated Neutrality toward Religion," 39 DePaul L. Rev. 993, 1005 (1990) ("Substantive
neutrality requires a baseline from which to measure encouragement or dis-
couragement [of religion]."); Paulsen, "Equal Protection Approach," 333 ("A
statement such as 'the state should be neutral' is completely vacuous; it
says nothing about that with respect to which the state is supposed to be
neutral.").
74. Gianella, "Nonestablishment Principle," 522.
75. Id. at 523; accord Laycock, "Neutrality," 1001.
76. See, e.g., Galanter, "Turning Point," 268 ("Older views stressed governmental abstention as a condition (if not the substance) of freedom. But
increasingly, affirmative governmental intervention is invoked to provide
resources and opportunities for desired freedoms."); Gianella, "Nonestablishment Principle," 526 ("[T]he continually expanding public sector acquires
many of the attributes of a collectivized society, so that unqualified adherence to the no-aid principal will tend to have a destructive impact on vol-
untarism."); Paulsen, "Equal Protection Approach," 355 ("In this age of the
affirmative state and 'unconstitutional conditions,' unemployment compensation, tax exemption, and scores of other policies of the fisc are now, for
better or worse, *quasi-entitlements*, the deprivation of which for reasons of
religious belief, affiliation, or profession is the functional equivalent of a tax
imposed on the free exercise of religion.") (emphasis in original).

77. Cf. Gianella, "Nonestablishment Principle," 524 (discussing Quick Bear v. Leupp, 210 U.S. 50 [1908]) ("Congress could only justify its involvement with [Native American] religious schools because of the Government's responsibility for totally sustaining Indian life. Absent this responsibility, it is difficult to see how the federal government could undertake to hold and apply funds in trust for the religious schooling of Indians."").

78. School Dist. v. Schempp, 374 U.S. 203, 296–97 (1963) (Brennan, J., concurring); id. at 309 (Stewart, J., dissenting).

79. Galanter, "Turning Point," 279; accord John Valauri, "The Concept of Neutrality in Establishment Clause Doctrine," 48 U. Pitt. L. Rev. 83, 121 (1986) (a "neutralizing aid" to religion is justified when it corrects for "burdens on religion created by the government's own activity").

80. See Gianella, "Nonestablishment Principle," 570–71. The Court rejected this argument in McCollum v. Board of Education, 333 U.S. 203, 225–26 (1948).

81. Stephen L. Carter, *The Culture of Disbelief: How American Politics and Law Trivialize Religious Devotion* (New York: Basic Books, 1993), 144. See also Valauri, "Concept of Neutrality," 99 (a policy that aids neither religion nor nonreligion "would be feasible only in a country with no public education, no public transportation, no public health and safety programs— in short, a libertarian, caretaker state").

82. Choper, "Parochial Schools," 285; Johnson, "Concepts and Compromise," 844; McConnell & Posner, "Economic Analysis," 24; Paulsen, "Equal Protection Approach," 359.

83. Johnson, "Concepts and Compromise," 822; Paulsen, "Equal Protection Approach," 356, 358 & n.210.

84. See Giannella, "Nonestablishment Principle," 572, 575. See also Phillip B. Kurland, *Religion and the Law: Of Church and State and the Supreme Court* (Chicago: University of Chicago Press, 1961), 9 ("Aid to parochial schools is not unconstitutional, so long as it takes a nondiscriminatory form."); Choper, "Parochial Schools," 270 (arguing that under Professor Kurland's doctrine prohibiting the use of religion as a legislative classification, "government could constitutionally finance the entire operational costs of all state-accredited educational institutions, including those controlled by a religious organization, because the classification—state-accredited educational institutions—which includes most parochial schools, is not in the religious terms his doctrine forbids"); Johnson, "Concepts and Compromise," 845 ("To the extent that programs of aid to private education are seen as meeting a widespread desire for alternatives to publicly administered education, permitting religious schools to participate may seem more like avoiding

discrimination against religion, rather than creating a religious establishment.").

85. See McCollum v. Board of Educ., 333 U.S. 203 (1948); Gianella, "Nonestablishment Principle," 571.

86. Alan Schwarz, "No Imposition of Religion: The Establishment Clause Value," 77 Yale L.J. 692, 700 (1968). See also id. at 698–99 ("[I]t seems absurd, except with respect to all-encompassing activities such as education, to equate a nonreligious, secular viewpoint with antireligion, or to characterize it as a competing secular religionism.").

87. 343 U.S. 306 (1952).

88. Cf. Schwarz, "No Imposition," 701: "The state . . . cannot be neutral in its operation of the public schools: It must either give equal time to a religious perspective upon so-called secular subject matter, in which case a discrimination between religions is inevitably effected, or it must limit itself to secular frames of reference, thereby belittling religion and offering itself as religion's competitor."

89. See 333 U.S. 203, 225–26 (1948).

Chapter 4. The Religious as Secular:
Government Appropriation of Religion

1. 343 U.S. 306, 313–14 (1952).

2. School Dist. v. Schempp, 374 U.S. 203 (1963); Engel v. Vitale, 370 U.S. 599 (1962).

3. Epperson v. Arkansas, 393 U.S. 97 (1968).

4. See, e.g., Wolman v. Walter, 433 U.S. 229 (1977); Meek v. Pittenger, 421 U.S. 349 (1975); Committee for Pub. Educ. v. Nyquist, 413 U.S. 756 (1973); Lemon v. Kurtzman, 403 U.S. 602 (1971); Board of Education v. Allen, 392 U.S. 236 (1968).

5. See, e.g., Lee v. Weisman, 112 S. Ct. 2649 (1992) (school sponsored graduation prayer violates establishment clause); Edwards v. Aguillard, 482 U.S. 578 (1987) (prohibition on teaching evolution in public schools unless accompanied by teaching of creationism violates establishment clause); Wallace v. Jaffree, 472 U.S. 38 (1985) (moment of silence at the beginning of the public school day to encourage personal prayer violates establishment clause). See also Stone v. Graham, 449 U.S. 39 (1980) (classroom display of the Ten Commandments violates establishment clause).

6. McGowan v. Maryland, 366 U.S. 420 (1961).

7. Marsh v. Chambers, 463 U.S. 783 (1983).

8. County of Allegheny v. ACLU, 492 U.S. 573 (1989); Lynch v. Donnelly, 465 U.S. 668 (1984).

9. E.g. Bowen v. Kendrick, 487 U.S. 589 (1988); Hunt v. McNair 413 U.S. 734 (1973).

10. Walz v. Tax Comm'n, 397 U.S. 664 (1970).

11. Compare Norman Dorsen & Charles Sims, "The Nativity Scene Case: An Error of Judgment," 1985 U. Ill. L. Rev. 837 (Court failed to stress the importance of separation of church and state in crèche case) with Peter Berger, "Religion in Post-Protestant America," 81 Commentary 41, 41–42 (May 1986) (separation of church and state does not require separation of religion from politics and culture).

12. 333 U.S. 203 (1948). The term "released-time" derives from an interpretation of compulsory public schooling, under which each child is compelled to cede a certain amount of time to the state for secular instruction, but some of it is "released" back to the student on the condition that it be spent in religious instruction. See *Zorach*, 343 U.S. at 323–24 (Jackson, J., dissenting).

13. *McCollum*, 333 U.S. at 209.

14. Id. at 212; accord id. at 209–10: "The operation of the State's compulsory education system thus assists and is integrated with the program of religious instruction carried on by separate religious sects. Pupils compelled by law to go to school for secular education are released in part from their legal duty upon the condition that they attend the religious classes. This is beyond all question a utilization of the tax-established and tax-supported public school system to aid religious groups to spread their faith."

15. 343 U.S. at 308.

16. Id.

17. Id. at 314. See also id. at 313–14 ("When the state encourages religious instruction or cooperates with religious authorities by adjusting the schedule of public events to sectarian needs, it follows the best of our traditions. For it then respects the religious nature of our people and accommodates the public service to their spiritual needs.").

18. Id. at 314.

19. Compare *Zorach*, 343 U.S. at 308 & n.1 with *McCollum*, 333 U.S. at 209, 212. Justice Douglas suggested in *Zorach* that public schools did not discipline students not attending the religious instruction to which they had been released, 343 U.S. at 311 n.6, but it is difficult to believe that released-time truancy had no consequences.

20. See, e.g., *Zorach*, 343 U.S. at 323–24 (Jackson, J., dissenting); Douglas Laycock, "A Survey of Religious Liberty in the United States," 47 Ohio St.

L.J. 409, 422 (1986). See also *Zorach,* 343 U.S. at 316–17 (Black, J., dissenting) ("I see no significant difference between the invalid Illinois system and that of New York here sustained. Except for the use of the school buildings in Illinois, there is no difference which I consider even worthy of mention."); William P. Marshall, " 'We Know It When We See It': The Supreme Court and Establishment," 59 S. Cal. L. Rev. 495, 525 (1986) ("Only in its use of a public building does *McCollum* pose more of an establishment problem [than *Zorach*], and that is a distinction in form rather than substance.").

21. *Zorach,* 343 U.S. at 319 (Black, J., dissenting) (quoting Thomas Jefferson Wertenbaker, *The Puritan Oligarchy* [New York: Grosset & Dunlap, 1947] [emphasis in original]).

22. 343 U.S. at 314.

23. School Dist. v. Schempp, 374 U.S. 203, 225 (1963).

24. 366 U.S. 420 (1961).

25. 370 U.S. 421 (1962).

26. 374 U.S. 203 (1963).

27. 366 U.S. at 422–24.

28. Id. at 431.

29. Id. at 431–32.

30. Id. at 445.

31. Id. at 449.

32. See id. at 452

33. 343 U.S. at 314.

34. Compare id. at 313 ("The teacher . . . cooperates in a religious program to the extent of making it possible for her students to participate in it.") with id. at 317 (Black, J., dissenting) ("*McCollum* . . . held that Illinois could not constitutionally manipulate the compelled classroom hours of its compulsory school machinery so as to channel children into sectarian classes. Yet that is exactly what the Court holds New York can do."); id. at 321 (Frankfurter, J., dissenting) ("The pith of the case is that formalized religious instruction is substituted for other school activity which those who do not participate in the released-time program are compelled to attend."); id. at 323–24 (Jackson, J., dissenting): "If public education were taking so much of the pupils' time as to injure the public or the students' welfare by encroaching upon their religious opportunity, simply shortening everyone's school day would facilitate voluntary and optional attendance at Church classes. But that suggestion is rejected upon the ground that if they are made free many students will not go to the Church. Hence, they must be deprived of their freedom for this period, with Church attendance put to them as one of two permissible ways of using it."

35. Cf. *Zorach*, 343 U.S. at 320 (Frankfurter, J., dissenting): "There is all the difference in the world between letting the children out of school and letting some of them out of school into religious classes. If every one is free to make what use he will of time wholly unconnected from schooling required by law—those who wish sectarian instruction devoting it to that purpose, those who have ethical instruction at home, to that, those who study music, to that—then, of course there is no conflict with the Fourteenth Amendment." Of course, this analysis would not have accounted for those provisions of Sunday closing laws that proscribed certain leisure activities on Sunday, such as hunting, fishing, dancing, and drinking. See *McGowan*, 366 U.S. at 423.

36. Justice Black concurred in Chief Justice Warren's majority opinion upholding the closing laws, and Justice Frankfurter wrote separately in defense of the laws.

37. Id. at 431.

38. 370 U.S. at 422–23. The text of the prayer was "Almighty God, we acknowledge our dependence upon Thee, and we beg Thy blessings upon us, our parents, our teachers, and our Country." Id. at 422.

39. 374 U.S. at 205–8, 211–12.

40. *Schempp*, 374 U.S. at 207, 211–12 & n.4; *Engel*, 370 U.S. at 423 & n.2, 430.

41. 370 U.S. at 425. See also id. at 424 ("[T]he Regents' prayer is a religious activity."); id. at 425 ("[The prayer] was composed by governmental officials as part of a governmental program to further religious beliefs."); id. at 435 & n.21 (characterizing prayer as a "purely religious function" and an "unquestioned religious exercise").

42. 374 U.S. at 225. See also id. at 223 (reading the Bible and reciting the Lord's Prayer "is a religious ceremony and was intended by the State to be so").

43. 374 U.S. at 223.

44. Id. at 224.

45. See Marc Galanter, "Religious Freedom in the United States: A Turning Point?," 1966 Wis. L. Rev. 216, 222–23.

46. Id. at 222.

47. See Lemon v. Kurtzman, 403 U.S. 602, 612–13 (1971).

48. See Church of the Lukumi Babalu Aye, Inc. v. City of Hialeah, 113 S. Ct. 2217, 2228 (1993); *McGowan*, 366 U.S. at 467 (opinion of Frankfurter, J.); Scott Bice, "Rationality Analysis in Constitutional Law," 65 Minn. L. Rev. 1, 19 (1980). See also Gomillion v. Lightfoot, 364 U.S. 339 (1960) (complaint properly pled cause of action under the Fifteenth Amendment

by alleging that city boundaries were redrawn from a perfect square into an "uncouth," "strangely irregular," twenty-eight sided figure that excluded virtually all of the previous black residents, but not one of the previous white residents).

49. 366 U.S. at 453 (dictum) (emphasis added).

50. 449 U.S. 39 (1980).

51. Id. at 41.

52. Cf. *Schempp*, 374 U.S. at 225 (approving the study of the Bible as literature).

53. 449 U.S. at 42.

54. See 393 U.S. 97, 98, 107 nn. 15 & 16 (1968).

55. See, e.g., Washington v. Davis, 426 U.S. 229 (1976); Palmer v. Thompson, 403 U.S. 217 (1971); United States v. O'Brien, 391 U.S. 367 (1968). But see Reitman v. Mulkey, 387 U.S. 369 (1967) (state law enacted by initiative which purported to exempt private parties from antidiscrimination provisions regarding sale of residential real estate held unconstitutional involvement of state in private racial discrimination).

56. See *Epperson*, 393 U.S. at 106–7 ("The State may not adopt programs or practices in its public schools or colleges which 'aid or oppose' any religion. This prohibition is absolute. It forbids alike the preference of a religious doctrine or the prohibition of theory which is deemed antagonistic to a particular dogma."); id. at 109: "Arkansas' law cannot be defended as an act of religious neutrality. Arkansas did not seek to excise from the curricula of its schools and universities all discussion of the origin of man. The law's effort was confined to an attempt to blot out a particular theory because of its supposed conflict with the biblical account, literally read."

57. Id. at 111–14 (Black, J., concurring).

58. Marshall, "Establishment," 527.

59. 482 U.S. 578 (1987).

60. Id. at 581. It can be argued that creationism is not the "intellectual competitor" of evolution because, notwithstanding any validity it might have as theology, it has no standing as science. This argument illustrates the privileging of objectivity over subjectivity discussed at length in chap. 2.

61. 393 U.S. at 109 (dictum). See also id. at 111 (Black, J., concurring) ("It is plain that a state law prohibiting all teaching of human development or biology is constitutionally quite different from a law that compels a teacher to teach as true only one theory of a given doctrine.").

62. 482 U.S. at 586–87, 590–92, 593–94.

63. Cf. Wallace v. Jaffree, 472 U.S. 38, 69–70 (1985) (O'Connor, J., concurring in the judgment) ("A statute that ostensibly promotes a secular inter-

est often has an incidental or even a primary effect of helping or hindering a sectarian belief. Chaos would ensue if every such statute were invalid under the Establishment Clause."").

64. 465 U.S. 665 (1984).

65. 472 U.S. 38 (1985).

66. *Lynch*, 465 U.S. at 688 (O'Connor, J., concurring), cited with approval in *Wallace*, 472 U.S. at 69 (O'Connor, J., concurring in the judgment).

67. *Lynch*, 465 U.S. at 690; accord *Wallace*, 472 U.S. at 69 (O'Connor, J., concurring in the judgment) (*"Lemon*'s inquiry as to the purpose and effect of a statute requires courts to examine whether government's purpose is to endorse religion and whether the statute actually conveys a message of endorsement.").

68. *Wallace*, 472 U.S. at 76.

69. See, e.g., Donald L. Beschle, "The Conservative as Liberal: The Religion Clauses, Liberal Neutrality, and the Approach of Justice O'Connor," 62 Notre Dame L. Rev. 151 (1987); Benjamine D. Feder, "And a Child Shall Lead Them: Justice O'Connor, The Principle of Religious Liberty and Its Practical Application," 8 Pace L. Rev. 249 (1988); Arnold H. Loewy, "Rethinking Government Neutrality towards Religion under the Establishment Clause: The Untapped Potential of Justice O'Connor's Insight," 64 N.C. L. Rev. 1049 (1986); Christopher S. Nesbit, Note, "County of Allegheny v. ACLU: Justice O'Connor's Endorsement Test," 68 N.C. L. Rev. 590 (1990); Note, "Developments in the Law—Religion and the State," 100 Harv. L. Rev. 1607, 1647 (1987).

70. 472 U.S. 38, 56 (1985).

71. Edwards v. Aguillard, 482 U.S. 578, 585–94 (1986); Witters v. Washington Dep't of Services for the Blind, 474 U.S. 481, 488–89 (1986); Grand Rapids School Dist. v. Ball, 473 U.S. 373, 389–92 (1985).

72. Although there was no majority opinion in *Allegheny*, five Justices agreed that the endorsement test was the proper doctrinal measure of the establishment clause questions in the case. See 492 U.S. at 589–94 (opinion of Blackmun, J., joined by Brennan, Marshall, Stevens, and O'Connor, J., with respect to part III-A).

73. For a general attack on the test, see Steven D. Smith, "Symbols, Perceptions, and Doctrinal Illusions: Establishment Clause Neutrality and the 'No Endorsement' Test," 86 Mich. L. Rev. 266 (1987).

74. See, e.g., Board of Educ. v. Mergens, 496 U.S. 226 (1990); *County of Allegheny*, 492 U.S. at 623; Corporation of the Presiding Bishop v. Amos, 483 U.S. 327 (1987); Estate of Thorton v. Calder, 472 U.S. 703 (1985); *Wallace*, 472 U.S. at 67; *Lynch*, 465 U.S. at 687.

75. See, e.g., Phillip Kurland, "The Religion Clauses and the Burger Court," 34 Cath. U. L. Rev. 1 (1984); William Van Alstyne, "Trends in the Supreme Court: Mr. Jefferson's Crumbling Wall—A Comment on *Lynch v. Donnelly*," 1984 Duke L.J. 770.

76. Smith, "Doctrinal Illusions," 301.

77. Mark V. Tushnet, " 'Of Church and State and the Supreme Court': Kurland Revisited," 1989 Sup. Ct. Rev. 373, 397–98. Tushnet himself is a critic of the test.

78. See Braunfeld v. Brown, 366 U.S. 599, 616 (Stewart, J., dissenting).

79. *McGowan*, 366 U.S. at 448. See also id. at 434 ("Further secular justifications have been advanced for making Sunday a day of rest, a day when people may recover from the labors of the week just passed and may physically and mentally prepare for the week's work to come."); id. at 450: "The State's purpose is not merely to provide a one-day-in-seven work stoppage. In addition to this, the State seeks to set one day apart from all others as a day of rest, repose, recreation and tranquility—a day which all members of the family and community have the opportunity to spend and enjoy together, a day on which there exists relative quiet and disassociation from the everyday intensity of commercial activities, a day on which people may visit friends and relatives who are not available during working days."

80. Id. at 452.

81. Id.

82. Tushnet, "Kurland Revisited," 399. See also Marshall, "Establishment," 508, 509 (Court has "distinguished, distorted, or failed to apply establishment doctrine" in order to "reconcile anti-establishment principles with a 'de facto establishment' reality.").

83. 465 U.S. at 671.

84. Id. at 681.

85. Id. at 683.

86. 492 U.S. 581, 587 (1989).

87. Justice Blackmun, announcing the judgment of the Court, found that the crèche, standing alone in the city-county building, was an unconstitutional endorsement of religion, but the menorah was not such an endorsement because it was displayed with a Christmas tree and a sign promoting liberty. Justice O'Connor concurred in both judgments. Justices Brennan, Marshall, and Stevens agreed that the crèche was an unconstitutional endorsement, but argued that the menorah was, too. Chief Justice Rehnquist and Justices Kennedy, White, and Scalia argued that no establishment clause violation can occur in the absence of a coercive effect. Accordingly, they concurred in the judgment that display of the menorah did not violate the

establishment clause, but dissented from the judgment that display of the crèche did violate the clause.

88. 492 U.S. at 598; accord id. at 580–81 (opinion of Blackmun, J.) ("No figures of Santa Claus or other decorations appeared" near the crèche.); id. at 626 (O'Connor, J., concurring in part and concurring in the judgment) ("In contrast to the crèche in *Lynch*, which was displayed in a private park in the city's commercial district as part of a broader display of secular symbols of the holiday season, this crèche stands alone in the county courthouse.").

89. See id. at 617 (opinion of Blackmun, J.); id. at 633 (O'Connor, J., concurring in part and concurring in the judgment).

90. Id. at 664–65 (Kennedy, J., joined by Rehnquist, C.J., and White and Scalia, J.J., concurring in the judgment in part and dissenting in part).

91. 465 U.S. at 711 (Brennan, J., dissenting). See also id. at 708 ("The nativity scene . . . is the chief symbol of the characteristically Christian belief that a divine Savior was brought into the world and that the purpose of this miraculous birth was to illuminate a path toward salvation and redemption. For Christians, that path is exclusive, precious, and holy.").

92. 492 U.S. at 643 (Brennan, J., concurring in part and dissenting in part).

93. Id. at 654 & n.15 (Stevens, J., concurring in part and dissenting in part).

94. 465 U.S. at 681, 685. See also Marshall, "Establishment," 515 (The Court in *Lynch* basically argued "that Christmas and nativity scenes had been sufficiently 'secularized' by our history and culture" that they did not violate *Lemon*'s prohibitions of religious purpose and primary religious effect.).

95. 465 U.S. at 691 (O'Connor, J., concurring); accord id. at 693 (Long-standing and common public acknowledgements of religion by government serve "the legitimate secular purposes of solemnizing public occasions, expressing confidence in the future, and encouraging the recognition of what is worthy of appreciation in our society."). See also Marshall, "Establishment," 532–33: "Justice O'Connor['s] opinion is simply a straightforward syllogism: Christmas is an unquestioned part of our heritage. Some celebration of the holiday is acceptable, and the nativity scene, combined with other common seasonal items, is a traditional form of the celebration. Therefore, the crèche will not be perceived as anything more than celebration of the holiday."

96. 492 U.S. at 613, 615 (opinion of Blackmun, J.). See also id. at 618 (describing the display as a "secular celebration of Christmas coupled with an acknowledgement of Chanukah as a contemporary alternative tradition").

97. Id. at 616, 617 (opinion of Blackmun, J.)
98. Id. at 633–35 (O'Connor, J., concurring in part and concurring in the judgment).
99. Hans W. Frei, *The Eclipse of Biblical Narrative: A Study in Eighteenth and Nineteenth Century Hermeneutics* (New Haven: Yale University Press, 1974).
100. Id. at 265.
101. Id. at 313–15.
102. *County of Allegheny*, 492 U.S. at 601.
103. *Lynch*, 465 U.S. at 727 (Blackmun, J., dissenting). Curiously, Justice Blackmun was apparently not so troubled by the comparable secularization of the menorah in *Allegheny*. See 494 U.S. at 587 n.34, 613–21.
104. See *Lynch*, 465 U.S. at 683.

Chapter 5. The Religious as Afterthought: Financial Aid and Tax Exemptions for Religion

1. Roemer v. Board of Pub. Works, 426 U.S. 736 (1976); Hunt v. McNair, 413 U.S. 734 (1973); Tilton v. Richardson, 403 U.S. 672 (1971).
2. Roemer v. Board of Pub. Works, 426 U.S. 736, 745 (1976) (plurality opinion). See also Hunt v. McNair, 413 U.S. 734, 741 (1973) (program granting tax-exempt bonding privileges "to all institutions of higher education . . . , whether or not having a religious affiliation"); Tilton v. Richardson, 403 U.S. 672, 676–77 (1971) (plurality opinion) (program funding capital improvements on college campuses was "intended . . . to include all colleges and universities regardless of any affiliation with or sponsorship by a religious body").
3. See Roemer v. Board of Pub. Works, 426 U.S. 736, 746 (1976) (plurality opinion) ("Religious institutions need not be quarantined from public benefits that are neutrally available to all").
4. 487 U.S. 589, 595–96 (1988).
5. Id. at 608.
6. Id. at 609.
7. 397 U.S. 664, 671 (1970).
8. See chap. 3, text at nn.69–70.
9. See Roemer v. Board of Pub. Works, 426 U.S. 736, 750, 751 (1976) (plurality opinion); Tilton v. Richardson, 403 U.S. 672, 681–82 (1971) (plurality opinion).
10. See Roemer v. Board of Pub. Works, 426 U.S. 736, 750 (1976) (plu-

rality opinion); Tilton v. Richardson, 403 U.S. 672, 685–86 (1971) (plurality opinion).

11. Roemer v. Board of Pub. Works, 426 U.S. 736, 758–59 (1976) (plurality opinion); Tilton v. Richardson, 403 U.S. 672, 681, 687 (1971) (plurality opinion).

12. 487 U.S. at 610–11.

13. Compare Grand Rapids School Dist. v. Ball, 473 U.S. 373, 386–87 (1985) (enrichment and extracurricular courses taught in parochial school classrooms by public school employees violated establishment clause because, inter alia, the courses were not monitored for religious content) and Leavitt v. Committee for Pub. Educ., 413 U.S. 472, 479–80 (1973) (program of reimbursement for state-mandated achievement tests prepared by parochial school teachers violated establishment clause because program provided no means of ensuring that the tests would be free of religious influence) with Roemer v. Board of Pub. Works, 426 U.S. 736, 762 (1976) (plurality opinion) (inspections to ensure that aid is not used to advance religion were not necessary).

14. Roemer v. Board of Pub. Works, 426 U.S. 736, 762 (1976) (plurality opinion)

15. Compare Aguilar v. Felton, 473 U.S. 402 (1973) (monitoring state employees providing remedial help to parochial school students to ensure that they do not teach religion held an excessive entanglement with religion) with Hunt v. McNair, 413 U.S. 734, 747–48 (1973) (bonding authority's powers to assess and collect fees against and to establish rules and regulations for the use of religious colleges' buildings constructed under its auspices held not an excessive entanglement) and Tilton v. Richardson, 403 U.S. 672, 675, 680 (1971) (plurality opinion) (conducting periodic on-site inspections and requiring religious colleges to disgorge benefits when violations of secular conditions are discovered held not an excessive entanglement).

16. Compare Grand Rapids School Dist. v. Ball, 473 U.S. 373 (1985) (pervasively sectarian environment of the parochial school presents the risk that state employees will alter their secular behavior to conform to and endorse sectarian beliefs and practices); Wolman v. Walter, 433 U.S. 229, 247 (1977) (same); and Meek v. Pittenger, 421 U.S. 349, 372 (1975) (same) with *Bowen*, 487 U.S. at 612 ("[N]othing in our prior cases warrants the presumption . . . that AFLA grantees are not capable of carrying out their functions under the AFLA in a lawful, secular manner.").

17. See Andrew M. Greeley, *Catholic High Schools and Minority Students* (New Brunswick, N.J.: Transaction, 1982), 54 (50 percent of black students

and 8 percent of white students attending Catholic schools are not Catholic); Jon Diefenthaler, "Lutheran Schools in America" in *Religious Schooling in America*, ed. James C. Carper (Birmingham, Ala.: Religious Education, 1984), 35, 53 (40.6 percent of the students at Lutheran schools are not Lutheran, and 9.1 percent of these lack any religion at all). See also Donald Oppewal & Peter DeBoer, "Calvinist Day Schools: Roots and Branches" in *Religious Schooling*, 58, 78 ("The student population of [Calvinist or Reformed Church] schools in the last ten years has changed from a predominantly Dutch, white, middle-class and Christian Reformed population to one that is much more diversified, both denominationally and racially.").

18. Compare Greeley, *Catholic High Schools*, 54 (50 percent of black students attending Catholic parochial schools are not Catholic) with Marilyn M. McMillan, *Diversity of Private Schools* (Washington, D.C.: U.S. Department of Education, 1991), Table 2 (minority enrollment ranges from 19 percent to 32 percent in Catholic parochial schools and from 11 percent to 16 percent in other private religious schools). See also Donald A. Erickson, *Private Schools in Contemporary Perspective* (Palo Alto, Cal.: Institute for Research on Educational Finance and Governance, 1983), 23 (both Catholic and non-Catholic blacks attend Catholic high schools to a disproportionate extent). See generally National Catholic Education Association, *Catholic High Schools: Their Impact on Low-Income Students* (1986); *Private Schools and the Public Good*, ed. Edward McGlynn Gaffney Jr. (New Brunswick, N.J.: Transaction, 1981), 6–48.

19. During the 1981–82 school year, 25.9 percent of teachers of Catholic parochial schools belonged to religious orders. Thomas C. Hunt & Norlene M. Kunkel, "Catholic Schools: The Nation's Largest Alternative School System" in *Religious Schooling*, 1, 17, 18. By 1991, the percentage had declined to 12.8 percent. Telephone interview with Fred Brigham of the National Catholic Education Association (Oct. 30 & Nov. 2, 1992).

20. See, e.g., Eduardo Rauch, "The Jewish Day School in America: A Critical History and Contemporary Dilemmas" in *Religious Schooling*, 130, 145 (noting that many of the teachers in the general studies departments of Jewish Day schools are not Jewish).

21. 413 U.S. 734, 743–44 (1973).

22. Telephone interview with Michael Garvey, Notre Dame University Public Relations Office (November 2, 1992).

23. Cf. Stephen V. Monsma, *Positive Neutrality: Letting Religious Freedom Ring* (Westport, Conn.: Greenwood, 1993), 45 (suggesting that the presumed secular nature of religious colleges and universities is often no more than a "convenient fiction").

24. Note, "Developments in the Law—Religion and the State," 100 Harv. L. Rev. 1606, 1687 (1987).

25. See, e.g., Hunt & Kunkel, "Catholic Schools," 24; George R. Knight, "Seventh-Day Adventist Education: A Historical Sketch and Profile" in *Religious Schooling*, 85, 103.

26. Cf. Michael A. Paulsen, "Religion, Equality, and the Constitution: An Equal Protection Approach to Establishment Clause Adjudication," 61 Notre Dame L. Rev. 311, 360 (1986) (advancement of religion unlikely to occur in remedial arithmetic classes); Rauch, "Jewish Day School," 145–46 (describing the rigid compartmentalization of secular and religious studies in the typical Jewish day school). Jesse Choper suggests that teachers in parochial schools might be more likely to use religiously informed examples to illustrate their subjects than would teachers in public schools, but does not find this constitutionally objectionable. Jesse Choper, "The Establishment Clause and Aid to Parochial Schools," 56 Cal. L. Rev. 260, 301 (1968).

27. See, e.g., Senate Task Force on Critical Problems, *Educational Partnership: Nonpublic and Public Elementary and Secondary Education in New York State* 161–66 (Albany: New York Senate Research Service, 1983), Appendix E (detailing components of elementary science, physical science, biology, chemistry and physics taught in Christian schools); James C. Carper, "The Christian Day School" in *Religious Schooling*, 110, 113–14 (noting that although science is taught from a creationist perspective in Christian day schools, evolution receives "some attention"); Rauch, "Jewish Day School," 133 (one educational objective of Jewish day schools is "to encourage participation in American society, based on a conscious awareness of the relationship between Jewish tradition and democracy"); id. at 145 (the general curriculum at Jewish day schools tracks that recommended by the local state board of education, and teachers generally use the same textbooks and materials that are used in public schools).

28. See, e.g., Erickson, *Private Schools*, 31; Diefenthaler, "Lutheran Schools," 53; Michael W. McConnell & Richard A. Posner, "An Economic Approach to Issues of Religious Freedom," 56 U. Chi. L. Rev. 1, 24 (1989); Rauch, "Jewish Day School," 145. See also Erickson, *Private Schools*, 25–26 ("It appears that the lowest status patrons of private schools (inner-city black & Latino patrons of Catholic and Lutheran schools and minority scholarship students in high-tuition schools, for example) have chosen these schools because they have unusually strong mobility aspirations for their children and because they view available public schools as inadequate avenues of mobility."); McMillan, *Diversity*, Table 2 (pupil-teacher ratios range from 12 to 21 in private religious schools versus 30 or more in most pub-

lic schools); Hunt & Kunkel, "Catholic Schools," 25 (summarizing research concluding that "although the original purpose of Catholic education was to serve religious ends, the contemporary Catholic educational system is primarily secular and specifically oriented to facilitating the social mobility of selected Catholic youth," and speculating that Catholic high schools "may become religious in name only"); Phillip E. Johnson, "Concepts and Compromise in First Amendment Religious Doctrine," 72 Cal. L. Rev. 817, 844 (1984) ("[A] high percentage of [parochial school] students in some cities are non-Catholics whose parents were presumably attracted by the quality of education rather than by any program of religious indoctrination.").

29. This finding was first reported for Catholic parochial schools by James S. Coleman, Thomas Haffer & Sally Kilgore, *High School Achievement* (New York: Basic Books, 1982), and confirmed by Greeley, *Catholic High Schools*, though it remains controversial. Subsequent studies have reported results ranging from no difference between Catholic and public school students to disproportionately high academic achievement by Catholic students; there are apparently no studies showing Catholic students as a group doing more poorly than public school students as a group. A number of studies are summarized in 2 *Comparing Public and Private Schools: School Achievement*, ed. Edward H. Haertel, Thomas James, & Henry M. Levin (New York: Falmer, 1987).

The data are more ambiguous with respect to Protestant schools. Compare Oppewal & DeBoer, "Calvinist Day Schools," 74 (noting that a goal of Calvinist education "is neither evangelization for church membership nor neutral value-free information giving, but preparing the learner for living a Christian lifestyle in contemporary society") and id. at 76–77 (explaining the Calvinist effort to integrate a religious outlook with secular curricular materials) with Carper, "Christian Day School," 120: "Although there is some evidence that students attending [Christian day] schools outperform their public school counterparts on standardized tests, several observers have lamented the poor academic standards evident in some schools. Other critics have deplored the 'super-patriotism' which characterizes a number of Christian schools. Commentators have also suggested that these schools may shelter students and thus fail to prepare them for life in the 'real world.'" Stephen Carter reached similar conclusions on this point in his review of the data. See Stephen L. Carter, *The Culture of Disbelief: How American Politics and Law Trivialize Religious Devotion* (New York: Basic Books, 1993), 195–97.

30. Choper, "Parochial Schools," 294–95. See also Donald A. Gianella, "Religious Liberty, Nonestablishment, and Doctrinal Development—Part II:

The Nonestablishment Principle," 81 Harv. L. Rev. 513, 573–74 (1968) (suggesting that although a "strong religious atmosphere" is maintained at most parochial schools, the "lingering suspicion that religious perspectives pervade the entire curriculum . . . is probably unfounded with respect to certain subjects").

31. McConnell & Posner, "Economic Analysis," 23.

32. See, e.g., 473 U.S. 373, 386 (1985).

33. Cf. William P. Marshall, " 'We Know It When We See It': The Supreme Court and Establishment," 59 S. Cal. L. Rev. 495, 525–26 (1986) (characterizing as "absurd" the view that "providing counseling services in a particular building as opposed to across the street" affects the behavior of school counselors).

34. Grand Rapids, 473 U.S. at 388; Aguilar, 473 U.S. at 428 (O'Connor, J., dissenting).

35. See John Garvey, "Another Way of Looking at School Aid," 1985 Sup. Ct. Rev. 61, 77.

36. See chap. 3, text at nn.44–48.

37. Garvey, "Another Way," 77. Garvey concedes that the cases might be distinguished on the ground that parochial schools are pervasively sectarian whereas colleges are generally not pervasively chauvinistic, thus relieving the Court in the latter situation from worrying about regulatory entanglement. This, however, still does not explain the Court's application of the entanglement analysis in cases such as Aguilar in which "it is hard to see a threat of government entanglement in the government supervising its own employees." Id.

38. Id. at 88.

39. Note, "Developments," 1686. See also Diefenthaler, "Lutheran Schools," 53 ("The 'Christian' aspects of the training offered in Lutheran schools no doubt appeals to certain evangelical Protestants, especially those who believe that America is on the brink of moral bankruptcy."); Carper, "Christian Day School," 115 (The proliferation of Christian day schools is in part a reaction by parents and students to "widespread uncertainty concerning sources of authority, dissolution of standards, loosening of custom and constraint, waning of evangelicalism as a culture-shaping force, scientism, and government social engineering.").

40. See Choper, "Parochial Schools," 298.

41. See Note, "Developments," 1691. Alan Schwarz argued that aid to parochial schools, which the Court rarely permits, presents far less a danger of religious coercion than aid to religious social service organizations, which the Court often allows; aid to religious social service organizations

"may be used to influence a nonbeliever's or other-believer's religious choice, whereas in the parochial school situation the affected parties generally attend the school because they desire the religious effect." See Alan Schwarz, "The Nonestablishment Principle: A Reply to Professor Gianella," 81 Harv. L. Rev. 1465, 1478 (1968).

42. See chap. 3, text at nn.41–42.

43. Garvey, "Another Way," 92. But see chap. 3, text at nn. 66–67.

44. See generally John Witte Jr., "Tax Exemption of Church Property: Historical Anomaly or Valid Constitutional Practice?," 64 S. Cal. L. Rev. 363 (1991).

45. 397 U.S. 664 (1970).

46. See 397 U.S. at 673, 674; Paul G. Kauper, "The *Walz* Decision: More on the Religion Clauses of the First Amendment," 69 Mich. L. Rev. 179, 183–84 (1970).

47. Id. at 703 (Douglas, J., dissenting). See also id. at 701 (Douglas, J., dissenting) ("In common understanding one of the best ways to 'establish' one or more religions is to subsidize them, which a tax exemption does."). In fact, property owned by the Anglican establishment that was dedicated to religious uses was exempt from property taxation at common law. See Arvo Van Alstyne, "Tax Exemption of Church Property," 20 Ohio St. L.J. 461, 462 (1959); Witte, "Historical Anomaly," 370–71.

48. See, e.g., 397 U.S. at 668 ("[F]or the men who wrote the Religion Clauses of the First Amendment the 'establishment' of a religion connoted sponsorship, financial support, and active involvement of the sovereign in religious activity"); id. at 672 (reading the Court's religion clause precedents as having "preserved the autonomy and freedom of religious bodies while avoiding any semblance of established religion"); id. at 674 (characterizing the ultimate issue as whether "the end result—the effect—is not an excessive government entanglement with religion").

49. See id. at 672–73.

50. See chap. 4, text at nn.15–23.

51. Id. at 675.

52. See id. at 673. See also Kauper, "*Walz* Decision," 197 ("The impact on religion of government acts and programs assumes a central place in [*Walz*].").

53. Van Alstyne, "Church Property," 462–66 (quoting John Stuart Mill, *Representative Government* [Chicago: University of Chicago Press, 1952], 337). See also Marshall, "Establishment," 501 (*Walz* did not require "that the religious organization justify its contribution to the community by any

secular-based criteria such as charitable works or community involvement. Religion was supported as religion and received favorable treatment on that ground alone."); Kauper, "*Walz* Decision," 197, 198: "Neutrality plays a large part in the Chief Justice's opinion; but his is the neutrality of accommodation and a neutrality which, by according a central place to religious liberty, permits a preferential treatment for religion . . . . According to Burger, benevolent neutrality is a neutrality which . . . permits a deliberate favoring of religion in order to free religion from possible intrusions by and entanglements with governmental authority."

54. Id. at 674–75. The empirical validity of this conclusion is doubtful. See, e.g., Witte, "Historical Anomaly," 266, 267: "The Court argues that [property tax exemption] interactions will result in an unconstitutional 'entanglement' between church and state. But the constitutionality of more intrusive and immediate interactions between the two institutions has been consistently upheld against establishment clause challenges, when, for example, church properties are zoned, church buildings are landmarked, church societies are incorporated, church employers are audited, church broadcasters and publishers are regulated, and intrachurch disputes are adjudicated . . . . The incidental and isolated interaction that would result from the taxation of church property is trivial by comparison."

55. 397 U.S. at 687–89.

56. Id. at 689. See also id. at 693 ("All churches by their nature contribute to the diversity of association, viewpoint, and enterprise so highly valued by all of us.").

57. Id. at 692. See also id. ("[E]xemptions do not 'serve the essentially religious activities of religious institutions.' Their principal effect is to carry out secular purposes—the encouragement of public service activities and of a pluralistic society.").

58. Id. at 696, 697 (opinion of Harlan, J.).

59. Id. at 674.

60. 489 U.S. 1 (1990).

61. Id. at 17 (plurality opinion by Brennan, J., joined by Marshall and Stevens, J.J.) ("Texas' sales tax exemption for periodicals promulgating the teaching of any religious sect lacks a secular objective that would justify this preference along with similar benefits for nonreligious publications or groups, and . . . effectively endorses religious belief."); id. at 28 (Blackman, J., concurring in the judgment, joined by O'Connor, J.) ("[A] tax exemption *limited to* the sale of religious literature by religious organizations violates the Establishment Clause.") (emphasis in original).

62. *Walz,* 397 U.S. at 673.

63. 489 U.S. at 14–15 (quoting Bob Jones University v. United States, 461 U.S. 574, 591 [1983]) (citation omitted).

64. 489 U.S. at 15 (plurality opinion).

65. See chap. 3, text at nn.37–38 & 49–71. This difference between religious communitarian and secular individualist analyses of tax exemptions recalls an analogous difference between the rationale for church property exemptions at common law and at equity in colonial America. The common law exempted the religiously dedicated properties of the established church as a quid pro quo for the established church's undertaking the religious responsibilities of the state. See Witte, "Historical Anomaly," 375, 379. Even in the post-disestablishment era, the religious activities of churches generally were thought to contribute important benefits to society which justified the exemption. See id. at 387. At equity, however, church-owned property was exempted only to the extent that it was dedicated to general "charitable" uses, id. at 375–76, 379, thereby relieving the state of social welfare burdens by their charitable activities, id. at 388. See also Van Alstyne, "Church Property," 462 (a theory for church tax exemption cannot be constructed by analogy to eleemosynary institutions "which, unlike churches, perform quasi-public functions that government would presumably be required to assume in their absence").

66. 489 U.S. at 11 (plurality opinion).

67. Monsma, *Positive Neutrality,* 11.

Chapter 6. The Religious as Irrelevant: Free Exercise Exemptions

1. 374 U.S. 398 (1963).

2. 406 U.S. 205 (1972).

3. 494 U.S. 872 (1990).

4. 98 U.S. 145, 166–67 (1878).

5. Id. at 164. See also chap. 1, text at nn.48–52.

6. 98 U.S. at 166.

7. See, e.g., Late Corp. of the Church of Jesus Christ of Latter-Day Saints v. United States, 136 U.S. 1, 48, 49 (1890); Davis v. Beason, 133 U.S. 333, 341 (1890); Murphy v. Ramsey, 114 U.S. 15, 45 (1885). See generally Marc Galanter, "Religious Freedom in the United States: A Turning Point?," 1966 Wis. L. Rev. 216, 234 (reporting that he could find only one reported decision before 1940 in which a claim of religious liberty was accepted as a defense to criminal liability).

8. 310 U.S. 296, 303–4 (1940).

9. See Galanter, "Turning Point," 235.

10. 366 U.S. 599, 601–2 (1961).

11. Id. at 607.

12. Id. at 614 (Brennan, J., dissenting) (citations omitted). See also id. at 615–16 ("In fine, the Court, in my view, has exalted administrative convenience to a constitutional level high enough to justify making one religion economically disadvantageous.").

13. Id. at 616 (Stewart, J., dissenting).

14. 374 U.S. 398, 410 (1963).

15. Id. at 407.

16. Id. at 403, 406–7.

17. See Galanter, "Turning Point," 252, 282–83.

18. See J. Morris Clark, "Guidelines for the Free Exercise Clause," 83 Harv. L. Rev. 327, 334–35, 360 (1969) (citing Braunfeld); Donald A. Giannella, "Religious Liberty, Nonestablishment, and Doctrinal Development—Part I: The Religious Liberty Guarantee," 80 Harv. L. Rev. 1381, 1403, 1409 (1967) (citing the Polygamy Cases). However, Professor Gianella argued that only crimes mala prohibita should be subjected to balancing; in his view, the classification of a religious practice as a crime mala in se constituted an absolute justification for prohibiting the practice. See id. at 1403, 1407.

19. 366 U.S. at 407.

20. Id. at 408–9.

21. Id. at 404, 410.

22. See, e.g., Scott H. Bice, "Rationality Analysis in Constitutional Law," 65 Minn. L. Rev. 1, 37–38 (1980) (citing, as an example, Dean Milk Co. v. City of Madison, 340 U.S. 349 [1951]).

23. See, e.g., Giannella, "Religious Liberty," 1411.

24. Bice, "Rationality Analysis," 38–39.

25. Clark, "Guidelines," 331.

26. Cf. Galanter, "Turning Point," 216 (noting the "immense prestige of the general notion of religious liberty").

27. Stephen Pepper, "Taking the Free Exercise Clause Seriously," 1986 B.Y.U. L. Rev. 299, 335.

28. 374 U.S. at 408–9.

29. See Galanter, "Turning Point," 279; Giannella, "Religious Liberty," 1401.

30. See 366 U.S. at 611 (Brennan, J., dissenting).

31. Giannella, "Religious Liberty," 1406–7.

32. 406 U.S. 205 (1972).

33. Id. at 234.

34. Id. at 221, 226–27, 236; id. at 238 (White, J., concurring).

35. Pepper, "Free Exercise Clause," 310.

36. See id. at 308.

37. E.g., Frazee v. Illinois Dep't of Employment Sec., 489 U.S. 829 (1989); Hobbie v. Unemployment Appeals Comm'n, 480 U.S. 136 (1987); Thomas v. Review Bd, 450 U.S. 707 (1981).

38. Galanter, "Turning Point," 267–68. But see Giannella, "Religious Liberty," 1419 (although the Supreme Court has formally disclaimed the existence of general standards for measuring the importance to the claimant of the religious practices burdened, "this cannot possibly mean that the claimant's assessment of the religious importance of his claim must always be taken at face value").

39. 450 U.S. 707 (1981).

40. See, e.g., id. at 715 ("Thomas' statements reveal no more than that he found work in the roll foundry sufficiently insulated from producing weapons of war. We see, therefore, that Thomas drew a line, and it is not for us to say that the line he drew was an unreasonable one."); id. at 716 ("[I]t is not within the judicial function and judicial competence to inquire whether the petitioner or his fellow worker more correctly perceived the commands of their common faith. Courts are not arbiters of scriptural interpretation.").

41. 489 U.S. 829, 832–33 (1989).

42. 322 U.S. 78, 86 (1944). See also id. at 87 (although the religious beliefs of respondents "might seem incredible, if not preposterous, to most people," the truth or falsity of such beliefs may not constituionally be made an issue in a criminal trial).

43. William Marshall, "The Case against the Constitutionally Compelled Free Exercise Exemption," 40 Case W. Res. L. Rev. 357, 359 (1990). See also Galanter, "Turning Point," 270 ("[W]hen this forbearance toward religious objection is combined with the new permissiveness in defining religion, other kinds of possibilities come into view. Dissidents of all kinds—nudists, LSD users, racists, utopians, and groups as yet unimagined—can be expected to present claims for religious freedom."); Michael W. McConnell, "Accommodation of Religion," 1985 Sup. Ct. Rev. 1, 53 ("The fear [of Sunday closing law exemptions] is less that the statute might induce someone actually to adopt a faith that recognizes a Sabbath than that some might feign such a religion in order to be guaranteed a particular weekend day off."). Gerard Bradley notes that most religions require sufficiently rigorous commitments and sacrifices that ascertaining the sincerity of an exemption claim is rarely

very difficult. Gerard V. Bradley, "Beguiled: Free Exercise Exemptions and the Siren Song of Liberalism," 20 Hofstra L. Rev. 245, 313 (1991).

44. See Pepper, "Free Exercise Clause," 326; cf. Ferdinand F. Fernandez, "The Free Exercise of Religion," 36 S. Cal. L. Rev. 546, 547 (1963) (the definition of religion is not important when an individual receives little benefit from asserting that his or her motives are religious).

45. Frazee v. Illinois Employment Securitiy Department, 489 U.S. 829, 835 (1989)

46. 455 U.S. 252 (1982).

47. Id. at 260.

48. Clark, "Guidelines," 335; Giannella, "Religious Liberty," 1398, 1409; Pepper, "Free Exercise Clause," 326, 327.

49. See chap. 2, text at n.98.

50. Douglas Laycock, "The Remnants of Free Exercise," 1990 Sup. Ct. Rev. 1, 17.

51. See, e.g. *Sherbert*, 374 U.S. at 408–9 (exemptions to the Sunday closing laws at issue in *Braunfeld* "appeared to present an administrative problem of such magnitude, or to afford the exempted class so great a competitive advantage, that such a requirement would have rendered the entire statutory scheme unworkable"); Clark, "Guidelines," 332 ("[T]he cost to the government frequently depends on the number of persons who can lay claim to the exemption."). Galanter, "Turning Point," 284 ("Often the probability of adverse effects is a question of numbers. An exemption may be harmless precisely because few people avail themselves of it."); Gianella, "Religious Liberty," 1392 (noting that denial of vaccination exemptions will not represent a threat to others so long as the number claiming the exemption remains low).

52. Cf. Pepper, "Free Exercise Clause," 314: "The smaller the minority, the more likely the majority will inadvertently impose on its religious interests, and therefore the greater need for protection under the free exercise clause. Conversely, the larger the minority, the more likely that the restraint of the establishment clause will be appropriate rather than the protection of the free exercise clause."

53. Cf. Laycock, "Remnants," 68 (noting that protection of religious exercise from "hostile or indifferent consequences of the political process" has long been thought to be one of the principal functions of judicial review under the free exercise clause).

54. 475 U.S. 503 (1986).

55. 485 U.S. 439 (1988).

56. 493 U.S. 378, 392 (1990).

57. Bowen v. Roy, 476 U.S. 693, 707–8 (1986) (opinion of Burger, C.J., joined by Powell and Rehnquist, J.J.).

58. See Mark Tushnet, *Red, White, and Blue: A Critical Analysis of Constitutional Law* (Cambridge, Mass.: Harvard University Press, 1988), 249.

59. 494 U.S. 872 (1990).

60. See chap. 2, text at n.78.

61. 494 U.S. at 882.

62. Id. at 884.

63. Id. at 881.

64. 494 U.S. at 877–78. See also id. at 882 ("There being no contention that Oregon's drug law represents an attempt to regulate religious beliefs, the communication of religious beliefs, or the raising of one's children in those beliefs, the rule to which we have adhered ever since *Reynolds* [i.e., the belief-action doctrine] plainly controls.").

65. 456 U.S. 228 (1982). See also McDaniel v. Paty, 435 U.S. 618, 632, 635 n.8, 639 (1978) (Brennan, J., concurring in the judgment) (prohibition of clergy from holding certain state public offices violates both free exercise and establishment clauses).

66. James D. Gordon III, "Free Exercise on the Mountaintop," 79 Cal. L. Rev. 91, 114, 115 (1991). See also Michael W. McConnell, "Accommodation of Religion: An Update and Response to the Critics," 60 Geo. Wash. L. Rev. 685, 691 (1992) ("Just as the Establishment Clause is more than a ban on a compulsory official church, the Free Exercise Clause is more than a ban on the Inquisition."). The Court's latest pronouncement on free exercise, Church of the Lukumi Babalu Aye, Inc. v. City of Hialeah, 113 S. Ct. 2217 (1993), hints that *Smith* may not be the last word on free exercise doctrine. In *Hialeah*, the Court examined, inter alia, the "effect" of a series of municipal ordinances to conclude that they had been enacted with the intent of criminalizing the sacrificial rituals of the Santeria church. See id. at 2228. A holding that strict scrutiny is required whenever facially neutral government action burdens religious exercise would have essentially restored the *Sherbert-Yoder* doctrine while overruling *Smith* sub rosa. *Hialeah* did not accomplish this, since it was not clear that the text of the ordinances there at issue was facially neutral, see id. at 2227–28, and at the same time it *was* clear that the text operated as a religious gerrymander, see, e.g., id. at 2228. Still, the Court's willingness to determine constitutionality by looking behind the text to the effect of government action on a religious complainant suggests that *Smith* may not be the last word on free exercise exemptions. See generally id. at 2240–50 (Souter, J., concurring in part and concurring in the

judgment) (arguing that *Smith* could be reexamined and overruled consistent with principles of stare decisis); Stephen L. Carter, "The Resurrection of Religious Freedom?," 107 Harv. L. Rev. 118 (1993) (speculating that *Lukumi Babalu Aye* and Lamb's Chapel v. Center Moriches Union Free School Dist., 113 S. Ct. 2141 [1993], indicate the Court's willingness to revisit *Smith*).

67. Compare W. Cole Durham Jr. & Alexander Dushku, "Traditionalism, Secularism, and the Transformative Dimension of Religious Institutions," 1993 B.Y.U. L. Rev. 421, 451 (noting that under the *Sherbert-Yoder* doctrine numerous free exercise claims were vindicated by state and lower federal courts, and lower-level officials were deterred from exercising discretion in favor of encroachments upon religious liberty) with Milner S. Ball, "The Unfree Exercise of Religion," 20 Cap. L. Rev. 39, 50–51 (1991) (arguing that restoration of the compelling interest test will not protect Native American religious practices) and Bradley, "Siren Song," 247 n.14 (reporting that in a random survey of one hundred reported pre-*Smith* exemption decisions, the plaintiffs prevailed in only seven cases, one of which was subsequently reversed on appeal).

68. Bradley, "Siren Song," 248.

69. See chap. 1, text at nn.45–53.

70. See Kent Greenawalt, *Religious Convictions and Political Choice* (New York: Oxford, 1988), 94. See also Church of the Lukumi Babalu Aye, Inc. v. City of Hialeah, 113 S. Ct. 2217, 2225 (1993) ("Although the practice of animal sacrifice may seem abhorrent to some, 'religious beliefs need not be acceptable, logical, consistent, or comprehensible to others in order to merit First Amendment protection.'") (quoting *Thomas*, 450 U.S. at 714). But see generally Bowers v. Hardwick, 478 U.S. 186 (1986) (declining to declare state antisodomy law unconstitutional as violation of constitutional privacy rights of homosexuals).

71. See, e.g., Church of the Lukumi Babalu Aye, Inc. v. City of Hialeah, 113 S.Ct. 2217 (1993); Larson v. Valente, 456 U.S. 228 (1982); McDaniel v. Paty, 435 U.S. 618 (1978).

72. See chap. 3, text at nn.49–67.

73. See, e.g., Zobrist v. Catalina Foothills School Dist., 113 S. Ct. 2462, 2466–67, 2469 (1993); Lamb's Chapel v. Center Moriches School Dist., 113 S. Ct. 2141, 2148 (1993); Westside Comm. Bd. of Educ. v. Mergens, 496 U.S. 226, 250, 252 (1990) (plurality opinion); Witters v. Dept. of Servs. for the Blind, 474 U.S. 481, 482–83, 487–88 (1986); Mueller v. Allen, 463 U.S. 388, 399–400 (1983); Widmar v. Vincent, 454 U.S. 263, 270–72, 273–74 (1981).

74. Phillip B. Kurland, *Religion and the Law: Of Church and State and*

the Supreme Court (Chicago: University of Chicago Press, 1961), 41. Professor McConnell concedes that exemptions benefit only believers, McConnell, "Accomodation of Religion" (1985), 11, but argues that this does not distort the preexisting pattern of religious choice because decisions to engage in religious conduct are always made independent of whether such conduct is exempt from government regulation or prohibition, McConnell, "Update," 686, 688, 716–17. However, it seems intuitively implausible that criminal prohibition and punishment of religious practices would have *no* effect on decisions by believers whether to engage in such practices. For example, nineteenth-century Mormons practiced polygamy at declining rates as federal persecution increased, and such persecution eventually forced the Mormons to abandon the practice completely as the price of institutional survival. See generally Frederick Mark Gedicks, "The Integrity of Survival: A Mormon Response to Stanley Hauerwas," 42 DePaul L. Rev. 167 (1992).

75. See Fernandez, "Free Exercise of Religion," 589; Jonathan Weiss, "Privilege, Posture and Protection: 'Religion' in the Law," 73 Yale L.J. 593, 618 (1964). See also Kurland, *Religion and the Law,* 22 ("To permit individuals to be excused from compliance with the law solely on the basis of religious beliefs is to subject others to punishment for failure to subscribe to those same beliefs."); Weiss, "Privilege," 623: "The task is to discern whether religion forms a variable in the statute's formulation or application by seeing whether an assumption or decision on a perspective of belief is called for. If so, then the statute is unconstitutional. If not, then religion can form neither a defense to its application nor a justification after application for calling the statute unconstitutional."

76. See, e.g., Branzberg v. Hayes, 408 U.S. 665 (1972) (reporter does not have constitutional privilege to refuse to reveal news sources when testifying before a grand jury).

77. 494 U.S. at 878 (quoting the text of the religion and press clauses of the First Amendment).

78. See, e.g., Heffron v. International Soc. for Krishna Consciousness, Inc., 452 U.S. 640, 652–53 (1981).

79. Compare Walz v. Tax Comm'n, 397 U.S. 664, 687–89, 693 (1970) (Brennan, J., concurring) (religious property tax exemption does not violate establishment clause when comparable exemptions are also granted to secular nonprofit organizations) with Texas Monthly v. Bullock, 489 U.S. 1 (1990) (sales tax exemption granted only to religious magazines violates establishment clause). See also Ira C. Lupu, "Reconstructing the Establishment Clause: The Case against Discretionary Accomodation of Religion," 140 U. Pa. L. Rev. 555, 592 (1991) ("The Court tends to uphold [programs

of aid to religious organizations] only if they exhibit a breadth of coverage sufficient to include nonreligous organizations."). But see Corporation of the Presiding Bishop v. Amos, 483 U.S. 327 (1987) (exemption of nonprofit activities of churches and other religious organizations from the Civil Rights Act of 1964 does not violate establishment clause). The Court's upholding a religiously defined exemption in *Amos* can be understood as its acquiescence in Congress's perception that such an exemption was constitutionally required under the *Sherbert-Yoder* doctrine, which was the constitutional law of free exercise both at the time the Act was passed and when *Amos* was decided.

80. 430 U.S. 705 (1977) (Jehovah's Witness not required to display state license plate that included the slogan "Live free or die").

81. 319 U.S. 624 (1943) (Jehovah's Witness not required to participate in compulsory flag salute).

82. See William P. Marshall, "Solving the Free Exercise Dilemma: Free Exercise as Expression," 67 Minn. L. Rev. 545, 560 (1983); Pepper, "Free Exercise Clause," 307–8.

83. See Pierce v. Society of Sisters, 268 U.S. 510 (1925); Meyer v. Nebraska, 262 U.S. 390 (1923).

84. 483 U.S. 327 (1987).

85. See 42 U.S.C. § 2000e-1 (1972).

86. 483 U.S. at 337.

87. Id. at 347 (O'Connor, J., concurring in the judgment). See also chap. 3, text at nn. 11–23.

88. The exemption provides that Title VII of the Civil Rights Act of 1964 shall not apply "to a religious corporation, association, educational institution, or society with respect to the employment of individuals of a particular religion to perform work connected with the carrying on by such corporation, association, educational institution, or society of its activities." 42 U.S.C. § 2000e-1 (1972).

89. 483 U.S at 337 n.15 ("Undoubtedly, [the employee]'s freedom of choice in religious matters was impinged upon.").

90. Cf. id. at 340 n.1 (Brennan, J., concurring in the judgment) (citation omitted) (emphasis in original): "The fact that a religious organization is permitted, rather than required, to impose this burden is irrelevant; what is significant is that the burden is the effect of the exemption. An exemption by its nature merely permits certain behavior, but that has never stopped this Court from examining the *effect* of exemptions that would free religion from regulation placed on others."

91. Id. at 341–46. See also id. at 336 (majority opinion): "It is a significant

burden on a religious organization to require it, on pain of substantial liability, to predict which of its activities a secular court will consider religious.
The line is hardly a bright one, and an organization might understandably be
concerned that a judge would not understand its religious tenets and sense
of mission." I explored this argument in detail in Frederick Mark Gedicks,
"Toward a Constitutional Jurisprudence of Religious Group Rights," 1989
Wis. L. Rev. 99.

92. See 430 U.S. at 342 (Brennan, J., concurring): "For many individuals, religious activity derives meaning in large measure from participation
in a larger religious community. Such a community represents an ongoing
tradition of shared beliefs, an organic activity not reducible to a mere aggregation of individuals. Determining that certain activities are in furtherance
of an organization's religious mission, and that only those committed to that
mission should conduct them, is thus a means by which a religious community defines itself. Solicitude for a church's ability to do so reflects the idea
that furtherance of the autonomy of religious organizations often furthers
individual religious freedom as well."

93. See 494 U.S. at 890 (dictum). Professor McConnell suggests that
Smith's tone of judicial restraint may augur an expansion of the zone of permissible accommodation even as the decision eliminated the zone of mandatory accomodation. McConnell, "Update," 710–12.

94. Compare Walz v. Tax Comm'n, 397 U.S. 664, 687–89, 693 (1970)
(Brennan, J., concurring) (religious property tax exemption does not violate establishment clause when comparable exemptions are also granted to
secular nonprofit organizations) with Texas Monthly v. Bullock, 489 U.S. 1
(1990) (sales tax exemption granted only to religious magazines violates
establishment clause).

95. Galanter, "Turning Point," 290–91; Pepper, "Free Exercise Clause,"
314. See also Stephen L. Carter, *The Culture of Disbelief: How American Politics and Law Trivialize Religious Devotion* (New York: Basic Books, 1993), 125
("It must not be missed that 'laws that apply to everybody else' often reflect,
albeit implicitly, the values and teachings of the nation's dominant religious
traditions."); Laycock, "Remnants," 15 ("Even if the Court were to forbid
legislated exemptions, the majority would rarely be required to violate its
deeply held beliefs, because the majority's deeply held beliefs will normally
be reflected in legislation without an exemption."); McConnell, "Update,"
734 ("Of course, truly mainstream religions have little need for accommoda-
tions at all. Given their influence on the culture, it is unlikely that the laws
will conflict in any serious way with deeply held principles.").

96. See, e.g., *Braunfeld*, 366 U.S. at 599. See also Lynch v. Donnelly, 465

U.S. 665 (1984) (publicly funded depiction of Jesus's birth did not violate establishment clause); Marsh v. Chambers, 463 U.S. 783 (1983) (nondenominational legislative prayers delivered in traditional manner by Protestant minister did not violate establishment clause).

97. Galanter, "Turning Point," 290–91. See also Pepper, "Free Exercise Clause," 314 ("While the majority is unlikely to disadvantage itself intentionally in religious matters, it is also highly unlikely to do so inadvertently. To truly equalize the minority and the majority, the religion clauses must reach not only purposeful favoring or disfavoring, but also the inadvertent.").

98. Lupu, "Discretionary Accommodation," 601–6.

99. See, e.g., Hebert Wechsler, "Toward Neutral Principles of Constitutional Law," 73 Harv. L. Rev. 1, 19 (1959). See also H. Jefferson Powell, *The Moral Tradition of American Consitutionalism: A Theological Interpretation* (Durham, N.C.: Duke University Press, 1993), 168 (In the American constitutional tradition, "a court's exercise of its legal jurisdiction was legitimate only if it could and did offer a reasoned and rationally persuasive justification for the decision, employing the agreed-upon modes of legal argument.").

100. See Stephen Monsma, *Positive Neutrality: Letting Religious Freedom Ring* (Westport, Conn.: Greenwood, 1993), 39. Curiously, Lupu himself concludes that these differences *preclude* legislatures from enacting permissive exemptions. Lupu, "Discretionary Accommodation," 606–7.

101. See Lyng v. Northwest Indian Cemetery Protective Ass'n, 485 U.S. 439 (1988) (free exercise clause does not prevent federal government from implementing land use plan that would destroy Native American religion); O'Lone v. Estate of Shabazz, 482 U.S. 342 (1987) (denying Muslim prison inmates exemption from policy that prevented them from attending worship services); Bowen v. Roy, 476 U.S. 693 (1986) (free exercise clause does not prevent government from assigning and using social security number to Native American child in violation of parent's religious beliefs); Goldman v. Weinberger, 475 U.S. 503 (1986) (denying Orthodox Jewish serviceman exemption from uniform regulation which prevented his wearing a yarmulke); Braunfeld v. Brown, 366 U.S. 599 (1961) (denying Orthodox Jewish merchant exemption from Sunday closing law that threatened economic viability of his business). See also Heffron v. International Soc. of Krishna Consciousness, 452 U.S. 640 (1981) (members of Eastern sect that requires distribution and sale of religious literature as a matter of belief not exempt from content neutral speech regulations). But see Torcaso v. Watkins, 367 U.S. 488 (1961) (atheist not required to profess belief in God as condition of receiving notary commission); United States v. Ballard, 322 U.S. 78 (1944) (determination of truth or falsity of "I Am" movement not within jury's competence).

102. Compare *Unemployment Compensation Cases*, 489 U.S. 829 (1989); 480 U.S. 136 (1987); 450 U.S. 707 (1981); 374 U.S. 398 (1963) (reversals of denials of unemployment benefits to nondenominational Christian, Jehovah's Witnesses, and Seventh-Day Adventist who lost or left employment for reasons of religious conscience) and Wisconsin v. Yoder, 406 U.S. 205 (1975) (Amish parents cannot be prosecuted for violation of compulsory school attendance statute) with Swaggart v. Board of Equalization, 493 U.S. 378 (1990) (denying television ministry exemption from general tax on sales of Bibles); Jensen v. Quaring, 472 U.S. 478 (1985) (affirming by equally divided Court denial of exemption from driver's license photograph requirement to person who believed photographs were "graven images" in violation of the Ten Commandments); Tony & Susan Alamo Found. v. Secretary of Labor, 471 U.S. 290 (1985) (denying religious foundation exemption from federal labor regulations); Bob Jones University v. United States, 461 U.S. 574 (1983) (denying Christian university exemption from regulation that denies tax exemption to racially discriminatory educational institutions); United States v. Lee, 455 U.S. 252 (1982) (denying Amish employer exemption from Social Security taxes); Minersville School Dist. v. Gobitis, 310 U.S. 586 (1940) (denying Jehovah's Witnesses exemption from public school requirement of saluting the flag), *overruled*, Board of Educ. v. Barnett, 319 U.S. 624, 642 (1943); Reynolds v. United States, 98 U.S. 145 (1879) (denying polygamous Mormon exemption from prosecution under antibigamy laws).

103. Cf. Galanter, "Turning Point," 268 ("[G]overnment tends to make majority notions into normative standards; enjoyment of benefits and sometimes avoidance of penalties are conditional upon acceptance of prevailing notions about health, education, hours of work, age of retirement, and the like."); Giannella, "Religious Liberty," 1385 (the Court's decisions under the free exercise clause have tended to vindicate the morality of majoritarian religion).

104. See, e.g., *Unemployment Compensation Cases*, 489 U.S. 829 (1989); 480 U.S. 136 (1987); 450 U.S. 707 (1981); 374 U.S. 398 (1963) (reversals of denials of unemployment benefits to nondenominational Christian, Jehovah's Witnesses, and Seventh-Day Adventist who lost or left employment for reasons of religious conscience); Wisconsin v. Yoder, 406 U.S. 205 (1975) (Amish parents cannot be prosecuted for violation of compulsory school attendance statute). See also West Va. Bd. of Educ. v. Barnett, 319 U.S. 624 (1943) (Jehovah's Witness cannot be disciplined for refusing to salute the flag).

105. Lupu, "Discretionary Accommodation," 586. See also Carter, *Cul-*

ture of Disbelief, 9 ("Religions that most need protection seem to receive it least.").

Conclusion: Death of a Discourse?

1. 112 S. Ct. 2469, 2655–59 (1992). The prayers at issue in *Weisman* were the following:

INVOCATION

God of the Free, Hope of the Brave:

For the legacy of America where diversity is celebrated and the rights of minorities are protected, we thank You. May these young men and women grow up to enrich it.

For the liberty of America, we thank You. May these new graduates grow up to guard it.

For the political process of America in which all its citizens may participate, for its court system where all may seek justice we thank You. May those we honor this morning always turn to it in trust.

For the destiny of America we thank You. May the graduates of Nathan Bishop Middle School so live that they might help to share it.

May our aspirations for our country and for these young people, who are our hope for the future, be richly fulfilled.

AMEN

BENEDICTION

O God, we are grateful to You for having endowed us with the capacity for learning which we have celebrated on this joyous commencement.

Happy families give thanks for seeing their children achieve an important milestone. Send Your blessings upon the teachers and administrators who helped prepare them.

The graduates now need strength and guidance for the future, help them to understand that we are not complete with academic knowledge alone. We must each strive to fulfill what You require of us all: To do justly, to love mercy, to walk humbly.

We give thanks to You, Lord, for keeping us alive, sustaining us and allowing us to reach this special, happy occasion.

AMEN

2. See 485 U.S. 439, 451 (1988) (citation to record omitted): "The Gov-

ernment does not dispute, and we have no reason to doubt, that the logging and road-building projects at issue in this case could have devastating effects on the traditional Indian religious practices . . . . To be sure, the Indians themselves were far from unanimous in opposing the . . . road, and it seems less than certain that construction of the road will be so disruptive that it will doom their religion."

3. Id. at 451–52 (quoting opinion below, 795 F.2d 688, 693 [9th Cir. 1986]). See also 485 U.S. at 451 ("We can assume that the threat to the efficacy of at least some religious practices is extremely grave.").

4. See Ronald Brownstein, "Dissatisfied Americans May Spell Democrat Losses," *L.A. Times,* July 28, 1994, at A1, cols. 5–6, A19 cols. 1–6 (Orange County ed.). Brownstein reports the results of a *Los Angeles Times* poll that found that 53 percent of all American adults and 60 percent of white Protestant "fundamentalists" (defined as those who believe that "the Bible is the literal word of God") think that "a moral climate that hurts community standards" is more threatening than economic strain; 70 percent and 82 percent, respectively, of the same two groups think that the "traditional family structure" is always best;, 61 percent and 87 percent think that "homosexual relations are always wrong"; and 76 percent and 94 percent favor prayer in public schools. Moreover, whereas 12 percent of adult Americans see religious conservatives as representing a greater danger to society than "liberal feminists" and "gay activists," more than three times as many, or 38 percent, see the latter two groups as a greater social threat than religious conservatives (43 percent saw neither or both as a danger). Finally, 64 percent of all Americans say that religious conservative activism in the Republican Party has not made them less likely to vote for Republican candidates, and another 13 percent says that such activism makes it more likely that they will vote Republican. Fundamentalists were reported to have diverged from all Americans on the issue of working women; 65 percent of fundamentalists think that men should be the "achievers" and women the "homemakers," whereas only 42 percent—still a surprisingly large number—of all Americans think so. Responses to questions on abortion showed that it is overwhelmingly opposed by fundamentalists, while all Americans are closely divided on the issue; only 18 percent of fundamentalists favored legalized abortion, compared to 45 percent of all Americans.

With respect to evolution, the Gallup Poll has reported that 44 percent of Americans believe in the creationist view that God created humanity and the world simultaneously, 49 percent believe in creation by an evolutionary process guided by God, and 9 percent believe in the classic neo-Darwinist account of human creation as the result of random physiobiological encounters occurring over millions of years (the figures exceed 100 percent because of decimal rounding). See Dennis A. Gilbert, *Compendium of American Public Opinion* 314 (New York: Facts on File, 1988). Although Gilbert interprets this as evidence that 58 percent of Americans accept evolution—49 percent plus 9 percent—it is at least as accurate, if not more so, to interpret the data as showing that the overwhelming majority of Americans—93 percent, or 44 percent plus 49 percent—reject the neo-Darwinist account.

5. Stephen L. Carter, "The Resurrection of Religious Freedom?," 107 Harv. L. Rev. 118, 132–33 (1993).

6. H. Jefferson Powell, *The Moral Tradition of American Constitutionalism: A Theological Interpretation* (Durham, N.C.: Duke University Press, 1993), 10; accord id. at 204 ("The advocates of a continued active role for the Court . . . cannot reconcile their desire for the Court to enforce libertarian and egalitarian values with allegiance to democratic decisionmaking). See also Stephen V. Monsma, *Positive Neutrality: Letting Religious Freedom Ring* (Westport, Conn.: Greenwood, 1993), 68–73 (detailing the antireligious bias of public and elite culture in the United States).

7. See Carter, "Resurrection," 119, 131; Monsma, *Positive Neutrality*, 50.

8. Eisenstadt v. Baird, 405 U.S. 438 (1972) (distinction between married and unmarried persons in statutory prohibition on purchase of contraceptives by unmarried persons lacks minimum rationality required by equal protection clause of the Fourteenth Amendment): Griswold v. Connecticut, 381 U.S. 479 (1965) (criminalization of use of contraceptives by married couples violates penumbral right to privacy implied by explicit limits on government action set forth in the Bill of Rights); id. at 500 (Harlan, J., concurring) (incorporating by reference Poe v. Ullman, 367 U.S. 497, 551 [1961] [Harlan, J., dissenting] [same, but locating privacy right in the due process clause of the Fourteenth Amendment]); id. at 487 (Goldberg, J., concurring) (same, but locating privacy right in the Ninth Amendment). See also Skinner v. Oklahoma, 316 U.S. 535 (1942) (forced sterilization of convicted felon violates fundamental right to procreation protected by the equal protection clause of the Fourteenth Amendment).

9. See, e.g., Alexander Meiklejohn, *Political Freedom* (New York: Harper, 1960); Vincent Blasi, "The Checking Value in First Amendment Theory," 1977 Am. B. Found. Res. J. 521.

10. See, e.g., United States v. Eichman, 496 U.S. 310 (1990) (Congress may not punish flag desecration on the basis of its likely communicative impact); Texas v. Johnson, 491 U.S. 397 (1989) (state may not punish flag-burning intended to convey contempt for United States simply because it finds the act and the message offensive); Spence v. Washington, 418 U.S.

405 (1974) (affixing peace symbol to flag in protest of then-current foreign and domestic policies of United States is protected expression under the First Amendment); Street v. New York, 394 U.S. 576 (1969) (state statute outlawing flag desecration held unconstitutional because it permitted punishment for speaking contemptuous words about the flag).

11. Cf. Steven D. Smith, *Foreordained Failure: The Quest for a Constitutional Principle of Religious Freedom* (New York: Oxford, 1995), 68 ("The problem, simply put, is that theories of religious freedom seek to reconcile or to mediate among competing religious and secular positions within a society, but those competing postions disagree about the very background beliefs on which a theory of religious freedom must rest.").

12. Stephen L. Carter, *The Culture of Disbelief: How American Politics and Law Trivialize Religious Devotion* (New York: Basic Books, 1993), 23–43. I should note here that I once made the identical argument, which is, of course, equally subject to the criticism in text. See Frederick Mark Gedicks, "Toward a Constitutional Jurisprudence of Religious Group Rights," 1989 Wis. L. Rev. 99.

13. See, e.g., Ronald Garet, "Communality and Existence: The Rights of Groups," 56 S. Cal. L. Rev. 1001 (1983) (arguing for constitutional recognition of religious group rights implied by, inter alia, Wisconsin v. Yoder, 406 U.S. 205 [1972]); Gedicks, "Religious Group Rights" (same with respect to Corporation of the Presiding Bishop v. Amos, 483 U.S. 327 [1987]); Mark De Wolfe Howe, "The Supreme Court, 1952 Term—Foreword: Political Theory and the Nature of Liberty," 67 Harv. L. Rev. 91 (1953) (same with respect to Kedroff v. St. Nicholas Cathedral, 344 U.S. 94 [1952]); Douglas Laycock, "Towards a General Theory of the Religion Clauses: The Case of Church Labor Relations and the Right to Church Autonomy," 81 Colum. L. Rev. 1373 (1981) (same with respect to NLRB v. Catholic Bishop, 440 U.S. 490 [1979]).

14. C. S. Lewis, *The Discarded Image* (Cambridge: Cambridge University Press, 1967), 221.

15. Id. at 222–23.

16. Cf. Stanley Fish, *Doing What Comes Naturally: Change, Rhetoric, and the Practice of Theory in Literary and Legal Studies* (Durham, N.C.: Duke University Press, 1989), 155 ("A theoretical pronouncement is always an articulation of a shift that has in large part already occurred; it announces a rationale for practices already in force.").

Index

· · · · ·

Frederick Mark Gedicks is Professor of Law at
Brigham Young University. He is coauthor with
Roger Hendrix of *Choosing the Dream: The Future
of Religion in American Public Life.*

Library of Congress Cataloging-in-Publication Data

Gedicks, Frederick Mark.
The rhetoric of church and state : a critical analysis of religion clause
jurisprudence / Frederick Mark Gedicks
p.   cm.
Includes bibliographical references and index.
ISBN 0-8223-1654-4 (cl : acid-free paper). — ISBN 0-8223-1666-8
(pa : acid-free paper)
1. Church and state—United States.   2. Freedom of religion—United
States.   3. United Sta
I. Title.
KF4865.G43   1995
342.73'0852—dc20
[347.302852]   95-10337